READINGS ON LA RAZA
The Twentieth Century

Also by Matt S. Meier and Feliciano Rivera

The Chicanos: A History of Mexican Americans

READINGS ON
LA RAZA
The Twentieth Century

Edited by

MATT S. MEIER &
FELICIANO RIVERA

American Century Series

HILL AND WANG   New York
A division of Farrar, Straus and Giroux

We dedicate this volume
to the memory of the late
PROFESSOR GEORGE I. SÁNCHEZ,
universally revered as dean of
Mexican American scholars.

CONTENTS

EDITORS' PREFACE

Readings on La Raza were chosen on the basis of our experience and personal interest to illuminate and illustrate salient aspects of what has happened to Chicanos since 1900. These selections from available period literature provide a chronologically and topically balanced information source for Chicano history in the twentieth century. By combining primary and secondary sources and by presenting a variety of perspectives, we hope to arouse concern and stimulate thoughtful reflection on the part of you, the reader.

While a broad survey of Chicano history, such as our *The Chicanos: A History of Mexican Americans*, is extremely valuable in obtaining a synthetic overall view of the Chicano experience, contemporary documents give the reader a "feel" for what really happened. Contained in this volume is only a part of what occurred, and the reader should be aware that it is neither the whole record nor always the "real" record. However, it does present the more important and controversial events and issues relating to Chicano history and touches upon the many aspects of society in which Mexican Americans have found themselves in conflict.

A few words should be said about one particular theme in this collection of readings. Appearing throughout its six sections are a number of selections dealing with immigration. While this movement of Mexicans north from Mexico is not the only important factor in Chicano history, we feel that it is sufficiently significant to be dealt with in considerable detail.

Headnotes are used to place the article in historical context, to emphasize particular points in an article, or to supply information on the contributing author. Footnotes in the readings have been deleted.

INTRODUCTION: BACKGROUND

In predominantly Anglo America, Chicanos form an ethnic group whose antecedents predate the founding of Jamestown in 1607. Today they constitute the second largest ethnic minority in the United States, numbering 7 million. They are concentrated primarily in California and Texas; these two states have more than 2 million each. Considerable concentrations also live in the states of Arizona, Colorado, and New Mexico, and since 1920 sizable communities have developed in Washington, Utah, Illinois, Michigan, Pennsylvania, and other states.

For many reasons it would be inaccurate to consider Chicanos to be like other immigrants to the United States. Having had a markedly different social, political, and economic history, they have had an experience distinct from other ethnic immigrant groups in American society. Analogies can be drawn between their experience and that of other poverty-stricken and exploited immigrants, especially those from southern and eastern Europe; however, the latter greatly improved their circumstances with the passage of time while Chicanos continued to fall further behind.

Racism, for example, has been directed with great violence against Chicanos in many regions of the Southwest and continues to be a most important factor in the struggle for Chicano liberation. Although their battles are far from over yet, Chicanos in the latter part of the twentieth century have begun to make progress in their struggle for social justice.

Chicanos have not lived in a vacuum. Although largely

unreported in textbooks, they have played important roles in Western history beginning with the Hispanic-Mexican period and continuing through the era of manifest destiny to the post-Civil War period of urbaniization and industrialization, down to the present.

Between 1530 and 1800, the Spanish undertook the exploration and development of the Southwest, and gradually clusters of frontier settlements took root and grew. Isolated from the center of their government and culture during both Spanish and Mexican periods, three separate and distinct groups developed in the north Mexican regions of New Mexico, Texas, and California. Varying geographic and economic conditions determined the way in which these unconnected areas developed. Early settlement efforts in New Mexico evolved around mining and missionary activities, while colonization in Texas and California was initiated by Spain principally to hold back rival colonial powers.

Settlements on Mexico's northern frontier, such as San Antonio, Santa Fe, Tucson, Los Angeles, and San Jose, remained isolated outposts through the eighteenth century—isolated from each other and from central Mexico. Serving as defenses against Indian raids and against potential foreign settlement, they survived in spite of a lack of concern by the government in Mexico. Consequently, they did not become dynamic centers of expansion, though some trade activity developed in New Mexico and California during the early nineteenth century. Northern frontier settlers, although Spanish (and after 1821, Mexican) citizens, had little awareness of what was occurring in Spain and Mexico, and thus their loyalties and allegiance did not lie with these entities.

Frontier attitudes during the Mexican revolution for independence, which broke out in 1810 under the leadership of Father Miguel Hidalgo y Costilla, illustrate this lack of concern. Although the northern provinces were aware of revolutionary events in central Mexico, they remained generally unconcerned with the movement for independence. Their aloofness from events in central Mexico continued through the period of Iturbide's empire in the early twenties to the later republican governments.

Rapid changes of government in Mexico City from empire to republican federation to centralist republic indicate the extensive chaos that permeated Mexican politics during this era. Various attempts by General Antonio López de Santa Anna to provide leadership during the thirties and forties met with abysmal failure. In Texas, the frontier region most affected by revolutionary federalist ideology, his efforts failed to turn the tide of separatism, fostered and led principally by disgruntled Anglo immigrants, legal and illegal. Texan revolutionaries, by defeating Santa Anna's army, ultimately succeeded in establishing their independence, and although Mexico refused to recognize it, she was unable to reassert her authority in the province. Thus began the disintegration of Mexico's northern provinces.

This breakup was purely political; it had little effect on the continuing evolution of a biological and cultural synthesis that dates to the sixteenth century. This amalgamation process began when Spanish conquistadores first encountered indigenous cultures in Mexico and on its northern frontiers. Out of the confrontation between Spaniard and Indian was born the mestizo Chicano.

Beginning in Tenochtitlán and extending to Indian groups of the north, there occurred a long and intricate process of blending that included a complex overlapping of races, cultures, and life styles. On the northern frontier, Spaniards, Mexicans, and Indians worked together, adapting and building on local Indian cultures, to create a tricultural mestizo society in an arid and hostile land. The essence of the Southwest today began during the colonial period with development of irrigated farming, sheep and cattle raising, and mining. Such a frontier economy attracted few members of the upper classes; however, throughout the colonial period, promises of land and other inducements continued to lure mestizos, mulattoes, and Indians from central Mexico.

Beginning in the early nineteenth century, this provincial Indo-Hispanic society began to be affected by the outside world. Increasing contacts between Mexicans and westward-pressing Anglos presaged the cultural and political conflict that soon developed and has persisted to the present. Politically, as early as the 1820's, the United States, influenced by expansionist attitudes of manifest destiny, put Mexico on the defensive by attempting to purchase parts of her northern frontier area. Unable to buy the desired territory, the United States pursued a policy of confrontation which finally ended in armed conflict when she declared war against Mexico in May 1846. This war proved disastrous for Mexico; unable to cope with American expansionism and aggression, she was forced to relinquish half of her national territory in the Treaty of Guadalupe Hidalgo. The Mexican war was merely part of a continuing political and cultural conflict that began years before and that continues to separate Anglo and Mexican Americans today.

In 1848, by ratification of the Treaty of Guadalupe Hidalgo, a new ethnic group was added to the American population. In a short time these new Americans found themselves a cultural minority in an Anglo-American world as they quickly became overwhelmed by waves of westward-moving Anglos. In California their disenfranchisement took place in the 1850's as a result of the unexpected discovery of a gold bonanza, while in New Mexico it was delayed until the advent of transcontinental railroads in the late 1870's.

Guaranteed citizenship, personal-property rights, and religious freedom under the Treaty of Guadalupe Hidalgo, Mexicans nevertheless soon found themselves strangers in their own land. Only the guarantee of religious freedom was honored by the conquerors, and within a few years other rights stipulated by the treaty became lost in the Anglicization of the Southwest. Change took place at such a rapid pace during this period that many rights of the newly conquered were ignored or rejected by ambitious and land-hungry Anglo migrants.

Economic advances in the West during the 1870's and 1880's put great pressure on the limited lands of this new Anglo frontier. Through intimidation, forced sales, legal maneuvers, and plain robbery, much of the land held by Chicanos had been taken over by Anglos by 1900. As a result, many Chicanos were dispossessed of lands which had been in their families for generations.

As the nineteenth century approached its end, conflict between the two peoples declined somewhat throughout the Southwest. An important facet of this change was a widespread tendency toward accommodation to Anglo society as Chicanos became an ever-smaller minority. However, at the turn of the century, this trend was abruptly interrupted by cataclysmic events in Mexico that culminated in the 1910 revolution, directly altering the future course of the older Mexican American population in the Southwest.

Readings on La Raza is organized into six chronological-topical sections, with an introduction and a brief afterword. Section I spans the period from 1900 to 1920 and introduces immigration as the starting point for the history of La Raza in this century. Large-scale migration from Mexico in the early twentieth century inundated and overwhelmed long-existing Mexican settlements in the United States, absorbing and greatly modifying their Mexican culture.

Section II, covering from 1920 to 1930, describes the expansion of Mexicans and Mexican Americans from their Southwest heartland to steel mills, packing plants, and *colonias* of the Midwest. Other selections address themselves to the development of a hostile attitude on the part of many Americans to the rising tide of Mexican immigration, this attitude exemplified in the Harris and Box bills in Congress.

Section III deals with repatriation in the 1930's. Threatened by economic realities of the Depression, various government agencies developed policies resulting in half a million people of Mexican descent leaving or being forced to leave the United States for Mexico during this decade. This period, a time of much labor-management conflict, witnessed an upsurge of agricultural-labor organizing attempts in California.

Section IV describes Chicano World War II experiences both at home and overseas. Although Chicanos were fighting valiantly in the armed services, a continuation of old stereotypical attitudes back home led to the Sleepy Lagoon verdict and "zoot-suit" riots. World War II introduced a new era in Mexico-United States relations, formalizing the use of bracero labor.

Section V traces continuing postwar demands for Mexican labor and the resultant increase in both braceros and mojados. Impact of this tremendous surge of workers eventually led to "Operation Wetback" and finally to termination of the bracero program in 1964. Elimination of braceros led to increased "commuter" traffic across the border to fill the persistent demand for low-wage labor in agriculture and industry.

Section VI encompasses a broad spectrum of contemporary Chicano activity and ideology. The 1960's ushered in a new era marked by increased and more aggressive political activity, represented by César Chávez, Rodolfo "Corky" Gonzales, Reies López Tijerina, and José Angel Gutiérrez. Also included are themes of Raza solidarity and Chicano nationalism, both arising out of politicization of Mexican Americans and their resultant radicalization in an urban environment.

These six sections are chronologically sequential, with some unavoidable overlap. Together they tell what has happened to La Raza from early 1900 to the present. In our afterword, "The Future," three leading Mexican Americans describe continuing problems of La Raza vis-à-vis the majority community.

Matt S. Meier
Feliciano Rivera

Santa Clara, February 21, 1973

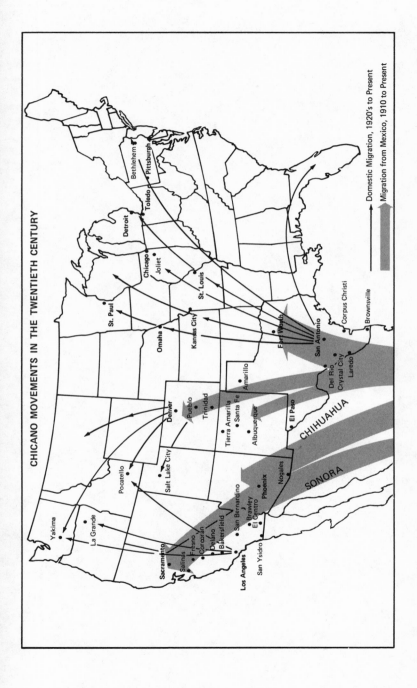

CHICANO MOVEMENTS IN THE TWENTIETH CENTURY

Domestic Migration, 1920's to Present

Migration from Mexico, 1910 to Present

READINGS ON LA RAZA
The Twentieth Century

I

NORTH FROM MEXICO

By 1900, Mexicans in the United States were rapidly being absorbed into the dominant Anglo culture. This trend toward acculturation and assimilation had existed since United States acquisition of the Southwest as a result of the Treaty of Guadalupe Hidalgo, which ended the war between Mexico and the United States in 1848. However, events in Mexico and in the United States at the turn of the century quickly altered this long-term development.

Deplorable political and economic conditions in Mexico, especially for the *peón* and Indian majority, unleashed a long bloody social revolution which gave birth to one of the greatest population movements in the Western Hemisphere and greatly modified the traditional Mexican American communities of the Southwest.

This movement north from Mexico originated as a direct result of the brutal social and economic conditions existing in that country immediately prior to the 1910 revolution. By 1900 a majority of Mexicans were landless, and when they obtained work, their wages amounted to but a few pennies a day. Widespread economic servitude bound a majority of agricultural workers to the land. With no hope for a better tomorrow or expectation of improving their miserable lot, peasants not only hungered for their own plots of ground but, most important, cried out for liberty and justice.

In the ensuing chaos of social and civil strife, beginning in 1900 and increasing in intensity till 1920, the peasantry, uprooted, either joined one of many revolutionary bands that ravaged rural Mexico or fled from the countryside. Many migrated to the larger towns and cities of Mexico; others migrated even farther—to "the land of milk and honey."

Mexico's inability to cope with her internal political problems impeded her from taking any direct action to prevent this exodus. Thus, although discouraging emigration, the Mexican government was unable to establish and implement a definite policy unilaterally or in concert with the United States. Consequently, the human flotsam of the revolution which flowed into the United States was left to fend for itself in a new and hostile environment.

At the same time that revolution was uprooting thousands of Mexicans from their rural complacency, in the Southwestern United States a rapidly increasing demand for workers attracted them northward. A number of coinciding factors created this phenomenon. By 1900, total farm acreage in Western agriculture had tripled in relation to what it had been a generation earlier; federal reclamation and irrigation programs had greatly expanded agricultural activity, which in turn increased demand for stoop labor. In addition, completion of railroad systems in the Southwest at this time also created an expanded need for unskilled track workers. This demand for labor quickly was filled by the flow of refugees from Mexico. Thus, "push-and-pull" factors in Mexico and the United States acted as a catalyst to set in motion a massive twentieth-century movement of people.

This migration from Mexico to the border region of the United States created economic pressures which set into motion a secondary migratory wave from Southwestern Mexican American communities. Moving north in a fanlike pattern, Mexican Americans inaugurated their own migration patterns from south central Texas. Using railroads as their chief means of transportation, sizable numbers soon appeared in almost every part of the United States except the South.

By 1920, Mexican Americans and Mexican nationals made up three fourths of Western agricultural labor, nearly all of Western railroad-track labor, and the majority of Western mining labor. In addition, smaller numbers had established themselves in industrial and transportation centers of the Midwest, such as Chicago, Detroit, Omaha, St. Louis, and Denver.

Another effect of this massive migration became apparent in the political arena and elsewhere in American society as anti-Mexican attitudes based on race began to be voiced. These attitudes would grow in intensity and finally climax in the congressional hearings of the 1920's on limitations to Mexican entrance into the United States.

Migration from Mexico to the United States between 1900 and 1920 numbered in the hundreds of thousands. Although it has been pointed out that many, perhaps the majority, entered this country illegally, legal or illegal, their contribution to the economic development of the United States is important and undeniable.

PAX PORFIRIANA

Migration north from Mexico beginning in the early 1900's had social, economic, and political causes. This migration took place primarily because of inhumane conditions existent in rural and urban Mexico immediately preceding the 1910 revolution. Stanley R. Ross paints a vivid picture of the life of the majority of Mexicans under the dictatorship of Porfirio Díaz.

. . . The price paid by the Mexican people for the accomplishments of the Porfirian system was high and constitutes a serious indictment of the regime. Opposition was ruthlessly suppressed. Behind the walls of Belém in the capital and in the military prison

From *Francisco I. Madero, Apostle of Mexican Democracy*, by Stanley R. Ross. New York: Columbia University Press, 1955, pp. 27–33. Copyright © 1955 by Columbia University Press. By permission of the publisher.

of San Juan de Ulúa the dictator endeavored to break the spirit of those who dared to oppose him. For more stubborn cases there was the penal colony of Quintana Roo, the most deadly territory in the nation. Persons assigned to jobs as well as those sentenced there rarely returned. Not all the opponents of the regime lived to experience the confines of the prisons. Many persons were victims of the *ley fuga* (law of flight). Summary executions were carried out, and the laconic notation, "Shot while trying to escape," served as acceptable explanation.

Forced conscription into the army, forced migrations, and forced labor were additional methods of persuasion and pacification. When troops were needed, each state had to provide a contingent. Consignment to arms, the *leva* (levy), was not universal or by lot but by administrative designation. As exercised by local officials the *leva* was developed into an instrument of persecution and vengeance. The Yaqui Indians of Sonora were transported at gun point from their homes to work as forced labor on the *henequén* (sisal hemp) plantations of Yucatán and in the tobacco fields of the Valle Nacional in Oaxaca as punishment and in the name of pacification. Mexico had peace, but the price included tyranny and suppression.

The peace, opportunity, and prosperity brought by the regime of Porfirio Díaz were reserved for the selected few. The political, social, and economic interests of the bulk of the Mexicans were treated with contemptuous disdain when considered at all. Not only was all political activity suppressed but Díaz failed to take advantage of his long tenure in office to prepare the people for democratic participation in their government. A political writer of the period observed that the Mexican people had "learned the habit of obedience, but still had to acquire that other fundamental lesson of civilization, consciousness of their own political rights." The people of Mexico also suffered from a lack of equity in the administration of justice. Justice, like security and opportunity, was the prerogative of the few. The state of public education was disgraceful. Schools were built, but the number was inadequate and the distribution uneven. Outside the capital and the key provincial cities, facilities were practically nonexistent. Even accepting official statistics, the illiteracy rate was shocking and showed only a slight decrease by the end of the period. In 1895, 86 percent of the population was unable to read and write, and at the close of the Díaz regime four out of every five persons were still illiterate. Health conditions were equally discouraging. There was a high incidence of enteritis, pneumonia, malaria, and venereal disease.

The heaviest burden of the Díaz era was imposed on the local and rural level, involving the overwhelming majority of the people. There the price of the system was highest, creating conditions which were certain to cause trouble. The generalized despotism of local authorities (caciquism) has already been noted. The local chieftain was converted into an instrument of the central government, a local tyrant without initiative and without local support. He had become an enemy of his own people and his own area. The rural area remained isolated, geographically and culturally, from national life. The great cities improved while the rural sections suffered from a lack of transportation and communication facilities, and the small towns and villages were neglected. Worst of all, the agrarian policy of the Díaz government reversed the efforts of the mid-nineteenth-century reform movement to destroy the feudal pattern of Mexican landholding, with serious consequences for the socio-economic equilibrium of the society.

A persistent theme in Mexican history has been the struggle between the privately owned estate, the semifeudal hacienda, and the communal landholding village. The reformers of the fifties, motivated by ideals of liberalism and individualism, lashed out against the feudal land system. The *Ley de desamortización* (Law of Expropriation) of 1856, later made part of the Constitution of 1857, was more than an attack on the economic holdings of the Church. It was a well-intentioned effort to advance the Indian economically by making him an owner of private property, to develop the ranchero (small farmer) class as a counterpoise to the large-estate owners, and, by achieving both these goals, to make possible real democracy in Mexico. The landholding villages came under the prohibition against corporate holdings, and it was soon apparent that the effects of the law were opposed by the Indians and, where applied, disastrous for the villages. As a result, the application of the law to villages was moderated until Porfirio Díaz came to power.

Starting with a theory that was a concoction of liberalism emphasizing modernization and industrialization and a brand of Spencerian dogma proclaiming survival of the fittest, the ideological architects of the Díaz period manifested disdain for the Indian mass and projected colonization through immigration. The communal village should be destroyed and the Indian reduced as an element in the population and replaced by a more desirable immigrant element. The policies directed to these ends facilitated the victory of the hacienda and generalized a form of agrarian feudalism throughout the country.

Díaz enforced the Reform Laws against the villages. Circulars in 1889 and 1890 decreed that all communal lands must be divided, and it was estimated that over $2\frac{1}{4}$ million acres were allotted to individuals, the major portion of which found its way, ultimately, into the hands of large landowners, speculators, and land companies. A series of colonization laws had similar objectives with the additional justification of an attempt to clarify land titles and to recover illegally alienated public lands. Surveying companies were authorized to search for, locate, and survey *terrenos baldíos* (national lands not legally alienated and considered, therefore, as "empty lands"). The company or individuals, usually government favorites, were entitled to one third of the lands outright as well as to the privilege of purchasing as much of the remainder desired at a ridiculously low price. Land could not be sold in units exceeding twenty-five hundred hectares (about sixty-two hundred acres), and there was a colonization requirement, but the companies could hold the land for speculative purposes and generally ignored their colonization commitment. The modifying law of 1894 permitted sale of tracts without size limitation and extended the area open to survey. The floodgates were thrown open for land absorption on a tremendous scale. The small landholder whose title was not adequate and the landholding village which could not legally hold land suffered. Wholesale denunciations of villages holding lands followed, with the Indians dispossessed or their villages incorporated into large estates.

When the inhabitants of the fertile Valley of Papantla in the state of Veracruz resisted the survey of their lands during the winter of 1890, the government responded with a full-scale invasion of the area and proceeded to a systematic extermination of the men, women, and children of the valley.

Indian villages were also deprived of their lands through the manipulation of water rights. By an act of 1888 the president received jurisdiction over water rights with authority to grant monopoly concessions. Control of water meant control of the land. Lastly, Indian tribes—for example, the Yaquis and Mayos of Sonora and the Mayas of Yucatán—were deprived of their lands as punishment for rebellion. In the name of peace and progress, just grievances were ignored, and cruel suppression, dispersal, and peonage awaited the Indians who protested or resisted. The basic element in the Mexican population was to be exploited and possibly eliminated in the name of the exalted goal, material progress.

This wholesale attack on the Indian village upset the equilibrium of native society and, consequently, depressed the well-being of the inhabitants. The principal fate awaiting the majority was a status of peonage on the large estates. By 1910 over 90 percent of the villages in the most heavily populated section of the country, the central plateau, had lost their lands. Through absorption of village lands and tremendous concessions of public domain, the hacienda system was confirmed and extended. The large estate rested on a foundation of debt peonage aggravated by pitifully low wages (12 to 18 cents daily), usually paid in kind, token, or credit, and by the exploitive operation of the *tienda de raya* (plantation store). While some of the new extractive plantations showed a degree of rough efficiency, the hacienda lands generally were not fully or effectively employed. Fertility declined, speculation increased, and land prices rose under this modern feudalism.

Although the number of individual landowners increased nearly threefold between 1854 and 1910, the percentage of land ownership was very small. The *hacendado*, favored by the government and avoiding and shifting the tax burden, enjoyed a distinct advantage over the small landholders. Probably no more than 3 percent of the total rural population owned any land at the end of the Díaz period. The hacienda, controlling about half the land and rural population and including over four fifths of the rural communities, dominated politically, economically, and socially the rural life of a predominantly rural nation. The fact that there were 834 *hacendados* and perhaps 9 million landless peasants living in miserable peonage makes understandable González Roa's assertion that the revolution was agrarian above all. To oppressive conditions was added the humiliation that much of the land had passed into foreign hands.

Foreign capitalism was superimposed on this feudal agrarian base. The forced, accelerated industrialization accentuated the colonial pattern of the Mexican economy, for the emphasis was on the extractive industries, especially mining. Foreigners built railroads under liberal conditions, ignoring the basic economic needs of the country and favoring external over domestic trade. The government, reversing Mexican legal patterns dating from colonial times, gave concessionaires unquestioned title to subsoil mineral deposits. Díaz boasted regularly of the new titles conceded to mining properties, for this was progress. Mexico received only long hours and low wages for her sons. Negligible revenues returned to the government. The foreigners were siphoning off the wealth, and in the process, the nation's resources lost their nationality. The foreigners were not only exploiting Mexico economically but enjoying influence greatly out of proportion to their numbers. Favorable consideration in the courts was assured. There was daily proof of the charge that Mexico under Díaz had become "the mother of foreigners and the stepmother of Mexicans."

The industrialization of Mexico and the vigorous exploitation of her wealth brought a new labor element on the scene. The growth of an independent industrial labor force free from the old controls and enjoying mobility of movement was of primary importance for future revolutionary development. Work on the railroads offered an alternative to the restrictive life of the plantation. Railroads facilitated emigration to the United States and contact with new ideas. Workers were made available to those selected to exploit the resources of Mexico, and the power of the government was employed to prevent industrial labor from making itself felt.

However, during the last decade of the dictatorship, strikes occurred at the Green Consolidated Mining Company in Cananea, Sonora, and at the textile mills in Río Blanco, Veracruz. While these outbreaks did not represent a serious threat to the regime, they were symptomatic of the increasing discontent. The role assumed by the government in the strife between capital and labor revealed once more, as in the case of the Indian wars, that bloody suppression was the Díaz remedy for the social ills of the people.

The most tragic aspect of the material progress and prosperity of the Porfirian era was the fact that the mass of the people did not participate. On the contrary, the industrial advance was made possible by the construction of tariff walls which raised prices to the Mexican consumer. The inefficient *hacendado* was protected from outside competition by duties on foodstuffs—at a time when food had to be imported! Food prices in Mexico, in contrast with those in the rest of the world, rose during this period. While industrial wages advanced somewhat, dollar wages of the rural workers remained approximately the same. Declining real wages inevitably meant a declining standard of living. . . .

THE GREAT INVASION

Unlike other ethnic groups in American society, the Chicano has received continued cultural reinforcement from the centers of Mexican society. At the beginning of the twentieth century, various push-and-pull factors greatly increased the movement of people north from Mexico. The magnitude of this exodus both reinforced and dramatically changed the pervasive Indo-Hispanic cultural ambience of the Southwest. Carey

From *The Mexicans in America*, by Carey McWilliams. New York: Teachers College Press, 1968, pp. 8–15. Copyright © 1968 by Teachers College, Columbia University. Reprinted, with deletions, by permission of the publisher.

*McWilliams discusses this most important movement of peoples in
twentieth-century America.*

By the 1890's Mexicans had become merely a "picturesque
element" in the life of the Southwest. They carried on, but in
minor roles and occupations, "colorful" representatives of a
subculture that was rapidly disappearing—or so everyone
thought. . . .

The land boom of the late 1880's in Southern California, which
engulfed the Mexicans and at the same time gave rise to a
booster-inspired legend of the past, also set in motion the invasion
of the Southwest by thousands of Spanish-speaking Mexicans who
returned to the land of their fathers in response to the demand for
labor. As a matter of fact, there had been a slow but steady influx
of Mexican immigrants prior to 1900. In that year, the Mexican
immigrant population of Texas was estimated at 71,061, of
Arizona at 14,172, of California at 8,096, and of New Mexico at
6,649. But between 1900 and 1964, 1.3 million Mexicans entered
the regions in two great waves; the first from 1900 to 1920, the
second from 1920 to 1930. It has been estimated that the number
of Mexicans entering the United States between 1900 and 1920
was roughly the equivalent of one tenth of the population of
Mexico.

The details of Mexican immigration to the United States are
quite complex and only the essential facts can be summarized
here. In all mass-migration movements, two sets of factors are at
work: "push" factors—those that set people in motion—and
"pull" factors—those that pull them to a particular place. There
were many push factors operating in the period from 1900 to
1964. In the first place, the portion of the old "borderlands"
immediately south of the U.S.-Mexican border offered no very
great inducements for people to stay there. Population was
expanding but economic opportunities were not. From this region
Mexicans could be easily induced to cross the border in search of
work, the more so since crossing the border involved no great
problems and the trip was not expensive. Then, too, in the period
from 1880 to 1910, railroad lines were constructed in northern

Mexico which made it possible for those seeking employment to travel "by coach" from such cities as Durango, Zacatecas, Chihuahua, and Sonora, to one or another of the communities on the American side. Another powerful push factor was, of course, the Mexican revolution, which, in the period from 1910 to 1920, resulted in a great deal of confusion, border troubles, and internal upheaval in Mexico. It was not so much that people fled to the States to avoid involvement in the revolution as that they were driven to the States in search of work and some means of earning a livelihood. Then, when some of the great objectives of the Mexican revolution, such as land redistribution, were not fully realized, many Mexicans left for the States out of a sense of frustration and disappointment.

The major pull factors, on the other hand, had to do with the rise of the Southwest as an economic empire. Originally it had been regarded as a largely arid region of little economic importance, but it was not long before its potentialities were perceived. Before its resources could be unlocked, rail lines had to be constructed. Mexicans, of course, had established the first trails which connected one Spanish outpost with another; they had also operated the pack trains that connected these outposts with points of settlement in Mexico. So it was quite appropriate, symbolically, that Mexican immigrants should have been imported to construct the new rail lines that ended the isolation of the region. It was no easy feat to push rail lines through the rugged, semidesert, mountainous terrain. There were few points at which materials could be assembled; the isolation of the region impeded construction. But fortunately, cheap Mexican labor, both resident and immigrant, was available in large quantities. Long after the major lines were completed, Mexicans continued to constitute 70 percent or more of the section crews and 90 percent of the extra gangs used in maintenance. Other lines, operating outside the region, also began to use Mexican labor. Once imported for this purpose, Mexican immigrants drifted into other types of work and their places were taken by new recruits from Mexico. Along the major rail lines of the Southwest, Mexican settlements sprang up, usually in the form of "boxcar" housing or, later, of rows of company housing. In the sparsely settled Southwest, rail lines were constructed well in advance of actual need and as a means of inducing newcomers to visit the region and, hopefully, to settle there. Construction of these lines would have taken much longer and would have cost much more if cheap Mexican labor had not been available in the desired volume. It was a type of labor, also, which was well adapted for work in the hot, rugged terrain. . . .

In all these industries—railroads, mines, sheep and cattle— Mexicans played a key role. But it was the emergence of the Southwest as an agricultural empire that brought the first waves of Mexican immigrants to the States. From the 1890's to 1910, the cattle industry began to give way to large-scale cotton farming, first in middle Texas and later in west Texas. As cotton pushed its way into the Southwest, Mexican labor came north to meet it. It so happened that the expansion of cotton farming coincided, roughly, with the inception of a period of revolutionary ferment in Mexico, which predisposed many Mexicans to "flee the revolution" and seek jobs in the States. Later, World War I greatly stimulated the expansion of the cotton industry in the Southwest by creating an active demand for long-staple cotton, which is best grown on the irrigated cotton farms in Arizona and California. In 1910, the year which marked the inception of the Mexican revolution, cotton was first planted in the Imperial Valley in California. Much of the new land that was devoted to cotton raising was brought into production through the use of large quantities of Mexican labor. . . .

Outside the Southwest, Mexicans were widely used in the sugar-beet industry, which began to expand after 1897, when a heavy tax was imposed on imported sugar. . . . Over the years some of these Mexican beet workers were either left stranded in the sugar-beet areas after the crop was harvested or decided to stay on, and in this way, small colonies of Mexican settlement sprang up. But by and large, Mexican immigration has been confined to the original fan of settlement, and as a consequence, the Spanish-Mexican influence has been massively re-enforced. In 1890 it seemed as though Mexicans were a vanishing element in the Southwest, but they are a large and expanding element there today.

Unlike European immigration, there has been an ebb-and-flow to Mexican immigration. To repeat a figure previously cited, between 1900 and 1964, 1.3 million Mexicans immigrated to the United States, but they have come in waves, and at different periods, many have returned. The first great wave, of 224,706, crossed the border between 1910 and 1920. The next large wave, of roughly 436,733, swept north between 1920 and 1930. Still a third wave, of 293,000, was recorded in the period from 1950 to 1960. But in the 1930–40 decade, only 27,937 immigrants crossed the border, and from 1940 to 1950 the number was 54,290. There is, of course, an explanation for the relative decline registered in these decades. The 1930's marked a period of depression. It was in this period, also, that tens of thousands of dust-bowl migrants, the so-called Okies and Arkies, came to Arizona and California and, to some extent, displaced the Mexicans in certain types of work. In the period from 1940 to 1950, with the demand for labor soaring, the number of Mexican "wetbacks," or illegal entrants, greatly increased, and this increase was not included in the immigration totals. In fact, the demand for labor during World War II and the Korean war became so great that the governments of the United States and Mexico entered into an agreement under which Mexican labor was imported, known as the bracero program. The braceros, or imported workers, were not included in the immigration total. They were imported, under contract, to work in certain crops and returned to Mexico once the crops were harvested. Generally speaking, when the demand for labor in the Southwest has increased, the volume of Mexican immigration has increased, but in depression years immigration has tapered off, and in some years, many immigrants have returned to Mexico. For example, during the Depression years welfare agencies in California deported thousands of Mexican aliens.

The wetback situation requires a word of comment. There have always been wetbacks in the border states and, in some periods, very large numbers indeed. During World War II, with the dust-bowl migrants being drawn into the shipyards and industrial plants, and with the Japanese-Americans being removed from the West Coast, the number of wetbacks zoomed. At the same time, thousands of braceros were imported (the first contingent arrived in Stockton, California, in September 1942). The demand for labor was so great that the wetback situation soon got out of control; the Border Patrol was not in a position to stop the influx even if it had wanted to. For every Mexican legally imported under the bracero program, at least four alien Mexicans or wetbacks were apprehended by the Border Patrol. Of the 875,000 apprehended in 1953, thousands were found to hold non-agricultural jobs. In fact, the wetback influx had such a demoralizing effect on wages and labor standards, and drained off so much purchasing power from local communities in the form of remittances sent to relatives in Mexico, that a determined effort was finally made to stop it. In 1953, the number of wetbacks rose to 1,035,282, but the next year the Border Patrol reported that the influx had been greatly reduced. Since then the border has been under fairly tight control. The bracero program continued, in one form or another, until it was permitted to lapse in December 1964. The number of workers imported under this program varied from year to year; 447,000 were imported in 1959, only 183,000 in 1964. The wetback problem, so troublesome and complex, is merely one of numerous aspects of Mexican immigration not to be found in the pattern of European immigration.

The years of heaviest Mexican immigration occurred *after* the peak of European immigration. Mexican immigration, in a word, has been a late chapter in the saga of immigration. The first restrictive immigration acts in the 1920's made an exception for immigration from the Western Hemisphere, so that Mexican immigration continued long after European immigration had, for all practical purposes, ceased to be important. Legislation adopted in 1965 for the first time fixed a quota of 120,000 per year for Mexican immigration. Mexican immigration, of course, continues. In 1965 it was estimated that in five of the eleven years since 1954, permanent visas issued to immigrants born in Mexico exceeded the number of immigrants from any other country. In the fiscal year ending June 30, 1965, 55,253 immigrants born in Mexico entered the United States under permanent immigrant visas. There is also a high and steadily mounting movement of people back and forth across the border; more Mexicans visit the

United States, more Americans visit Mexico. And since the Southwest is still expanding, it is reasonable to assume that Mexican immigration, in substantial volume, will continue for a long time. . . .

MEXICAN POLICY
TOWARD EMIGRATION

Turbulence and chaos marked Mexico's history in the first decades of the twentieth century, unleashing wave after wave of refugees who inundated the Southwest. Official Mexican policy on emigration was at once contradictory and confusing. Professor Juan R. Martínez describes the historical developments which affected the course of this vacillating policy.

. . . Indifference, approval, and disapproval were the three phases through which Mexican policy respecting emigration passed between 1910 and 1921. This period of eleven years in Mexico was filled with violence and commotion. Emigration grew in volume and therefore in significance, but the Mexican government was not free to take effective action to control the thousands abandoning their country at a time when the nation itself was rent in twain. . . .

In view of the chaotic conditions in Mexico at this time, perhaps it is inappropriate to say that the Mexican government was indifferent to emigration. In reality, the whole nation was absorbed in the revolution. It might even be said that at certain times, as in the years between Madero's fall in 1913 and Carranza's rise to power in 1915, there was no real government in Mexico. . . .

From "Mexican Emigration to the United States, 1910–1930," by Juan R. Martínez. Berkeley: Ph.D. diss., University of California, 1957. Reprinted, with deletions, by permission of the author.

Subsequently, Mexico's policy on the departure of its nationals to the United States became confusing and contradictory. Approval and then attempts to dissuade braceros from emigrating characterized this vacillating policy. This halting and reluctant attitude is explainable by the fact that basically the Mexican government really did not favor her people going to the United States. No nation is anxious to admit that her people must go abroad because a livelihood cannot be made at home. However, the revolution and chronic economic problems combined to gain reluctant permission, but when braceros became involved in difficulties of a serious nature, their government then expressed its basic disapproval and for a short time endeavored to discourage emigration to the United States. Presently the difficulty either passed or gave way to the same reasons that elicited original but reluctant approval of the emigration. This policy and reaction occurred several times and underlies the official government position from 1917 on.

Although the United States was not induced to assume responsibility for the fulfillment of promises to the braceros, Mexico consented to the emigration. In fact, the Departamento de Migración increased its personnel in various parts of Mexico to assist those who desired to go to the United States. In addition, President Carranza offered free passage on Mexican railroads to all who wanted to work across the border.

The apparent reasons for Mexico's cooperation were the bad economic conditions prevailing in Mexico as a result of the fighting during the revolution. Thousands were literally starving, and no other hope of employment or relief was in sight.

Another factor contributing to Mexico's willingness for her workers to emigrate was the material returns from such an exodus. The Mexican government required written contracts between the braceros and their employers. These agreements included a clause which obligated the workers to open a savings account with the United States Postal Savings Bank. Twelve and one half cents, United States currency, were deducted from each day's wages and deposited until fifty dollars were accumulated. This sum and the interest were returned to the bracero upon completion of contract when he returned to Mexico. . . .

In addition to the dollars flowing to Mexico and the technical knowledge and experience the braceros gained, Mexico was benefited by the total cultural effect that the emigration had upon the lower classes. This sentiment was accurately expressed in *El Universal* as follows: "In the United States they [the braceros] learn many good things, to be temperate, to dress well, to earn good wages, to live properly, to eat properly, to speak English and much of modern agriculture. That is, they become cultured and when they return to Mexico, they progress rapidly."

As the war came to an end in November 1918, the need for the Mexicans' services in the United States at the time seemed also to have come to an end. The anticipated consequences of the sudden return of tens of thousands of Mexicans to Mexico soon became an unwelcome reality. Ambassador Fletcher reported that Mexican newspapers complained that presently the United States government would order deportation of all Mexican laborers in the United States "with consequent hardships for the Mexican government and laborers." The State Department informed Ambassador Fletcher that no orders had been given to deport Mexican workers from the United States, but that the Department of Labor on December 18, 1918, had issued an order which stated that not only Mexicans but all additional foreign labor admitted for war purposes would be prohibited from entering after December 18, 1918. However, all those who entered before that date could remain through the following season. Ambassador Fletcher immediately made public the fact that his government had not ordered immediate deportation of Mexican laborers in the United States. Of course, this clarification only applied to Mexicans who had entered the United States legally. The illegal entrants were subject to deportation at any time.

These wetbacks began to be deported within a week after the war ended. Eagle Pass and Matamoros were two main centers through which the deportations were made. Thousands were forced to return to Mexico, and since many of them had no money, they gathered along the Mexican side of the border. Subsecretary of Foreign Relations Garza Pérez complained in a statement to *El Excelsior* that the deported Mexicans could not remain at the border, for there was nothing for them to do there.

He stated that trains would be made available to transport these people to the states of Chihuahua, Guanajuato, Durango, and Zacatecas, where it was hoped the mines could absorb them. *El Excelsior* protested that the braceros had been contracted for work when the United States needed them, but at the end of the war the United States was happy to be rid of them.

The burden and cost of repatriation of many thousands of practically indigent Mexicans fell to the Mexican government. As the task began, the government complained of the emigration, whereas previously only good results had been contemplated. The Secretaría de Relaciones Exteriores (Department of Foreign Relations) stated to *El Excelsior* that "these are the consequences of that kind of emigration. It is only after these workers are in trouble that they seek from their government food and passage back to Mexico and various other costs."

The burden the Mexican government was called upon to bear was not the only factor causing official discontent with the emigration. All during the war, braceros were reported to have been mistreated and abused by both American employers and American immigration officials. These facts, plus the difficulties of repatriation, caused Mexico to take an active interest and concern in the movement of its citizens to and from the United States. Regulation and control of emigration began to be considered in order to avoid a repetition of difficulties.

The hardships and abuses Mexicans were reported to suffer were many and varied. In 1917 *El Excelsior* declared that four thousand Mexicans were imprisoned in Arizona and New Mexico. It was reported in the Mexican press that these Mexicans were charged with having used violence in strikes against the mine operators instigated by the Industrial Workers of the World. In another part of the United States, the Mexican consul at Kansas City, Missouri, informed his government that the Mexicans in his area were, in general, abused and mistreated and that in some of the labor camps braceros were even forced to gamble. . . .

Since the Mexicans and their families were generally without resources when deported from the United States, they suffered greatly in the desert areas south of the border. Many died as a result of being thrust across the frontier. Fatigue and starvation took a sure toll. The Mexican Consul General at San Antonio, Texas, labored with some success to minimize this hardship. He persuaded some of the farmers who most needed and used braceros to pay the laborers' return passage to their homes in Mexico. He reported that often farmers hired wetbacks and their families, but when harvests were over the immigration officers were called in to deport them and the farmers thus avoided paying illegal entrants their money.

Nevertheless, Mexico was slow to take steps to control emigration. Yet there were some efforts in that direction as early as 1917. Since Mexico approved of the emigration during the war, these early efforts were only aimed at preventing excessive numbers of workers from leaving the country. No legislation was passed at this time concerning the emigration problems, but the government did try to discourage undue numbers of braceros from going to the United States. . . .

A more stringent measure to control emigration was the Mexican government's instructions, both during and after the war, to the governors to put a stop to the activities of *enganchistas*, or American labor contractors, within Mexico. These labor contractors were widely disliked. They were bold and often made promises with no intention of fulfilling them. . . .

Some governors of Mexican states attempted to keep their people at home and were somewhat more effective in controlling emigration than the national government. As emigration increased, the state of Jalisco became strict with her artisans but not with her laborers. . . . The governor of Sonora also attempted to discourage emigration by threatening to impose a head tax on every Mexican who wanted to leave for the United States. President Carranza, however, opposed this as being unconstitutional. . . .

As the braceros continued to leave Mexico in greater numbers, even the local authorities found they could not be restrained. "The governors of Jalisco and Tamaulipas urgently asked the Departamento de Gobernación to stop the emigration, for it was hurting their industries and agriculture." Gobernación only partly complied with the urgent request by issuing a circular warning braceros, as it had at previous times, that conditions were adverse for them in their neighbor country and that they should remain at home. But as usual, the counsel had little effect. . . .

Amid the clamor of the press and of some of the governors to put a stop to the drain on Mexico's "life blood," Pastor Rouaix, Secretary of Agriculture, in March 1920 issued a statement which drew intense criticism from the press. The secretary in an interview stated that "the emigration could not be an embarrassment to Mexico because the braceros' only thoughts were to return to Mexico." George Summerlin, Chargé d'Affaires at Mexico City, reported that because of such statements by Mexican government officials, the Mexican press clamored for effective control of the emigration. As a result, the Mexican government made an official statement to the press in an attempt to justify its position regarding emigration and the measures it had taken to regulate it. . . .

The Mexican government continued in its declared policy of trying to inform braceros of the difficulties to be encountered by emigrating. It was hoped that, in this way, legislation would be unnecessary. The governors on March 25, 1920, were instructed by the Departamento de Gobernación "to wage a publicity campaign to stop the emigration." Mexicans did not cease crossing the border, for by August 1920 El Universal declared "the situation from the Mexican point of view was profound and grave. The emigration ought to be stopped at all costs."

The main reason for not legislating on the emigration problem was made clear by Plutarco Elías Calles, who was Secretary of Gobernación and later succeeded Obregón as president. Calles pointed out that there were no existing laws prohibiting emigration, and the problem could not be solved by merely passing and promulgating laws because the hungry and unemployed would clandestinely cross the frontier anyway. . . .

MEXICAN LABOR
IN THE UNITED STATES

The changing nature of Mexican immigration to the United States was noted as early as the first decade of this century. Victor Clark, in his pioneering work on Mexican labor in the United States, discusses the far-reaching implications of the transition from an immigration of temporary laborers to one of permanent settlers.

So long as the Mexican immigration is transient it is not likely to have much influence upon the United States, except as it regulates the labor market in a limited number of occupations and probably within a restricted area; for transient labor is not likely to be largely employed beyond a certain radius from El Paso and the Rio Grande, or to enter lines of employment in which it competes with citizen labor. But the Mexicans are making their homes in the United States in increasing numbers and, being assimilated by the Spanish-speaking population of the Southwest, are forming the civic substratum of our border states. The proportion of the immigrants who ultimately take up a permanent residence north of the border is entirely a matter of estimate. As this immigration has assumed importance since the census of 1900, figures derived from the census reports do not indicate present conditions and tendencies.

Up to 1900 very few Mexicans had emigrated beyond the border states and territories. For instance, Colorado, which now employs several hundred Old Mexicans transiently, had but 274 residents of that nationality in the last census year. Louisiana had 488. Colorado, however, had 10,222 residents, mostly in the

From Bulletin #78, Bureau of Labor, by Victor Clark. Washington: U.S. Government Printing Office, 1908.

mining counties around Trinidad, who had been born in New Mexico.

Between 1880 and 1890, the Mexican-born population increased more slowly than the total population; but during the following decade it increased at a more rapid rate than the total population, both in the United States as a whole and in all the border districts except Arizona. In 1880, Mexicans comprised 1.01 percent of the total foreign-born population of the United States; in 1890, .9 percent; and in 1900, 1 percent, showing the same general tendency of variation as to the total population. Of the more than five thousand immigrants who passed through El Paso in September 1907, not one expressed the intention of becoming an American citizen. The only one of several score questioned at the immigration station who had this intention was a skilled mechanic, of quite a different class from the main body of immigrants. Nevertheless, Mexicans are settling permanently, especially in Texas and California. Two persons in a position to be unusually well informed upon the subject, one of them a general official of a railway carrying immigrants to the frontier, estimated that 50 percent of those who visited the United States finally made their home there. On the Mexican Central Railway, which moves more immigrants than any other single road in Mexico, the official estimate of third-class passengers (laborers) crossing the frontier northward during the twelve months ending with August 1907 was fifty thousand and the return traffic during the same period was estimated to be thirty-seven thousand. However, the proportion of those passing through El Paso who return is larger than of those crossing the lower Rio Grande, because so much of the former labor is employed on railways and in mines in the desert, where there is little temptation to make a permanent home. Immigrants through El Paso are seldom accompanied by their families, while many women and children cross at Laredo, especially to pick cotton. A prominent Mexican merchant in San Antonio, Texas, said, "Mexicans who have come to the United States seldom go back to stay, because conditions are better here, and because they are not kept down so much in this country." The superintendent of public instruction in Arizona stated that in the southern counties of that territory nearly one half the children enrolled in public schools have foreign-born parents, mostly Mexicans, but that very few of these children were born in Mexico. In California, Mexican laborers were said to be accompanied by their families, and to be settled in little colonies near a number of the larger towns; but in Colorado there was no evidence that the immigrant Mexicans have come to remain. An evidence of increasing settlement in Texas is the large number of excursionists that return to Mexico each year to attend the religious festivals in Aguascalientes and in Mexico City. These people, though Mexican-born, buy return tickets to Texas.

The transition in Texas from an immigration of temporary laborers to one of settlers was thus described by a railroad official who had observed it from the outset: "Ten years ago our Mexican immigrants were chiefly men. It was rare to see a woman among those who came through here from any distance down the line. About one thousand men who had been in the United States and returned to Mexico began to bring back their families with them. Usually they were also accompanied by a number of single men, or married men without their families, who had never before been in this country. Most of the men who had families with them did not go back the following season, but the men without their families did, and some of them in turn came back the next year with their families to remain permanently. So the process goes on, with, I believe, a larger proportion of women and children among the immigrants each year, and a larger proportion remaining in this country."

The Bishop of the Texas diocese (Roman Catholic) stated that many thousands of immigrants from Old Mexico were settling in his parishes, and that the increase of Mexican population was general throughout the southern part of the state.

Probably a conservative estimate of the proportion of immigrants remaining permanently in the United States would be from one fourth to one third. The number is probably in the neighborhood of twenty thousand per annum. With the lack of more definite data than is possessed at present, the number can only be estimated—and the estimate has possibly a wide margin of error—because this annual increment to the permanent Mexican population of the country settles over such a wide area that its presence is hardly perceptible except in large city colonies.

Americans of Mexican descent take an active part in local politics and have their bosses and machines like English-speaking Americans. In New Mexico they were said to make very fair citizens, though more apt to be loyal to personal leaders than to political parties. The immigrants, even if they make their home in this country, seldom become naturalized. The records at San Antonio show that before the federal naturalization law went into operation the number of persons with German names who became citizens was eight or nine times the number of those bearing Spanish names, though the Mexican population of Bexar County is over one third the total foreign-born residents. In the entire state in 1900, the Mexican population was 39.6 percent of the total foreign-born population, and doubtless has been increasing relatively since that year. Those Mexicans who become naturalized have usually resided in the United States for many years, sometimes for the greater part of their lives. It is not unusual for several persons of the same family name to acquire citizenship at the same time, probably to facilitate the settling of an estate or for some other legal purpose.

Spanish-speaking citizens consider themselves socially superior to the immigrants, and rather pride themselves on being Americans. There is for this reason less social intermingling than the identity of language, religion, and customs might lead one to expect. The "Americanization" of the Spanish-speaking population of the Southwest is proceeding much more rapidly at present than heretofore, partly because these people are themselves migrating temporarily or permanently to English-speaking sections of the country, and partly because of the large immigration from other parts of the union. The history of Las Vegas, New Mexico, indicates how this change affects civic ideals. The original Mexican town in the river valley antedates the advent of the American. When the railway was built, an American town grew up in its vicinity, possibly a mile from the center of the older village. Later the two places were incorporated as a single city. But this arrangement was unpopular with the Mexicans, used to more primitive political arrangements and averse to taxation, and through their influence the town was disincorporated. The American town then went ahead, incorporated separately, constructed public works, and built up an excellent system of public schools, including a high school, housed in fine buildings. After several years the Mexican town finally incorporated separately and now is following the example of its neighbor in the matter of improvements and school facilities. So the New Mexican and largely Spanish-speaking community is now taxing itself more heavily than many a town in the East for public education, and has issued bonds and erected creditable schoolhouses. This case is fairly representative of what is taking place wherever the railway and American example are bringing the influence of other sections of the country to bear upon the native population. An educational officer, who himself spoke Spanish fluently, whose duties made him familiar with conditions in the southern part of Colorado, said that a marked language change had occurred within ten years, so that while formerly it was comparatively rare to meet a person of Mexican race who spoke English, it was now rare to meet a young "Mexican" who was not familiar with that language.

These changes to American habits of life in the home and to American civic ideals in the community, coupled with the gradual acquisition of English in the public schools, are all recent. The public-school system of New Mexico is but fifteen years old, and railways have been in the territory less than a generation. They have as yet influenced appreciably only that part of the so-called Mexican population that has been born in the United States. At present, the immigrant Mexican does not seem likely to be assimilated by our own people; that is, actual fusion of blood appears to be remote. But barring this, which may not be permanent, he may learn to understand our institutions and adopt our habits of thought and action in public affairs.

THE MEXICAN IMMIGRANT

The implications of "race mingling" as it related to Mexican immigration periodically emerged as an issue in American politics. In 1921, the Honorable James L. Slayden, a Texas politician, warned of a potential threat to American society he saw in Mexican immigration. The racism expressed by Mr. Slayden was not limited to politicians or to Texas but represents an attitude prevalent throughout Southwestern Anglo society.

. . . The importance of the question of immigration from Mexico can hardly be overestimated. It has a direct bearing on the general subject of immigration which Congress has been considering for years and which has not yet been solved. It is tied up with the greatest of all of our problems, that of race mingling. It may be, roughly speaking, considered from three angles, economical, racial, and political.

Economically considered, the Mexican immigrant is usually well received. Until a very recent time there has been no real protest, for he nearly always went straight to the farms where his labor was most urgently needed, or into domestic service where clamorous housewives welcomed him in spite of his hopeless inefficiency. . . .

This steady incoming of an alien race, not altogether white, is welcomed by some Americans, tolerated by others, and utterly abhorred by those who look beyond the next cotton crop or the betterment of railway lines.

Large planters short of labor, because of the extraordinary hegira of Negroes in the last few years, know their value and welcome the Mexican immigrants as they would welcome fresh arrivals from the Congo, without a thought of the social and

From "Some Observations on Mexican Immigration," by James L. Slayden. *Annals of the American Academy of Political and Social Science* (January 1921).

political embarrassment to their country. On the other hand, the small Southern farmers (and they are the greater number) who cultivate their land with the help of their children do not want the Mexicans and would gladly see the movement of Negroes go on until the last one was settled in New England or Illinois or wherever they may be most happy, prosperous, and welcome.

But both Negroes and Mexicans are here yet in large numbers, and close observers begin to detect a feeling of jealousy and dislike between them. In Texas and other Southern states the Mexican is classed as white in public conveyances, hotels, and places of amusement, which does not make for good feeling between him and the Negro, and the Mexican, even of very low class, is not much inclined to social intimacy with the Negro.

That to substitute one for the other may be jumping from the frying pan into the fire is a thought that will intrude itself.

Racially speaking, the Mexican immigrant does carry an element of danger, for it cannot be denied that with the American masses who come in contact with him there exists a certain latent hostility. That this prejudice is mutual is amply shown day by day by the tone of Mexican newspapers, by the frantic appeals by the Mexican demagogue, by the testimony of travelers or American residents in Mexico, and by certain fantastic projects entertained from time to time in official circles during the administration of President Carranza. That he believed it possible to excite the American Negroes to revolt is quite true, and that his emissaries undertook to execute the foolish scheme cannot be doubted.

Less than eight years ago a party of Mexican revolutionists, as they called themselves, invaded Texas, declared the state reannexed to Mexico, proclaimed the "Plan of San Diego," and promised social and political supremacy to the Negroes. They killed a few citizens of the United States, derailed a train and murdered the passengers, and destroyed property (the invariable curtain raiser to a Mexican revolution), but some straight-shooting Texans soon convinced them of the error of their way, and those who could sit a horse hurried back to the southern side of the Rio Bravo.

Politically the Mexicans were vastly more important in Texas a few years ago than they are now. The white population has

increased much more rapidly than immigrants have come or
Mexican children been born. This has made them politically
impotent in spite of the fact that they are easily gathered into
clubs or "juntas" and voted solidly by their leaders. Amended
election laws also had a part in destroying their political power.
Every voter now pays a poll tax many months before the election
and must make his own ballot. Many Mexicans will not do the first
and cannot do the last. This may not be true of the next
generation, as they attend our public schools without cost and are
even provided with textbooks as freely as the children of our own
citizens. Until very recently citizens of Bexar County, just outside
of San Antonio, men of business in the city and taxpayers have
been compelled to pay a special fee if their children attended the
city schools, while those of Mexican refugees, driven from home
by revolutions, had textbooks and schooling without cost. This
condition had to be changed because of the growing indignation
on the part of the overburdened American taxpayers.

In Texas the word "Mexican" is used to indicate the race, not a
citizen or subject of the country. There are probably 250,000
Mexicans in Texas who were born in the state, but they are
"Mexicans," just as all blacks are Negroes though they may have
five generations of American ancestors.

Most Mexicans are Indians or mestizos (mixed white and Indian
blood), and between them and the other inhabitants of Mexico
there is a sharply defined social distinction. The upper classes, of
European ancestry, are frequently educated in Spain, France, or
the United States, and few of them become immigrants unless
forced out by revolutions, when they go to San Antonio, El Paso,
or Los Angeles. At home they are the merchants, big planters,
bankers, and professional men.

With rare exceptions these people stay at home, look after their
private affairs, and do not meddle with politics. They would make
good and useful citizens of any country. When one of them does
go in for politics (or revolution, which is the same thing in
Mexico), he does more mischief, because above his wicked heart is
a cleverer head. He easily becomes the leader of the low-browed,
poverty-stricken *peón* class, and by perfervid appeals to the
prejudice of the thoughtless and uneducated mass of Indians and

the promise of an impossible utopia quickly converts them into murderous bandits. Resounding phrases about the Constitution, whether that of 1857 or that of Querétaro, makes no difference—and the rights of the Indians, mixed with contemptuous remarks about the "gringos" and the hated "Colossus of the North" soon can make fiends of otherwise quiet and useful men.

Of all people trying to conduct government, the Mexican is most in need of wise and firm leaders. Of course it is perilous to say it at this time when the "uplifter" is abroad in the land, but to the writer (and to most others who know Mexico) it seems essential if the country is ever to be lifted out of carnage and chaos, to have some such man as Porfirio Díaz at the head of affairs. After fifty-six years of the most chaotic and bloody conditions, he did create an orderly and nation-building government, and that is what Mexico must have or perish. Many people who know him hope that such a man has been found in Alvaro Obregón.

These are the people, high and low, from whom thousands of immigrants are coming to the United States. What it may mean for Americans in the future no one can tell. Probably our safety and peace lie in the fact that as yet so few of them, comparatively, are coming.

II
MIGRANT TRAILS

Mexican Americans continued to be the mainstay of agricultural labor in the Western United States during the prosperity decade of the twenties. Need for their labor continued to be high, and by 1920 the Southwest, especially Texas, had become a vast reservoir of cheap, unskilled workers. In Texas the Mexican population jumped from about 125,000 in 1910 to more than 250,000 in 1920 and then to 680,000 in 1930.

From this area Mexican and Mexican American workers were recruited in the early 1920's by Midwestern railroads, agricultural interests, and industry. During this period beet growers, railroads, and steel companies began bringing Mexican workers north, either to fill their labor needs or to act as strikebreakers. Many of these people subsequently moved into such areas as meat packing, trucking, restaurants, dry cleaning, and other service industries; and as a result Detroit, Omaha, Kansas City, Chicago, St. Paul, and other Midwestern centers began to develop sizable Mexican barrios. By 1928 Illinois had nearly twenty thousand Mexicans, Minnesota had seven thousand, and Michigan about six thousand.

In California Governor Clement C. Young's Mexican Fact-Finding Committee, after two years of research, completed a detailed report which the governor characterized as "unquestionably . . . one of the most exhaustive and most valuable ever issued by any of the Departments of the California state government." This report indicated that, while the majority of Mexican Americans found employment in agriculture, many thousands also were working on railroads, in construction, in manufacturing, and in other such diverse industries as brick manufacturing, clothing, slaughterhouses, iron foundries, saw-mills, bakeries, and millinery. This exhaustive report originated from governmental concern about the effects of heavy Mexican immigration to California in the 1920's. Nationally, increased Mexican immigration and reports of large numbers of illegal aliens in the United States were also arousing wider interest and concern. Inevitably, this migration led to a rising tide of anti-Mexican feelings, as Mexicans became the largest, most recent flood of unskilled or low-skilled immigrant workers enter-ing the United States.

As a result, a negative stereotype developed and Mexican Americans became victims of discrimination in social intercourse as well as in employment. In Texas, for example, violence and discriminatory practices against Mexican Americans became so widespread that by the late 1920's the Secretary of State warned the governor that action would have to be taken to protect Mexican Americans.

During 1921 debate in Congress on immigration reform intro-duced discussion concerning the inclusion of Western Hemisphere countries in a general quota system. Then in 1924 a more thorough and careful revision of United States immigration policies was undertaken by Congress; at this time a concerted effort was made to place Mexican immigrants under quota. Hearings on immigration held during this period saw Western railroad and agricultural interests argue against such a quota, pleading for continuation of an open-border policy on Mexican workers. Only labor unions voiced strong opposition at this time to unlimited admission of Mexican immigrants. Although the 1924 Immigration Act did not limit Mexican immigration, establish-ment of a border patrol in the same year may be considered a small and partial victory for those Americans wishing to stem the flow of Mexicans. A second minor victory for this group came in 1929 when, after years of discussion and debate, Congress passed a bill making illegal entrance a criminal offense.

As greater numbers of Mexicans continued to swell cheap labor reservoirs, Anglo-American negative attitudes toward Mexicans and Mexican Americans spread. They were looked upon stereotypically as phlegmatic, docile, contented laborers who worked from sunup to sundown without complaint, as long as American farmers needed them, and who then quietly returned to their native Mexico or to San Antonio, El Paso, or Los Angeles. However, American opinion of Mexican workers was not uniform; in addition to those patronizing employers who saw them as faithful servitors, there were those who considered them an inferior but acceptable substitute for white Anglo-Saxon labor.

Increasing numbers of Mexican immigrants during the years 1927 and 1928 led the Immigration and Naturalization Service to institute a policy of administrative restriction. Early in 1929, American consuls in Mexico were instructed by the State Department to enforce more rigorously existing legislative restrictions on immigration. However, the stock-market crash of October 1929, with its succeeding economic depression, reversed the trend of Mexican immigration to the United States. This economic disaster accomplished the goals of the new, restrictive policy.

MEXICANS NORTH
OF THE RIO GRANDE

Mexicans have long played an essential role in Western farm labor; their early role in Midwestern and Eastern industrial centers has been less generally recognized. Paul S. Taylor, long-time expert and scholar of Mexican labor in the United States, traces the extension of Mexican labor, via the railroads, from its traditional Southwestern reservoirs to the colonias in the industrial centers of the United States.

From "Mexicans North of the Rio Grande," by Paul S. Taylor. *The Survey*, 66 (May 1, 1931).

The Mexicans are here—from California to Pennsylvania, from Texas to Minnesota. They are scattered on isolated sections along our Western railroads in clusters of from two to five families; they are established in colonies in the agricultural West and Southwest which form, in places, from one to two thirds of the local population. They have penetrated the heart of industrial America; in the steel region on the southern shore of Lake Michigan they are numbered in thousands; in Eastern industrial centers by hundreds. And they have made Los Angeles the second largest Mexican city in the world. . . .

A large part, probably the majority, of the Mexican population is migratory. It is the most mobile element in our labor supply. It moves in seasonal cycles covering hundreds, even thousands, of miles. . . .

The Southwest is the great reservoir of migratory Mexican labor. It winters there, or across the line in Mexico. Throughout the postwar years, the pull of the labor market of Wyoming and Pennsylvania was felt on the mesa central of Mexico, six or eight hundred miles below the Rio Grande. On the river, El Paso, Laredo, and Nogales form a secondary tier of labor centers—gateways to the United States. Every spring, from San Antonio, Fort Worth, Kansas City, Albuquerque, Phoenix, Los Angeles, and lately from Chicago, St. Louis, Omaha, Denver, Sacramento, and in smaller numbers from a score of other cities, Mexicans are gathered up by *los enganchistas* and shipped out for a summer's work on the tracks at from 35 to 40 cents an hour in Nevada, the Dakotas, Kansas, Illinois, Ohio, or Pennsylvania. For with the spring the railroads resume maintenance and construction work. Skeleton section crews are augmented, and large extra gangs of fifty, sixty, or more Mexican solos are organized for special projects. These men live in the converted boxcars so familiar to all who travel, rolling from job to job, working in places remote or near, town or desert, strumming their guitars of an evening and singing their Mexican songs.

In May the sugar beets of the North need thinning—and the Mexicans of the Southwest are called upon to furnish their quota of hand laborers, as the German-Russians who preceded them are no longer immigrating. For this work families—families as large as possible—are wanted. They are transported by the trainload to the Arkansas and South Platte Valleys and the Western Slope of Colorado, to Wyoming, Idaho, Montana, Nebraska, the Dakotas, Iowa, Minnesota, and Michigan. When they reach the beet fields they are scattered out on the farms, each family under contract to tend its allotted fields at from $23 to $25 an acre. . . . In the winter the tide of beet workers, like that of the railroad laborers, recedes. But an increasing number stay on, responding to the stimulation of beet farmers or of sugar companies who offer houses rent free, or of opportunities to build in colony tracts. In the valley of the South Platte, in northeastern Colorado, the number of Mexican families so remaining rose in six years from 537 to 2,084. Other families winter in increasing numbers in the cities of the North. Many drift into industry, particularly in Detroit.

The maturing cotton crop puts wheels under Mexican labor in Texas. They come down the Rio Grande in late June and July to Brownsville to chop and pick the first cotton of the season. In July and August seemingly most of the Mexicans of the state converge on Corpus Christi. . . . As the cotton season opens in other parts of the state, the Mexicans move on. Guided by the United States Employment Service, by the experience of other years, by correspondence with farmers, and by their own grapevine telegraph, they take to the highways by single families, groups of families, or by caravans led by *contratistas* who know enough English and have sufficient initiative and experience to take the lead in finding employment and making labor contracts for the others. . . . At San Antonio the stream of pickers divides. Some work westward with the cotton to San Angelo and Sweetwater. Others make their way northward by stages to Taylor and Waco, thence west to Dallas and across west Texas even as far as Amarillo in the Panhandle. By the latter part of the year the cotton of the state is harvested, and the cycle of migration is closed by the return of the Mexicans to the places they call home.

A similar flow and ebb recurs annually in California. In May the Mexicans move northward from the Imperial Valley. They "follow the fruit," thinning apricots and peaches, advancing as the season advances. They are joined by those who have delayed in order to harvest the cantaloupes, and together with thousands of Mexicans from all over Southern California they surge northward to practically all the valleys of the state. Most of them ascend the ridge of Tehachapi and pour over into the great valley of California. In cars of all makes and all ages, used Fords predominating, with the entire family inside and the washtub and lantern tied on outside, they move along the highways, stopping in the hot sun by the roadside to repair blowouts, on grades to let the engine cool, or under eucalyptus trees to camp for the night. From June to August the Mexicans are busy thinning fruit; then picking fruit. They work in the San Joaquin Valley, around Bakersfield, Hanford, and Fresno, or they cross the Pacheco Pass to Hollister and Gilroy; they invade the Santa Clara Valley at the southern end of San Francisco Bay, and tongues of the flood pass on northward to the Napa Valley above the bay, and up the Sacramento Valley into the northern interior of the state.

In late August the grape harvest, centering in Fresno, sucks into its vineyards Mexicans who have been dispersed in the fruit, together with the fresh recruits from over the ridge to the south, some even from the states lying southeast of California. Mexicans, Japanese, Filipinos, "whites" from California, Texas, and Oklahoma, a few Indians from the mountains, and Negroes, and still fewer Chinese and Hindus all enroll in the army of pickers which strips the vines. In the orchards under the fruit trees, down on the riverbanks by the roadside or in the town park, in tents on the ranches of their employers, with or without tents elsewhere—sometimes as well without because of the heat—with or without water and sanitary facilities at hand, amid clouds of flies, you can see them preparing their tortillas and frijoles over open fireplaces or on portable stoves, and heating large galvanized iron tubs of water in which to do the family washing.

By the end of September, leaving a large nucleus to finish the grape harvest, the pickers began to scatter. Many return to Los Angeles and Southern California for urban employment, and for the walnut and citrus harvests; others return to the Imperial Valley for the oncoming lettuce season or for cotton picking. The expansion of cotton in the San Joaquin Valley extends the season of employment in that region and, with the additional attractions of weatherproof housing and school facilities which are increasingly provided, operates to increase its year-round Mexican population. But most of the tide which moved across the Tehachapi recedes southward during the fall and winters in Southern California. In February, probably 80 percent or more of the Mexican population of the state is found there.

The American public has known that, since the war, Mexicans have been playing an important role in these hand-labor operations of our modern agriculture, but it has been less generally realized that important nuclei of Mexican immigrants are found in the industrial centers of the Midwest and East. . . .

Mexicans form a large proportion of track laborers in the Chicago-Calumet area; signs in Spanish advertising track work are general on Canal and Madison Streets, and Mexicans are conspicuous among those sauntering by, or loitering before, offices who are fair game for the "man-catchers." They form an important element in the common labor supply of the steel mills, rising in one case to 30 percent. To a lesser extent than in steel they are found in the packing industry. In considerable numbers Mexicans work in Michigan, not only in the beet fields but in the automobile and other industries of that state. Small outpost colonies of two hundred, three hundred, or perhaps more are scattered through the principal steel centers as far east as Ohio, Pennsylvania, New York, and New Jersey. . . .

The rapid influx of a large laboring class, migratory, prolific with primitive standards of living, different in race and culture, is bound to disturb the social equilibrium. Whether this disturbance raises "problems" depends upon one's point of view.

Take for instance the schooling of rural Mexican children. Is their non-attendance a problem? The farmers want their labor, the parents their children's earnings; it costs money and effort to put them into school and causes a lot of disturbance after they get there. If you think Mexican children should have the pressure of the American state behind their education, it is a problem. If you do not, their non-attendance may mitigate local difficulties in getting the kind of farm labor you have a hard time finding anyone else to do. Said an Imperial Valley farm manager:

> If they were miserable or unhappy, I would say, "All right, Mr. Educator, do your damndest." But the Mexicans are a happy people, happier than we are; they don't want responsibility, they want just to

float along, sing songs, smoke cigarettes. Education doesn't make them any happier; most of them continue the same sort of work at the same wages as if they had never attended school. It only makes them dissatisfied, and teaches them to read the wrong kind of literature (I.W.W.) and listen to the wrong kind of talk.

In the cotton belt of Texas and the sugar-beet fields of the North, non-attendance generally is not treated as a problem; in California and in cities elsewhere, it is, and Mexican children are generally checked up on and, if need be, compelled to go to school.

If Mexican children do go to school, Americans of almost all points of view see their presence as a problem. Differences of language, culture, class, race, standards of cleanliness, rates of educational progress between the children of the Mexican laborer and those of the American farmer or townsman raise difficulties. Shall their children be educated in the same schools, or shall they be separated? If separated, shall the separation continue through four grades or twelve? American communities answer these questions in the light of educational and hygienic considerations, financial and administrative expediency, and racial feeling. With such a diversity of viewpoints, the resulting situations are varied, as can be imagined. They range from separation through the first grade to separation through high school; from excellent school buildings and teaching staffs to inadequate shacks inadequately equipped and staffed; while the local American schools may be operated with the aid of state money allotted to the district because of the numerical count of its Mexican children. Sometimes no school at all is provided for the Mexicans. On the other hand, notably in larger cities and in rural communities under the adult-education system in California, men and women as well as children are reached by classes which are genuinely appreciated.

MEXICAN LABOR COLONY AT BETHLEHEM, PENNSYLVANIA

An early study of an Eastern Mexican industrial community, undertaken by Paul S. Taylor, indicates the difficulties encountered by Mexicans and Mexican Americans settling outside of their traditional cultural boundaries. A review of Taylor's study summarizes his research in this important Eastern colonia.

The Mexican colony in Bethlehem, Pennsylvania, was built up mainly by the transportation from the Southwest of Mexican workers under contract with the Bethlehem Steel Company. In 1923 the settlement reached its peak population of about one thousand. Since then its numbers have rapidly declined, and in 1929 there were probably 350 or 400 in the colony, with those arriving and leaving about balancing each other. A monograph dealing with this colony forms the sixth of the published researches made by Paul S. Taylor on a grant from the Social Science Research Council and issued by the University of California. He made three visits to Bethlehem—the first in the early part of 1928 and the last in the early part of 1930.

Previous to 1923 there were only a few Mexicans in Bethlehem. In the spring of that year, however, there was an industrial revival and the steel company's idle furnaces were again started up. In order to meet the increasing demand for labor, efforts were made to secure Mexicans, with the result that between April 6 and May 30, 1923, there were 912 Mexican men, 29 women, and 7 children transported from Texas to Bethlehem. Mexican workers were also sent to other plants of the company.

The recruiting was done through Texas employment agencies

From *Monthly Labor Review* (October 1931).

cooperating with the Mexican consulate general in San Antonio.
One of the company's Spanish employees was detailed to Texas to
aid in procuring and handling the desired labor. A representative
of the Bethlehem Steel Company and the Mexican consul general
in San Antonio signed the contract covering the Mexican nationals
shipped out of that city, as the latter wished to protect his
departing countrymen. . . .

The coming of the Mexicans was without doubt a shock to the
people of Bethlehem and gave rise to exaggerated statements
about this newly imported labor. It was rumored that these
workers were strikebreakers taking the places of natives who were
reported to have left the plant demanding higher wages. Some
weeks before there had been danger of serious labor disturbances.
The company representative, however, regarded these reports as
propaganda to keep Mexicans from coming to Bethlehem and
denied the existence of a strike. An investigation was made by the
Mexican consul at Philadelphia, who found conditions satisfactory
to the imported laborers.

In 1929 a minor official of the company said, in reference to the
attitude of the other workers toward the newcomers, "The other
employees knew there was a shortage of labor, so they accepted
the Mexicans." That the Bethlehem workers were not pleased at
the advent of the Mexicans is quite obvious, however, the writer
thinks, from a newspaper item published about the time of their
arrival. The claim that there was a dearth of labor at this period is
corroborated by the Pennsylvania State Employment Office
report under the date of March 15, 1923, that "in the iron and
steel industry it is impossible to supply the needs for unskilled
workers." . . .

Some Mexicans come to Bethlehem in search of work because
they hear of the large steel mills in that locality. If they get jobs
they stay; if not, they leave. Considerable numbers of them have
come to Bethlehem because they had relatives already employed
in the town. Frequently, money has been forwarded to Mexico or
Texas to enable them to make the long trip. A remarkable
instance is that of one of the group shipped from Texas in 1923
who has been followed by seven brothers and three sisters,

together with the families of those who were married, making a total of thirty persons.

As soon as the Mexicans reached Bethlehem in 1923, they began to scatter to look for more attractive jobs than the steel company offered. The greatest number on the payroll of that company in any month of those who were originally brought from Texas in 1923 was 790 in May of that year. By the middle of the summer there were 24 percent less, by November the number was 53 percent under the maximum, and by the close of the same year 71 percent.

In the spring of 1930 only forty-six Mexicans who were known to belong to the original group shipped in 1923 remained on the company's rolls. Estimates of the total number of Mexicans employed in 1930 range from 90 to 150. Including Mexicans born in the United States, the writer considers 125 a conservative figure.

> Upon arrival in Bethlehem the original contingents of Mexicans were concentrated in bunkhouses in a labor camp. In a little over a year, however, the scattering of Mexicans to other localities in the East, their return to the Southwest or Mexico, and their dispersion to other domiciles in Bethlehem depopulated the camp. The company then ceased to provide special arrangements for boarding Mexicans. Some of the solos were already boarding with Mexican families; now they are found boarding with Polish, Wendish, Slovak, Spanish, and Mexican families. Some of them live in groups, renting and housekeeping for themselves, each man buying his own food and doing his own cooking. Most of the Mexicans live in town houses, but a number, both of families and solos, still live in company-owned houses at the coke plant.

The greater number of the Mexicans of Bethlehem live scattered about the southern front of the works. They are not segregated in such clearly defined districts as characterize Mexican colonization in the Southwestern part of the country. . . .

Almost all of the Mexican employees of the steel company are laborers. There are, however, a very few skilled mechanics and semiskilled workers among them. According to a statement of a Mexican, there are artisans among the Mexican laborers—carpenters and machinists—but they are not asked to follow their trades. This informant added, however, that these men do not speak English.

On the whole, the comments of numbers of executives on the Mexicans' industrial qualities were favorable. One executive, who had more direct experience with Mexican labor than some of the other reporting officials, made the following statement:

> I don't think that the Mexicans are inherently different from other people. They are very easy to handle if they are given just treatment and are greeted with a smile. We rule them, but we are just. We tell them what to do and expect them to do it; but we don't worry them with what not to do. I take a personal interest in each Mexican, and have obtained their confidence. If they are sick or in trouble of any sort, they usually come and tell me. If they are sick, we send them to the hospital. . . .

Prejudice against Mexicans in Bethlehem because of their color apparently was not strong and only occasional, if it had any existence. No color distinction was reported in the case of the few Mexican children in the schools.

In 1927 a characteristic mutual-benefit society was organized but expired. It was succeeded by another, which in 1930 claimed a membership of 120. The initiation fee was 50 cents and the monthly dues $1. After a waiting period, sick benefits of $8 a week are paid for thirteen weeks and longer if the society votes approval. The death benefit is $100 plus a collection of $1 from each member.

Only a very small percentage of the Mexicans living in Bethlehem or in other parts of the United States have become American citizens, most of them expecting to return to Mexico. However, in Bethlehem they learn English more rapidly and adopt the characteristic American urban garb more readily than in the rural Southwest. In 1929 four Mexicans had bought homes in Bethlehem. The town also had a Mexican grocery, a barber shop, a pool hall, and a stand for selling Mexican newspapers. A considerable number of the Mexican workers buy company stock.

No criticisms were made in Bethlehem concerning the cleanliness of Mexicans, and the record of Mexican children in school, according to the reports of teachers and school officials, "was at least equal to that of the other children, a large proportion of whom were of European parentage."

Mexicans take little part in politics. Voting is restricted to the few, eighteen in number, according to a report made early in 1930, who are naturalized citizens or were born in this country.

Apart from their grievances against foremen of European stock, little friction existed between Mexicans and other nationalities except the Poles. Intermarriages of Mexican men with women of other nationalities were reported as comparatively frequent. None of the Mexican women had intermarried. The Mexicans have some sense of kinship with other Latin Americans living in Bethlehem. Some Mexicans were included among the members of a Spanish club. Spaniards were eligible for membership in the Mexican society, although when the inquiry was made in the early part of 1929 none had applied for admission. . . .

DETROIT MEXICANS

Midwestern Chicano communities expanded rapidly during the twenties, as increased industrialization and declining European immigration caused employers to seek new sources of labor. Norman D. Humphrey delineates development of the Detroit colonia.

Mexicans settled in the United States, especially after 1910, for two major reasons. They felt the pull of the economic advantages to be found north of the Rio Grande, with all their attendant stereotypes of wish-fulfillment, and they sought to flee from the dismal economic future and the political instability for Mexican peasants, which offered very little hope for political safety or economic security. In this connection Bogardus's comment is relevant: "The incentives to Mexicans to immigrate to the United

From "The Migration and Settlement of Detroit Mexicans," by Norman D. Humphrey. *Economic Geography*, 19 (October 1943).

States have been chiefly economic. The higher wages have been effective stimuli: three dollars a day, for instance, in 1929 looked large to a Mexican accustomed to receiving the equivalent of fifty cents. . . ."

The bulk of Mexican emigration to the United States came from the central part of Mexico. Michoacán, Guanajuato, Jalisco, and Zacatecas were the states which furnished more than 50 percent of the legal entries into the United States, even though they were not the most heavily populated. As a matter of fact, of the three states of the republic that have more than one million inhabitants, Jalisco is the only one to provide proportionally a high rate of emigration. The "Cristero Revolution" of the 1920's, with its attendant disorders, strongly stimulated Jaliscan emigration. For other sections of Mexico, however, the dynamic factor in the outward flow of population is to be found in the peonage system on the great estates that effectively precluded economic advancement for the vast majority. Peasants thus came to the United States primarily as unskilled laborers drawn from the underprivileged.

As high as 60 percent of the immigrants in 1926 were laborers, while thereafter fewer were unskilled, though the unskilled still constituted about one third of the total group. Persons having trades included butchers, cooks, bakers, shoemakers, tanners, masons, mechanics, molders, boilermakers, and miners. But even these individuals who had skills applicable to the Mexican economic milieu tended to become common laborers in the United States as a consequence of the specialized character of American production. The majority of immigrants were males. A typical migrant was young and in the "prime of life," a situation related to the fact that he usually married after coming to the country and that a majority of "first children" of Mexican immigrants were born in the United States. On the basis of using the place of birth of the first child as evidence of the point of origin of the family (as distinct from the individual), it may be concluded from the records of 420 families enumerated by the Detroit School Census of 1935 that only 70 had their origin in Mexico, while 350 originated in the United States. In 72 cases, the oldest child was born in Texas, while in 190 cases the first child was born in Detroit. It is clear from these data that most children of Mexican parents were born in the United States and also that most Mexican couples living in Detroit came to the United States as individuals outside of marriage, or else came previous to the birth of the first child. Opportunity beckoned to the young and venturesome. Migrants trickled slowly into this country prior to World War I; and after the stoppage of European immigration, they flowed in a veritable stream. This influx ran its course for a decade. The increment of Mexicans to the American population is illustrated by the facts that in 1920 the Mexican population in Michigan was twenty times greater than in 1910, and in 1930 the 1,422,533 Mexicans in the United States constituted one twelfth of the Mexican population of the world.

Significant in the stimulation of emigration were the facilitators of illegal entrance, the smugglers or "coyotes," the contractors or *enganchistas* who provided peons with jobs over the border, and, perhaps more basically, the farmers and railroads of the American Southwest and Midwest who required cheap labor for their enterprises. This included labor recruiting in Mexico and in Texas for beet-field work in the United States. Illustrative of the work of these *enganchistas* and coyotes are the following facts drawn from a welfare-case record:

> Mr. L. said that the first time he entered the United States (1915) he paid five cents for his bridge toll and that that was the only technicality encountered. The second time he sought entrance, however (in 1920), an American immigration authority attempted to assess him a head tax of $10.00. He did not have the money, and he turned back, but a "coyote" observed his predicament and put him in touch with an "enganchista" who offered Mr. L. a job. With a job assured, the "coyote" smuggled Mr. L. across the border.

Some indication of the ease with which a person might enter the United States illegally but without the aid of a coyote is shown in the following case:

> Mr. R. said that he crossed the bridge at El Paso, Texas, in 1924 and when he was asked from what town he came, he answered El Paso, but he did not explain that he came from El Paso, Mexico, and not from El Paso, Texas. He was allowed to go through and took the train to Colorado for work in the beet fields there.

Individual reasons and motives for Mexicans to come to the United States are naturally more diverse than the more societal factors enumerated above. A case suggesting such personal factors is the following:

> Mrs. B. was born on a farm in Tecolotlan, Jalisco. When she was a young girl, her three brothers left for the United States. Shortly thereafter her father tried to make her marry a man she did not like, and she tried to marry a man she had chosen. Her father resolved the disagreement by saying to her, "Here is the money. Go to the United States and stay with your brothers for six months. See all the things, have a good time, and then come back." She went and kept house for her brothers. But she married still another man and stayed eighteen years before she went back to Mexico for a visit.

The vast range of other personal motives and rationalizations for emigration includes revolutionary activities that destroyed individual security, promises of high wages and educational opportunities, financial inducements by relatives, sheer boredom, and desires for new experiences and adventures. How these compulsions and others became mixed in individual cases is brought out in the following interview summary:

> The son of an officer in the Mexican army, who lost his position in the revolution, left Mexico at the age of seventeen and came directly to Detroit to become a student at the Ford factory. He had received his appointment through a Ford representative in Mexico. He worked at Ford's for eight years and then returned for an eight-month visit to Mexico. He then came back to the United States, first to Houston and then to Ford's in Detroit.

The work of the *enganchistas* and of newspaper stories describing the Ford Motor Company's labor policies have been so effective that many Mexicans come to the United States with the sole object of working at Ford, seldom realizing beforehand that other large industrial plants make similar inducements. Most Mexicans, however, come to the United States with expectations for agricultural or railroad-track work.

From a national viewpoint Texas has been the main settling point of entering Mexicans, and in Texas itself, San Antonio is the largest Mexican center. From Texas a secondary migration has occurred to all parts of the United States. The other border states also became points of heavy settlement by Mexicans entering this country for the first time. The Mexican immigrants who finally landed in Detroit reached this destination after drifting through intermediate stops in Texas or other Western states.

The Mexican colony in Detroit first grew to noticeable size in 1918, when several hundred Mexicans came to the city to work in the motorcar factories as students. Later, laborers poured in to replace workmen who had enlisted to fight in the American army. The members of the colony at this time were noted to be "unobtrusive, industrious and patriotic." In December 1920, the colony was estimated to have eight thousand members, but two months later the colony is reported to have dwindled to twenty-five hundred persons. "Most of those who left Detroit had worked in the sugar beet fields in the summer and came to Detroit for the winter at the promise of jobs," which then did not materialize. Such was a journalist's explanation of the startling drop in the population of the colony. The Mexican government helped the exodus by paying return fares to Mexico.

With better times the colony began to increase on a firmer basis. In 1923, Our Lady of Guadelupe Church was opened, indicating the formation of an institutional skeleton for a permanent Mexican body. In 1926 there were an estimated five thousand Mexicans in Detroit and fifteen hundred others in Michigan. The colony reached its maximum in 1928, when unsettled conditions in Mexico caused thousands to migrate to the United States. It is estimated that the colony at that time numbered fifteen thousand.

With the onset of the Depression of the 1930's the number declined. At first the Mexican consul, Ignacio Batiza, attempted to institute a relief program in Detroit for his charges; but eventually a repatriation program began to take form. On October 10, 1931, sixty-nine Mexicans left Detroit, and it was significantly the Detroit Department of Public Welfare in cooperation with the Mexican government that made their return possible.

Regarding the group which left, Batiza said, "The Mexican colony of Detroit is young. The majority of the fifteen thousand Mexicans have not been in the United States more than five years.

They have not yet adapted themselves to the American ways and have been hit hard by the current depression." He estimated that five sixths of the fifty thousand Mexicans had gone from the area by the end of 1932, "more than half of whom returned to Mexico." Actually, by the end of 1932, fifteen hundred Mexicans had been sent from Michigan, and lesser numbers went back from other nearby states. Most of these removals were made as voluntary repatriations.

The motives for returning to Mexico were primarily economic. Unable to find employment in Detroit, the breadwinner who was willing to return felt certain that he would obtain agricultural work in Mexico. The Mexican government offered to supply repatriates with land and with the tools to work it. Such were the main incentives operating on the Mexican to return to the homeland. In addition to this force pulling the immigrant, there was a strong force pushing him out, which took one form in hostility manifested toward him by relief workers.

The exact Mexican population of Detroit at any one time is difficult to ascertain. The most accurate figure is that of the federal census, which in 1930 enumerated 6,515 Mexicans in Detroit. The official estimate of the Detroit Board of Education Statistical Bureau for 1934 (the estimate including all Mexican children whether born in the United States or in Mexico) stated that 278 families were enumerated and that the total population was 1,946 persons. In the same year Consul Batiza placed their number at 4,000. In the 1935 school census of Detroit 456 families were enumerated, containing in all 2,220 persons. The same figure was given for the Mexican population in 1936 by A. H. Navarro, then consul.

The changes in population obviously are reflections of changing economic opportunities during this period, better times attracting migrants. On the other hand, Detroit Mexicans have not been as mobile as have the notoriously mobile Mexican farm laborers in the Western United States. The 1935 school census of the 456 enumerated Mexican families in Detroit showed that 76 percent of the children born of Mexicans in Detroit were from families which came into Detroit in 1930 or before. Using the place of birth of children as the criterion of geographic mobility or immobility, we may conclude that the families in Detroit in 1930 who were not repatriated tended to remain here for at least five years subsequent to that date. While this statement takes no account of single individuals, the fact that only eight of the 456 families did not have children indicates that there was little childlessness among married couples, which would become a factor promoting permanence. Within Detroit, however, mobility is great, with constant movement from less desirable to more desirable homes within a neighborhood. . . .

CHICAGO'S MEXICAN COLONIES

Chicago was one of the first Midwestern industrial centers to which Mexican workers migrated in fair numbers. Anita Jones describes the daily realities of life in the three Mexican colonias of Chicago during the 1920's.

. . . The Mexicans in Chicago live for the most part either in railroad camps or in well-defined colonies. . . . The most important colonies are those which may be described as the Hull House colony, the University of Chicago Settlement colony, the South Chicago colony. In addition, there are other groups not so definitely concentrated, scattered in small settlements near these communities. . . .

The Hull House neighborhood is one of the oldest and perhaps one of the poorest in Chicago. For the past fifty years it has been receiving the newly arrived immigrants. At present, the Mexicans constitute the bulk of the new arrivals. It is here that they find low rents, employment agencies, nearness to work, and other Mexicans.

From "Conditions Surrounding Mexicans in Chicago," by Anita E. Jones. Chicago: M.A. thesis, University of Chicago, 1928.

Hull House reports the first contact with a Mexican family more than twenty years ago. This family came from Mexico to the St. Louis World's Fair, where the father was an exhibitor of feather work. From St. Louis they went to Boston and after a short time came to Chicago. The young child in the family was enrolled in the Hull House kindergarten. The members of this family served as interpreters later when the general Mexican immigration reached Chicago. All the children in this family are grown now and have bought homes in Chicago.

The University of Chicago Settlement colony is younger than that near Hull House. Miss Mary McDowell does not know how the first Mexicans found their way to the district. They were suddenly discovered by the settlement residents after the war in 1919. A year later Swift and Company had ninety-seven Mexican names on its payroll.

The Mexican colony of South Chicago is the newest of the three. It began in 1923, when, European immigration having been cut off by the Quota Act, the steel mills found it necessary to go south to bring in the first gang of Mexican laborers. Before that time a few had worked in the mills but there was no colony. . . .

A great many of the Mexicans who live in the Hull House neighborhood are recent arrivals and are unemployed except at the best season of employment. Many of the Mexican families go to the beet fields of Michigan and Minnesota, and instead of returning to their southern homes at the close of the season, come to Chicago. They seldom have more than a few dollars, and work is always scarce in the winter. The first winter here is a hard one. Those already established lend a neighborly hand and do all they can to alleviate the suffering. The cold weather adds to the suffering, for the supply of clothing, bedding, and furniture is very meager. The Mexican consul tried to prevent this suffering last winter by inserting a notice in the chief Mexican papers warning his people not to come to Chicago in the winter expecting to find work. Many, however, did not see this notice. Most of those who have work are at the Illinois Central Freight House, the bedding factories on Roosevelt Road, at the Cracker Jack factory, other candy factories, and at the hotels in the Loop. All this work is irregular and during periods of depression many of the Mexicans lose their places.

In the University of Chicago Settlement district, the railroads and the packing companies furnish work for the Mexicans. When any of these industries reduces labor, it is the Mexican who suffers most. They are the last to arrive and the first to be laid off. The Mexicans who have been here through more than one winter have learned to save money for the slack time. The People's Stock Yards Bank, 47th and Ashland Avenue, reported more than one thousand Mexican depositors, and the bank across the street, the Depositor's State Bank, reported 150 Mexican depositors. The packing companies hire their own men, as do most of the railroads in the neighborhood. There were formerly two labor agencies on Halstead Street, but both went out of business during the industrial depression of the winter (1928).

The South Chicago Mexicans are largely employed by the steel mills. Each mill has its own employment office. Men are employed and given work numbers. The Mexicans have a custom of selling or lending these numbers to other Mexicans when they wish to leave the work. Sometimes they sell the numbers outright, and again they charge a fee for their use while the rightful owner makes a trip to Mexico or tries his luck in other employment. The foremen do not seem to be aware of this practice. Perhaps all the Mexicans look alike to them. When it is necessary to check on the Mexican's work record, his assumed name must be known. When Mexicans get into trouble, they give the names under which they are employed and not their own names.

The hours of work in the steel mills are as follows: in the Illinois steel mills, laborers work from seven in the morning to five-thirty in the afternoon; others work in shifts from eleven at night to seven the next morning, seven in the morning to three in the afternoon, and three in the afternoon to 11 p.m. In the Wisconsin steel mills, all men work eight hours per day. Their shifts are from 2 p.m. to 10 p.m.; 10 p.m. to 6 a.m.; 6 a.m. to 2 p.m. Both these mills change shifts every week.

The wages of the Mexicans in the steel industries vary from 42½ cents per hour for a ten-hour day for common laborers to 54 cents per hour for eight hours per day and one half day on Saturday received by molders. When mills lay off for long periods, the men generally ship out for somewhere else. A few who have families provide for unemployment by saving during employment. Generally the men do not bring their families until they have a regular job. The Illinois steel mills have what is known as a Good Fellows Club. The employees pay a small weekly fee which entitles them to borrow money from the club or to be taken care of in case of necessity. All employees are of course protected by Workmen's Compensation administered by state law. The company also fosters a group-insurance policy whereby the employees receive a death benefit by the payment of a small weekly premium. . . .

The railroad camps in and around Chicago were the first homes of many of the Mexican immigrants. These camps multiplied rapidly at first, then began to disappear, diminish in size, and there are at present twenty. During the winter of 1927–8, 950 Mexican people were found living in twenty camps of whom 423 were men, 155 were women, and 372 children. Two of these camps numbered more than one hundred each in population.

Seven railroads have camps in and about Chicago; Atchison, Topeka & Santa Fe Railway, Chicago, Milwaukee, St. Paul & Pacific Railway Company, Chicago & North Western Railway, Burlington Northern Railroad, Belt Railroad Company of Chicago, Illinois Central System, Baltimore & Ohio Railroad Company.

These camps were first brought to the notice of the social agencies in February 1918, when the United Charities found the camp belonging to the Rock Island Lines, located at Burr Oak, in a deplorable condition; they reported the conditions to the Rock Island Lines, to the school superintendent, and to the Blue Island Health Department. . . .

There was a scarcity of houses in Blue Island at the time the camp was established (1917) and the railway company was forced to provide shelter for its employees. It is said that labor agents in Monterrey, Mexico, showed pictures of beautiful houses and represented that such would be the homes furnished by the railway company here. Whether this is true or false, the statement of one of the present tenants that work was plentiful when he came to Chicago, and that he took the Blue Island job only to secure a place for his family to live, seems to point to scarcity of houses. The other camps were also established about this time, as a result of the railroads' demand for labor and the workers' need of nearby homes. . . .

While the railway companies were rather solicitous of their employees' comfort when they first came, many have changed their policies. Coal was dumped at the camp in carload lots, water was furnished in tank cars, and rent was free when the camps were first established. Now at many camps coal and water must be carried long distances. In one camp, a charge is made for the coal. Two companies deduct a small rent charge from each man's pay. The pay per hour has been cut in several instances.

During seasons of unemployment, the residents of these camps are still quite stable, for although they are not working for the railroad they are allowed to occupy the houses in boxcars, and get an occasional day's work shoveling snow, etc. In many of the camps an intimate family relationship exists. The members intermarry, bring relatives north to jobs during good seasons, and all live in close proximity. This tie of blood or kinship, even to godparents of the children, often causes horrible overcrowding during periods of economic depression such as existed during the winter 1927–8. When the relatives lose their jobs and the demands of landlords become insistent, they move in with other Mexicans in their rent-free houses at the camps. . . .

The work at most of the camps is on the track. At El Proviso camp, part of the men work in the roundhouse. At the Rock Island Lines camp at 124th Street, all the men work at the shops. This last-named camp was to have been demolished in May, but a committee from the band appealed to the division superintendent and he stayed the order. A part of the men who live at the Bensonville camp of the Chicago, Milwaukee, St. Paul & Pacific Railway Company work at the roundhouse. . . .

Most of the companies would like to abolish these camps now, and many of them are reducing the members in the camp to only a gang of emergency men. . . .

CONDITIONS OF
MEXICANS IN CALIFORNIA

Mounting concern over expanding Mexican immigration characterized the 1920's. Recognizing the economic implications of increasing numbers of Mexican workers, state and federal agencies began to study what they considered a serious problem. In October 1930, an important report dealing with Mexicans in California was published by Governor Clement C. Young's Fact-Finding Committee. A review of this lengthy report follows.

It is conservatively estimated that between 1900 and 1920 approximately 200,000 Mexicans came into the United States illegally. The rush of Mexican immigration commenced during the period of the world war, doubtless as a result of the shortage of labor at that time. . . .

Under the existing Quota Act, more than 40 percent of all alien immigrants declaring California as their intended permanent residence are Mexicans. In brief, the principal immigrant race now coming to California is the Mexican. Neither Mexico's official statistics on emigration nor the United States's figures concerning Mexican immigration are complete. Beyond a doubt, there are now more than 1 million Mexicans in the United States, and under existing immigration legislation, the committee declares, unlimited numbers can continue to come in. More than 80 percent of the Mexicans residing in this country in 1920 were living in three states—Arizona, California, and Texas. The proportion residing in California rose from 7.8 percent of the total in the country in 1900 to 15.2 percent in 1910 and to 18.2 percent in 1920. . . .

In California manufacturing industries there are about eleven

From "Labor and Social Conditions of Mexicans in California." *Monthly Labor Review* (January 1931).

Mexicans in every one hundred wage earners. In factories where there are both Mexicans and other workers, the Mexicans constitute 17 percent of all the employees. The proportion of Mexicans in a number of industries ranges from 2.4 to 66.3 percent. Over 50 percent of all Mexicans in the industries in California are employed in establishments in Los Angeles County and only 10 percent in establishments in San Francisco County. There are probably about 28,000 Mexicans in the manufacturing industries of the state, and at the time of the enumeration there were 2,700 Mexicans in fruit and vegetable canneries.

Based on reports from 159 building and construction companies employing 20,650 workers on June 15, 1928, the proportion of Mexicans in all classes of construction is 16.4 percent. In May 1928, there were 10,706 Mexican laborers on the payrolls of six large interstate and interurban railroads in California. In brief, the report states, Mexicans have secured a strong foothold in the industries of the state and are certainly displacing other immigrant races and the native-born. . . .

In building and construction, Mexicans are employed mostly as common laborers, at pick-and-shovel work, at digging trenches, and in cesspool work; also at grading. Reports from representative building and construction concerns indicate that the hourly rates of Mexicans in the industry run from 40 to 50 cents, and daily wage rates from $3.50 to $5, the prevailing rates appearing to be 50 cents per hour and $4 per day. On railroads, Mexicans are used as "section and extra gang" laborers, their average rates being 38 cents per hour and $3.06 per day. . . .

The majority of Mexican alien immigrants who come to this country are "laborers," not "farmers and farm laborers."

Mexicans constitute the largest group of unskilled, low-paid labor in California, and they have come into the state willing to occupy the same economic level as in their own country. They have had little or no schooling and are unfamiliar with English. Before they came to this country, they lived on a meager diet, paying little attention to sanitation and hygiene. Their infant mortality rate is high, as is also the rate for tuberculosis and other communicable diseases. They have had a feudal relation toward authority, making it difficult for them to adjust themselves to

American traditions. Furthermore, the committee reports, there is
a racial prejudice against them, especially against those of
non-European stock who are not white and whose customs and
habits are so different from the American standard.

Mexicans in California have a tendency to live in colonies both
in urban and rural districts, and this retards their assimilation with
the native population. The housing facilities available to most of
the Mexicans are often poor and do not conform to proper
sanitation standards. Sales agreements frequently prohibit these
aliens from buying property in any but Mexican districts. The
existing ground-rent system in certain sections results in overcrowding and unhygienic conditions. . . . According to the Los
Angeles Health Department, the rate of communicable-diseases
cases among the Mexicans is above that of the general population. . . .

There is one Mexican among every ten children receiving state
aid in California. In 1928 the proportion of Mexican children in
the orphanages of the state was 7.8 percent, and in Los Angeles
County over 16 percent of all the children in institutions were of
the race in question. Five sixths of the Los Angeles [Community
Chest] agencies give no assistance to Mexicans. Those organizations which do serve these people give them a great part of their
service. . . .

A house-to-house investigation of Mexican families in Southern
California disclosed the fact that the majority of the males
included in the survey were unskilled laborers in agricultural
pursuits. Many semiskilled and skilled workers, such as black-
smiths, carpenters, electricians, and mechanics, were, however,
found among these immigrants.

Of 769 Mexican families covered by the investigation, 40.4
percent had three children or fewer; 54.7 percent, four children
or fewer; and 45.3 percent, five children or more. The average
number of children per family canvassed was 4.3.

Of the 701 Mexican families for which reports on average
monthly income were obtained, 69.2 percent averaged less than
$100 per month; 20.5 percent, $100 but under $150; 5.9 percent,
$150 but under $200; and only 4.4 percent, $200 or over.

According to a study of the total incomes for twelve consecutive months of 435 families, 47.1 percent had yearly incomes of less than $1,000; 31.5 percent, $1,000 but under $1,500; and 21.4 percent, $1,500 or over. The average yearly income of these 435 families was $1,156.15. Of the 403 families with children for whom data were secured in yearly incomes, 142 (35.2 percent) reported 250 children on full-time or part-time work, but mostly on part time.

IMPERIAL VALLEY
CANTALOUPE STRIKE

While the California Fact-Finding Committee was studying Mexican immigration to California, a strike occurred in the Imperial Valley during May 1928. Immediately, Mr. Will J. French, Department of Industrial Relations, initiated an investigation of the growers' labor problems. The following part of the investigator's report explains how the Mexican Mutual Aid Society of the Imperial Valley was organized.

Hon. Will J. French, Director
Department of Industrial Relations
State of California
State Building, San Francisco

Sir:

In compliance with your instructions, I visited the Imperial Valley to investigate the causes and conditions of employment which led to the strike of the cantaloupe pickers and to ascertain the facts surrounding the arrests of many Mexican laborers. In order to secure an impartial and unbiased account of facts which

From the Report of Governor C. C. Young's Fact-Finding Committee, *Mexicans in California.* San Francisco: 1930.

resulted in the incarceration and subsequent release of about sixty cantaloupe pickers, I interviewed Mr. Elmer W. Heald, district attorney of Imperial County; Mr. Charles L. Gillett, sheriff of Imperial County; officials of the Union of Workers of the Imperial Valley; officials, superintendents, and field men of employers; and several jailed workers. I also conferred with Messrs. Hermolao E. Torres, vice consul of Mexico, and Alfred Blaisdell, attorney for the vice consul and for the arrested Mexican workers.

While I hesitate burdening you with a lengthy report on a labor disturbance which already appears to have been practically settled, I feel that a thorough understanding of the origin of this labor trouble requires a detailed explanation of the working conditions of cantaloupe pickers, who are mostly immigrant alien Mexican laborers.

The picking of cantaloupes in the Imperial Valley begins early in May and lasts about eight weeks. Approximately between forty-five hundred and five thousand male workers are engaged in the harvesting of this crop. The preponderant majority of these men are Mexicans, but Filipinos and other Orientals are also working on some ranches as cantaloupe pickers. The bulk of the cantaloupe acreage is around Brawley, Westmorland, and Holtville.

Before the season's picking begins, the grower of the melons, who in most cases leases the land from an absentee landlord, enters into a picking agreement with a labor contractor. This contractor is usually a Mexican, but there are also Japanese, Filipino, and Hindu contractors. There is a standard picking agreement in the Imperial Valley which is used with slight variations by all growers, large or small. This agreement makes it obligatory upon the labor contractor to furnish sufficient help to harvest the crop in a workmanlike manner.

The grower obligates himself to make weekly payments to the labor contractor, who is referred to as the "picker," for all crates of melons accepted by the distributor, less 25 percent of the total amount of money which may become due to the contractor. This percentage is retained by the grower until the completion of the contract as a guarantee of the fulfillment of its conditions. The contract emphasizes the fact that the "picker" is an "independent contractor" and stipulates that the pickers hired by the contractor are his own employees, for whose acts or omissions the grower is not responsible. The contract further provides that the contractor, not the grower, must comply with the requirements of the Workmen's Compensation Act.

It is a fact that, in most cases, the labor contractor is financially no more responsible than are the Mexican laborers whom he hires to do the picking. If the contractor gets from the grower 13½ cents per standard crate of melons, he usually retains half a cent for his work of hiring others and for his responsibility of handling and distributing the money received from the grower. Some contractors board the pickers, and before paying them they make the proper deductions to cover the board bills. Several of the growers whom I interviewed professed that they did not know how the contractor distributed the money among his workers. It is more or less of a cooperative arrangement whereby the contractor acts as the intermediary between the growers and the pickers. It saves the grower the trouble of hiring each worker and of keeping a record of his account. At the end of the season, the grower pays the contractor for the last week's crates marketed plus the percentage held to ensure the completion of the contract.

The difficulties with the contract usually start toward the end of the season. Sometimes the contractor absconds with the last payment he receives from the grower and leaves his workers stranded without the wages for their last week's work and minus the 25 percent withheld from the season's wages. If the contractor is honest enough and willing to pay his workers, his intentions are sometimes checkmated by the failure of the grower to make the last payment to the contractor. The growers are often financed by other persons, and a bad market, poor management, or an unsuccessful crop leaves them without funds before the season is over. There is another aspect to this situation. In some cases the grower makes a contract with a Japanese contractor to cultivate, pick, and pack the crop. The Japanese contractor in turn lets out the picking and the packing contracts to other contractors. In some cases, this Japanese contractor fails to pay the picking or packing contractor to the detriment of their respective workers.

These defalcations are not infrequent, and the Mexican laborers in the Imperial Valley have suffered considerably on account of them. The records of the El Centro office of the Division of Labor Statistics and Law Enforcement are replete with cases of defaulting contractors. Where the contractor absconds with the last payment received from the grower, it is almost next to impossible to do anything for the laborers affected. The grower cannot be held responsible because it was the contractor, not the grower, who hired them and who was supposed to pay them their wages. If a crop failure, a bad market, or poor management is responsible for the financial reverses of the grower and the contractor does not get paid, the workers are deprived not only of their last week's pay but also of the 25 percent of the season's wages. The perennial defalcations of the contractors or of the growers have resulted in genuine dissatisfaction with the contract system on the part of Mexican laborers. Not only do they complain that they often do not get their wages at the end of the season but they also claim that the contractor often shorts them and pays them for less crates than they pick.

Although the labor contractor is not a new phenomenon in the Imperial Valley, at least one of the provisions of the picking agreement, and of similar agreements, is probably illegal. It is very doubtful whether the contractor who hires the picker on a piece-work basis may legally withhold 25 percent of every week's wages.

The difficulties which the Mexican laborers have been experiencing with the labor contractors are undoubtedly, in large measure, responsible for the organization of the Union of Workers of the Imperial Valley. I was told by Hermolao E. Torres, vice consul of Mexico, that Carlos V. Ariza, former consul of Mexico in Calexico, conceived the idea of organizing the Mexican laborers. Mr. Ariza was consul of Mexico in Calexico for several years and during his term of office he was frequently called upon by his countrymen to help them collect their wages from defaulting contractors. Mr. Ariza would naturally call upon the El Centro office of the Division of Labor Statistics and Law Enforcement for assistance in these matters. While our El Centro office collected many thousands of dollars for the Mexican laborers, in many instances our El Centro office was unable to collect the wages of workers of the Imperial Valley whose employers were irresponsible labor contractors or growers. Mr. Ariza was aware of the facts surrounding the working conditions of the Mexican workers in the Imperial Valley, and he apparently considered these conditions as justifying the formation of a Union of Mexican Workers. I was told by Mr. Torres that Mr. Ariza had addressed several organization meetings which resulted in the formation of La Union de Trabajadores del Valle Imperial.

When Carlos V. Ariza ceased to be consul of Mexico, he joined a firm of American attorneys in El Centro, to act as Spanish interpreter and to get an enlarged Mexican clientele. The services of this firm of attorneys were engaged to incorporate the union under the laws of the state of California. It is the belief of Elmer Heald, district attorney of Imperial County, that Mr. Ariza was not directly responsible for the strike which followed the organization of the union. From what I could gather on this subject, the former Mexican consul of Calexico decided that he would have nothing further to do with the union as soon as its members went on strike and a number of its members got into difficulties and public opinion was aroused against them. I am citing Mr. Ariza's part in the formation of the union only because many people in the Imperial Valley blamed him for the strike of the Mexican laborers. Personally, I believe that if it were not for Mr. Ariza, the union would probably have been organized anyway. I am basing my belief upon the fact that similar Mexican unions have been very recently organized throughout Southern California and that one of the principal aims of these unions is to do away with the labor-contracting system. (I am referring to the Confederación de Uniones Obreras Mexicanas.)

The union was organized in the latter part of April. Its board of directors was selected on April 22, 1928. Its birth was announced in the Imperial Valley under the name of the Mexican Labor Union of the Imperial Valley, Inc., or as the Union of United Workers of Imperial Valley. The original articles of incorporation as prepared by the firm of attorneys referred to in the preceding paragraph carried the name of Union of United Workers of the

Imperial Valley, Inc. But the original articles were returned by our Secretary of State because they did not specify under which civil code the incorporation was wanted. The attorneys took advantage of it and changed the name of the union to Mexican Mutual Aid Society of Imperial Valley. The revised articles of incorporation were sent to the Secretary of State at Sacramento on May 15, 1928. The objects of this society as set forth in Article II of the articles of incorporation are, among others, "to assist and protect the members in their dealings with other persons and to counsel and advise the members in all matters pertaining to their respective contracts of employment, and to assist the members in the collection of moneys and wages due the members as a result of their work and employment in Imperial Valley." The headquarters of this union are in El Centro, but the location of its largest local is in Brawley. Branches of the union were also organized in Westmorland and in Calipatria. The officers of the union claimed to have 1,220 members, as of May 4, 1928, in El Centro, Brawley, Westmorland, and Calipatria. Branches of the union have been organized in these places.

ATTITUDES
TOWARD THE MEXICAN

Passage of the 1924 Immigration Act, which reduced European immigration, sharply focused attention on the issue of Mexican immigrant labor. Both opponents and proponents of continued use of Mexican workers testified in support of their diverse viewpoints. Robert J. Lipshultz documents this discussion.

From "American Attitudes toward Mexican Immigration, 1924–1952," by Robert J. Lipshultz. Chicago: M.A. thesis, University of Chicago, 1962. Copyright © 1962 by Robert J. Lipshultz. Reprinted, with deletions, by permission of the author.

On July 1, 1924, the long-debated European immigration law finally passed and put into effect, America seemingly had only to assimilate what remained of her un-Americanized newcomers. But from the south arose a new threat, as Mexico fell into one of her periodic economic depressions, leaving millions of farmers and laborers without a source of income. These disinherited Mexicans turned their eyes northward to the booming Southwestern United States, whose large-scale agriculturists beckoned for cheap labor. Geared for mortal combat, gladiators on both sides of the question made haste for congressional committees, publishers, and editors. On both sides were formed opinions of every character, ranging from cold, logical statistics to passionate humanitarianism.

The corporate agriculturists of the Southwest, whose attitudes indicated a desire for unlimited Mexican immigration with astute reservations, formed the core of opposition for the lately triumphant restrictionists.

S. Parker Frisselle, representing the California Federated Farm Bureau, and the California Development Association, at a hearing before the House Committee on Immigration and Naturalization in 1926, stated the problem:

> We, gentlemen, are just as anxious as you are not to build the civilization of California or any other western district upon a Mexican foundation. We take him because there is nothing else available to us. . . .
>
> We would prefer white agricultural labor and we recognize the social problem incident to the importation of Mexicans. We are loath to burden our State with this type of immigrant, but . . . it seems that we have no choice in the matter. The Mexican seems to be our only available supply.

S. Maston Nixon, farmer of Robstown, Texas, assured the committee that "their entry into the United States will not in any way lower the standard of living of the working class, but on the other hand, will make possible the production of diversified agricultural products in a way that will reflect prosperity not only for the agricultural interests in the South and Southwest, but for the manufacturing in the North and Northeast." In the same year, George P. Clements, manager of the Agricultural Department,

Los Angeles Chamber of Commerce, pleaded with the growers that discretion be exercised with the Mexican laborer:

> The question is entirely economic. We cannot get along without the Mexican laborer. To get him we must offer just inducements and guarantee him security. To keep him we must foster him and cease to abuse him. To make the best use of him we must devise some means to make his service possible to agriculture and industry when needed, and be responsible for him until his term of employment is ended, then return him to his home, a living advertisement to others, that the supply may not fail us. . . .

The attitudes of other anti-restriction agriculturists during the twenties perhaps more closely approached the underlying motives of this group. A physical shortage of labor undeniably existed, as thousands of farm laborers left for higher-paying industrial jobs in urban centers. As the price of Anglo-American labor increased, corporate agriculture began to discern previously unrecognized qualities in this group. Suddenly, agricultural labor was unbefitting Anglo-Americans. The rugged, frontier-type settler of the past had graduated, to be replaced by a brown-skinned *peón* whose innate qualities destined him for a life of physical labor and meager salary.

Charles C. Teague, president of the California Fruit Growers' Exchange, presented an argument heard before in American history:

> Mexican casual labor fills the requirements of the California farm as no other labor has done in the past. The Mexican withstands the high temperatures of the Imperial and San Joaquin valleys. He is adapted to field conditions. . . . He does heavy field work—particularly in the so-called "stoop crops" and "knee crops" of vegetable and cantaloupe production—which white labor refuses to do and is constitutionally unsuited to perform.

The testimony of Representative Addison T. Smith of Idaho, questioned by Adolph J. Sabath of Illinois of the House Committee on Immigration and Naturalization, is revealing:

> MR. SABATH: Mr. Smith, if the sugar-beet growers should increase the wages of the laboring men who are employed in that work, could you not secure all the white men for this work that you need?

Mr. Smith: I do not think so, Judge Sabath, for the reason that it is very tiresome work for anyone except persons who are small in stature, because they have to get down on their knees a great deal of the time and crawl along the rows and weed out the extra plants, and a large man such as you or myself, figuratively speaking, would have a good deal of difficulty in engaging in that sort of work with any degree of comfort for probably more hours per day. We might stand it two hours. . . .

A farmer of Nueces County, Texas, interviewed by Professor Paul S. Taylor of the University of Southern California, insisted that the Mexican was created for agricultural labor:

You know what the Bible says about hewers of wood and drawers of water; the poor we always have with us; they're not progressive. You know how God created the Negro race to labor, and marked them so you'd know them. If He hadn't intended it, He'd have made them white, and the Mexicans, too. . . . We're short of labor now, and if they take more away, it will bankrupt the county. . . .

Truly, the prosperous twenties augured great things for the Anglo-American. "I want to say to you," said Fred Cummings, corporate farmer of Fort Collins, Colorado, "that there is not a white man of any intelligence in our country that will work an acre of beets."

I do not want to see the condition arise again when white men who are reared and educated in our schools have got to bend their backs and skin their fingers to pull those little beets. . . . You can let us have the only class of labor that will do the work, or close the beet factories, because our people will not do it, and I will say frankly I do not want them to do it. . . .

No words were spared in praise of the Mexican laborer during the twenties. The Mexican offered everything a farm operator could desire, if only properly handled. Under questioning from restrictionist Adolph J. Sabath of Illinois, J. T. Whitehead, farmer of Mitchell, Nebraska, voiced an oft-repeated view of the Mexican:

Mr. Sabath: Do you think the Mexican would make a much better neighbor than the European?

Mr. Whitehead: No sir; I would hardly say that, but the Mexican does not become a neighbor. The Mexican is a child, naturally.

MR. SABATH: Some of them are pretty tough children, are they not?
MR. WHITEHEAD: Some children need a good deal of discipline.

A farmer of Nueces County, Texas, interviewed by Professor Taylor, refused to hire white labor because "We can't handle them as we do the Mexicans. . . . Whites cannot be as easily dominated, led, directed as the Mexicans." Another preferred Mexicans to Negroes because "A nigger is unappreciative. Do little things for a Mexican. He's just like a dog; slap him and he'll lick your hand." A third farmer was ebullient in his praise:

> The Mexicans are a wonderful people; they are docile; I just love them. I was paying Pancho and his whole family 60 cents a day before the war [World War I]. There just were no hours; he worked from sun to sun.
> The situation is paradoxical. They are in command yet extremely subservient. Pancho's wife just won't let *Madama* do anything when she is sick; she comes to the house and demands that she be allowed to care for her. Pancho won't permit me to work; when it comes to that, he's my chief.
> Don't get to pitying the Mexican and depreciating the white people, holding him in subjection. He wouldn't have it any other way. The Mexican is a most honest man; and the damndest thief. But he figures "I'm his, and so what is his, is mine." It's just like the nigger: "Massa's nigger, Massa's watermelon," so it can't be stealing.
> You'll never find in any fine club the deep and true joy that you'll find in the evening after a day of cotton picking at that thatched home. That man is more civilized than we are. That thatched home—that's glory; go with John Burroughs and Thoreau and find out what life is! You can come down here and talk of subjection, but he's as free as a bird of the air.

Not only was the Mexican character amenable to peaceful labor-management relations but the little brown man was miraculously adapted to agricultural work. Said C. V. Maddux, Labor Commissioner of the Great Western Sugar Company of Denver, Colorado:

> It is a mental and it is a physical suitability. A man who is high-strung could never work beets, because there are five miles of row to every acre, and if a high-strung man would look down those rows and figure there are five miles to every acre he would be distraught. He could not

see the end. It takes a certain mental attitude, or whatever you call it, line of thinking and physical equipment to do this work.

Fred H. Bixby, representing various agricultural interests throughout the Southwest, praised the Mexican as an ideal laborer:

> I do not want a bunch of negroes out in my country, not the cotton-picking type, and I want the cotton-picking type of Mexicans, because they would just as soon pick cotton, thin beets, pick fruit, harvest grains, raise vegetables—anything; they will work all day or night and the next day without ever making a kick. I have had them do that time and time again, and they will work when you are in a big hurry and go in Sundays and work. The white man will not work, and will say "Sunday is my day off."

J. Frank Dobie, ranchman and instructor at the University of Texas, sang the praises of the Mexican vaquero, or cowboy:

> The average ranchman who knows Mexicans and can get them had rather work them than white "boys." They cost less, and demand less, and on the whole are more efficient. They have not yet taken on the softness of the "drugstore cowboy." . . . Truly they are hombres del campo (men of the camp).
>
> A *vaquero* never heard of being paid for "over-time." He knows no "over-time." His time is all day and all night, too, if necessity requires all night. For uncomplaining loyalty, he is probably an equal to the "befo' de wah" darky and as trustworthy. He takes infinite pride in the sayings, in the appearance, and in the possessions of his master.

And so it went throughout the twenties. . . .

UNRESTRICTED
MEXICAN IMMIGRATION

Continuing discussion of unrestricted Mexican immigration led to the expression of many different points of view. Jay S. Stowell, author of The Near Side of the Mexican Question *(1921), appeals for understanding and a sense of fair play in dealing with this complex issue.*

The number of Mexicans in this country is variously estimated at from 1 to 2 million and even higher; 1,200,000 is probably a conservative estimate based on actual information. They have so thoroughly incorporated themselves into the life of Texas, Arizona, and California that their sudden withdrawal would paralyze the industrial and economic life of large areas. To a smaller extent that is true of New Mexico, Colorado, and Kansas—in regard to specialized industries in other states.

The Mexican raises Bermuda onions by the thousands of bushels in Texas; he picks cotton, not only in Texas, but in Mississippi, Arkansas, and Tennessee, where he has in some communities replaced Negro labor for that purpose. The growers of the Great Western Sugar Company alone employ about two thousand Mexicans to grow 293,000 acres of beets. The amazing developments in the Salt River and Gila River Valleys of Arizona are Mexican products. In California the Mexican has made possible the development of the Imperial Valley, with its manifold productions. He dominates the lima-bean empire; he picks walnuts; he raises citrus fruit; he is particularly skilled in horticultural work and, in fact, has made himself indispensable to Southern California. In Pittsburgh, Pennsylvania, and a dozen other places he helps make steel, and in Alaska he cans salmon.

From "The Danger of Unrestricted Immigration," by Jay S. Stowell. *Current History*, 28 (August 1928).

There are thousands of Mexicans at work in Chicago. At least five thousand are employed in the beet fields of the North Platte Valley of Nebraska. Another substantial colony is engaged in similar work in the Red River Valley of North Dakota, and still another colony centers around the plants of the Colorado Fuel and Iron Company of Pueblo. Joliet, Illinois, has one thousand Mexicans and Aurora fourteen hundred. The Columbia Sugar Company of Michigan employs four hundred Mexican families. Toledo has a Mexican population of twenty-five hundred, and Newark, New Jersey, of two thousand. The places just mentioned are but typical of many more.

The Mexican has made an important place for himself in the railroads of the country. Thousands are employed by the Atchison, Topeka & Santa Fe Railroad on all its lines, and other thousands on the Rock Island. From information available we estimate nearly ten thousand Mexicans on these two systems alone. The Denver & Rio Grande Western Railroad reports three thousand; the Great Northern Railroad from five hundred to one thousand (varying with the season); the Southern Pacific Lines, 4,276 in Texas and Louisiana alone; the Northern Pacific several hundred and the Pennsylvania Lines 1,290 regular Mexican employees and several hundred additional seasonal workers.

In spite of the popular impression, which often points to the contrary, the Mexican is a good worker, but that does not mean a perfect worker. He is sensitive, and sometimes he fails to appear the next day if his foreman has been unduly abusive. He has no watch and may be late for work. He is often undernourished and poorly housed, and he has had little training in thrift.

Probably no single group in the United States is suffering more seriously from the evils of seasonal employment than is the Mexican. The beet-sugar industry, in which so many of them are employed, is typical. Technically, the beet season begins in the early spring and the beet harvest is not completed until well into November. Actually the working period is very limited, although it extends over six or seven months from May to November. The hand work in the beet fields is done by contract, and the price per acre in 1926 in Colorado, which is the most important sugar-beet-producing state, ranged from $21 to $24. One Mexican can usually care for about ten acres. During the slack periods the Mexican is free to seek other work if he can find it, but he must be on hand to care for the beets when his help is needed. From the last of November till the next May he is likely to be unemployed.

The living conditions growing out of this system of seasonal employment have at times been very bad, although employers are coming to see that crude, unsanitary shacks are in the long run a poor business investment as well as a social menace. A study made in 1925 by the National Child Labor Committee of 330 families on the Western Slope of Colorado showed that the children were retarded in every way and that boys and girls of school age were employed at arduous labor. It has been the custom in the beet country to recruit workers each spring from border towns or from Spanish-American groups in New Mexico. There is a growing conviction, however, that such a labor turnover is poor economy, and definite efforts are being made to care for the workers during the winter so that they will be on hand for the next crop.

In California there is a marked tendency for agricultural workers to congregate in Los Angeles during the "off" seasons. San Antonio and El Paso are favorite rallying centers in Texas. Many, of course, go to Mexico for a limited period and return with the arrival of spring. If they do not remain longer than six months in Mexico, they are treated as visitors and may return to the United States without legal difficulty.

Although the Mexican has moved about a great deal since coming to the United States, he shows a marked tendency toward stabilization. A striking illustration is to be found in Los Angeles, probably the greatest single Mexican center in the country. Here, during the past five or six years, as soon as his economic status permitted, the Mexican has been deserting the downtown Plaza district for the suburbs, where tens of thousands of Mexicans are now living in their own little homes hedged in with colorful flower gardens. Their children attend modern public schools, and they and their children's children will color California history for generations to come.

Legally the Mexican is a "white" man; yet a few communities

insist that his children shall be enrolled in the colored schools, and in cases where there is no such school, separate Mexican schools are sometimes maintained.

Racial prejudice takes many forms. Not many months ago a capable young man of Mexican parentage walked into the office of a Mexican consul in Texas and asked if he could renounce his United States citizenship and gain a Mexican status. He had been born in Texas, had grown up in the public schools of the state, and had served with the army overseas. Recently he was drawn on a jury panel and then rejected by one of the lawyers in the case involved because of his Mexican extraction. "I was good enough to fight," said he, "but I am insulted when drawn on a jury."

Probably most friction in Texas is produced by labor contracts. Many cases of dishonest dealing with Mexicans, particularly on the part of cotton growers, have created a scandalous situation. An organization, known as La Comisión Honorífica, has come into existence for the purpose of assisting Mexican laborers to obtain satisfaction from their employers. One trick played by employers is to get the Mexican deported just as the crop which he has raised and in which he is supposed to share comes to harvest. In all dealings the American, of course, has the advantage, and his contracts are full of loopholes which can be used for his advantage. Nothing is of greater urgency than fair business dealings with the Mexican. At present he is exploited by employers and by ruthless agents who persuade him to buy useless articles at exorbitant prices. There are, however, some large concerns that have already gained a reputation for honesty with Mexicans. . . .

The Mexican rarely becomes a naturalized American citizen. There are at least two reasons for this. One is that the homeland is never far away; the other that he is not sure whether he would be fairly treated if he threw his lot permanently with this country. He sees too much injustice meted out to his people. Last year in one consular district alone in Texas, twenty-two young men, born and educated in the United States, walked into the Mexican consul's office and declared themselves citizens of Mexico. These young men had just reached twenty-one years of age. They had never lived in Mexico, but they were so doubtful that they would receive just treatment in the United States that they did not have faith enough to inspire them to remain citizens of the United States but preferred to risk the future as Mexicans.

The situation along our Mexican border is complex and it will never be anything else. It demands mutual understanding and a sense of fair play. Difference in language is a handicap to fraternity. We need desperately a genuinely bilingual border. Any progress in teaching Spanish to citizens of the United States and teaching English to Mexicans is a real social gain. The Mexican is here to stay, and his children's children will be with us so long as the United States is a country. A man may desert his wife and abandon his children, but the United States can never run away from Mexico. If we try, we shall find Mexico worthy of better understanding and abiding friendship.

THE MEXICAN ALIEN
RESIDENT PROBLEM

The seriousness of American reaction, pro and con, to Mexican immigration in the 1920's is illustrated in the following selection. The article ends on a somewhat pessimistic note concerning future Mexican immigration to the United States.

The variety and seriousness of the situations created by Mexican migration are such that ever since the quota laws for Europe took effect there has been talk of restricting Mexicans. The outcries of the restrictionists—legislators, schoolteachers, small tenant farmers, social workers, organized labor in Mexico and the United States—have been quite as vociferously balanced by the demands

From *Survey of American Foreign Relations*, C. P. Howland, ed. New Haven, Conn.: Council on Foreign Relations, Yale University Press, 1931.

of the anti-restrictionists—those controlling the large-scale agricultural interests in the Southwest, the railways, the sugar-beet, lumber, and other industries looking to Mexicans for their labor supply. The arguments of both sides, and the data assembled to support them, that confront the observer in a period of acute unemployment and depression are no doubt exaggerated and unweighed. But there stand out certain consequences of Mexican immigration which are not the fiction of partisan tongues. . . .

The arguments in favor of administrative as against legislative action to limit Mexican immigration would seem decisive. Should the quota be applied to Mexico alone, that country would have good reason for feeling discrimination, and yet to put all countries of the Western Hemisphere under quota restrictions would be superfluous and unreasonable, since Mexico is the only one which presents an immigration problem. Administrative regulation is efficient in gaining reductions and preventing importation of cheap labor, while retaining a certain flexibility, and secures a uniform immigration policy for all the Western Hemisphere, while not inflicting what would be taken as an insult by withdrawing quota-exemption privileges extended since 1921. Beyond this, while the Mexican government does not oppose strict adherence to existing American immigration laws, it would resent further statutory restriction as an offense to its people and a contradiction of assertions of friendliness on the part of the United States. More distasteful to Mexico than legislative action in itself is the nature of some of the arguments used in the process of restriction, such as racial and moral inferiority. The quiet formulation of a permanent administrative policy is thus important, since it does away with this type of agitation.

Administrative restriction, meanwhile, did not forestall congressional discussion. For while steady decreases in Mexican immigration followed within a few months after the consular conference in Mexico City, the administrative measures which accomplished these reductions are judged by some of the more ardent advocates of restriction as an insufficient, undependable, or temporary solution of the problem. At the beginning of 1930, the Johnson and Box bills in particular were being discussed in the House, the Harris bill in the Senate. Since none of these has become law up to the present writing, it would not be pertinent to discuss them at length.

The Johnson bill, bearing the name of the representative from Washington, Chairman of the House Committee on Immigration and Naturalization, and reported favorably from that committee in March 1930, aims to limit immigration from the entire Western Hemisphere including Mexico, and for this purpose divides the whole region into immigration units grouped within geographical areas, of which Mexico and islands politically dependent form one. It provides "that the maximum number of immigrants eligible for entry into the United States under the immigration laws which may be admitted in any fiscal year from each immigration unit shall not exceed a number equal to three times the number of United States citizens who have departed for such immigration unit for permanent residence in the fiscal year 1929"; as the author explained blandly before the House, "The method is simplicity itself and involves no discrimination or arbitrary features which could offend the sensibility of our dear neighbors, be they near or distant, in North or South America . . . that is to say to our American hemisphere alien friend that we will accept three times as many of your native-born citizens as immigrants as you have received from us last year [1929]." Since 725 United States citizens emigrated to Mexico during the fiscal year of 1929, the Mexican quota would be 2,175. The bill further provides "that the Secretary of Labor shall select from applicants for immigration visas as quota immigrants persons whose mental, moral, physical and hereditary characteristics shall tend to assimilate readily and develop a homogeneous population in the United States." All preferences after those under the immigration laws had been granted were to be given to persons speaking and writing the English language. . . .

The outcome of congressional agitation on Mexican immigration is still uncertain at the present writing. The Department of Labor and the Bureau of Immigration continue to ignore in their publications the reductions resulting from administrative restriction. Senator Harris, on October 2, 1930, declared his intention of renewing the fight for the Mexican quota. Although he admitted that the recently announced decrease in Mexican immigration was indicative of a more active interest in enforcing the law, he feared that if his measure failed of passage in the House, the Administration would "become lax in enforcement." More pressing issues before Congress, on the other hand, may relegate decision on Mexican immigration to the indefinite future. Meanwhile, consideration of this particular problem may be absorbed into the immigration question as a whole, if the proposal of Senator Reed to suspend for two years all new immigration for permanent residence should go through. Secretary of State Stimson pointed out to the Senate Committee on Immigration the effects of the strict control of quota immigration from Europe (not unlike that in force for Mexico since 1929) operative since October 1, 1930, following the announcement in this regard by the President on September 8, 1930, and based upon a report prepared at his request by the Department of State. Under this policy consular officers were informed that in view of the existing unemployment in the United States, particular care should be taken before issuing immigration visas to determine whether the applicants might become public charges at any time during a period considerably after arrival, and were ordered to withhold visas to applicants with no reasonable prospect of prompt employment. But the secretary, while believing that the department had practically accomplished the purpose of the Reed bill, declared that far from opposing such legislation, "we should be relieved if the responsibility for that effort [to meet changes in the United States brought on by the Depression] should be taken by the Congress," or in the words of President Hoover to Congress, December 3, 1930, "There is need for revision of our immigration laws upon a more limited and more selective basis flexible to the needs of the country." Thus, it is possible that the problem of Mexican immigration may become merged into the larger economic problem involving immigration from all countries.

Any attempt at conjecturing the effect of the decline of Mexican immigration on American industry and agriculture would be useless at the present writing, especially since agricultural and industrial depression closed in upon the inauguration of the restrictive policy. There is no telling the effect of the cutting off of the labor supply in Southwestern truck farming, the sugar-beet districts, in the meat-packing and steel plants, or on the railroads. If, and when, more nearly normal times return, there may once more be heard the call for Mexican labor. At that future date, internal industrial reconstruction, agrarian reform, and internal colonization of sparsely settled regions may be so well along in Mexico, internal labor demands so greatly increased, that there will be no unemployed to fill American needs.

One result of limiting Mexican immigration, either by administrative or legislative means, is that it tends to increase the permanent resident population in the United States, an eventuality little welcomed by either country. The class of persons hitherto entering the United States annually, or remaining for a longer period sooner or later to return to Mexico, were in 1930 coming with their wives and families. It seemed advisable to them to risk the new life together rather than face the possibility of separation, or the probability that their breadwinner would be barred in the future from his source of livelihood. "Women and children," it is reported, "now comprise a larger proportion of the immigrants of the Mexican race than was the case a year ago. In the preceding fiscal year 23,842, or 61 per cent of the total, were women and children under twenty-one years of age, as compared with 8,415 or 71 percent for the year 1930." Those who heretofore were entering and residing illegally in the United States are, now that it may be in the future difficult for them to return to this country, regularizing their status, impelled perhaps by fear of deportation on criminal charges or by the desire to meet naturalization requirements. The Mexican government is not averse to seasonal and temporary migration of its citizens to the United States as casual labor, but permanent departure is regarded as a calamity. For the United States, on the other hand, the increase of Mexican *peón* residents introduces a host of problems including diplomatic embarrassments which might surround naturalization in the future. Should Mexican immigration ever become an issue between Mexico and the United States, it is to be supposed that some solution of seasonal immigration could be found satisfactory to both governments, whereby labor needs will be met in the north, without insulting our southern neighbor, or denuding its population. . . .

III
HARVEST OF DESPAIR

Problems of the Depression were not the exclusive burden of Mexican Americans; nevertheless, as a group they lived a different experience during the 1930's than did other groups in American society.

When disaster struck the American economy in the 1930's, Mexican Americans and Mexicans, historically that part of the work force last hired and first fired, found themselves reaping a harvest of despair. Traditionally ill paid and without financial reserves, large numbers quickly went on welfare programs or became recipients of relief. However, many soon became victims of discrimination as they were singled out racially by city, county, state, and federal agencies in an effort to pare welfare costs.

Defended by government officials as humane and fair, this effort, indiscriminately carried out, was a move to alleviate a labor surplus and to reduce relief rolls. As a result, thousands of Mexicans returned, or were forced to return, to their home villages in Mexico. No one knows how many Mexicans returned to Mexico either voluntarily or under duress between 1929 and 1940; a reasonable estimate would be over one third of a million.

No longer welcomed in the United States because of their poverty and the rising levels of relief costs to maintain them, in the early 1930's Mexican families began an exodus that was to endure until World War II revived the American economy. From Michigan and Wisconsin as well as California and Texas, the pattern was much the same, as Mexican families, goods piled on their secondhand cars or trucks or loaded on repatriation trains, made their way back to the border.

Basically this migration followed one of three patterns. It was made up of those who left voluntarily when job opportunities dried up, of those (a relatively small number) who were legally deported by immigration officials, and finally of those, illegally in the United States, who returned because they were threatened with official action if they did not leave voluntarily. This last group probably made up a majority of repatriates, who often had all or part of the costs of their return to Mexico paid by various public and private welfare agencies.

Numerically most repatriates came from Texas and California, but on a basis of percentages, a majority came from the more industrialized Midwestern states of Michigan, Wisconsin, Illinois, and Indiana. In these states over half of the Spanish-speaking population was repatriated. New Mexico and Colorado, areas with the lowest Mexican immigration rates, lost only a small part of their Spanish-speaking, both in percentage and gross numbers.

Problems of the repatriates did not, of course, end with their return to Mexico, whose economy was also suffering from effects of the worldwide Depression. Despite some interest in helping resettle and re-establish its returning sons, the Mexican government was in no financial position to undertake any extensive programs of settling and reintegrating repatriates into her national life. Mexico did establish some resettlement colonies in which, it hoped, the United States experience and skills of the repatriates might be put to good use, but with little success. Modest American efforts to settle small numbers of returnees also achieved little.

The Depression cut deeply into whatever economic and social gains Mexican Americans had been able to achieve since 1900. Anti-Mexican feeling was widespread in the Southwest, and job competition from Oklahoma and Arkansas dust-bowl refugees became intense in the early 1930's. Signs asserting ONLY WHITE LABOR EMPLOYED were aimed at Mexican Americans as well as blacks. During this time of extreme job discrimination, the economic status of Mexican Americans reached an all-time low.

Arising out of depressed economic conditions, a mounting tide of labor unrest and strikes formed a second theme of the thirties.

In an effort to improve their conditions, Mexican Americans turned toward labor unionization based on their organizing experiences of the 1920's and on outside radical leadership. In California the years between 1929 and 1935 witnessed an especially large number of agricultural strikes. Most important of these labor disputes was the Corcoran cotton strike in the central valley during early fall 1933. In many ways—size, location, techniques—it was a prototype of César Chávez's Delano grape strike of three decades later. It also helped lead to formation of the Associated Farmers of California, a powerful grower organization dedicated to opposing unionization of farm workers. Not all growers accepted the views expressed by the majority via the Associated Farmers, and a handful even dared to speak out for the right of Mexican farm workers to organize.

Outside of California, relatively little Mexican American union organizing occurred. In southwestern New Mexico and southeastern Arizona some Mexican union activity developed in the copper mines, and a temporarily successful Spanish-Speaking Labor League was established in the mines around Gallup, New Mexico. Texas, on the other hand, had virtually no Mexican union development at this time.

As the 1930's came to an end, Mexican Americans continued to suffer from low educational levels and desperate poverty. They remained largely rural, poor, and limited to back-breaking, dirty, low-paid jobs. Their low socio-economic levels and the racist views held by Anglo-Americans continued to exclude them from sharing in the benefits of American society.

GOODBYE, VICENTE

"Repatriation" meant different things to different people. Length of stay in the United States and degree of acculturation resulted in great variations of reaction among repatriates to their uprooting. Robert N. McLean gives his personal view of this unfortunate occurrence.

Vicente is going home!

On Monday, the sixth of April, I crossed the bridge from El Paso, Texas, into Juárez. On both sides of the street in front of the immigration office were parked the cars of homesick Mexicans. Mexicans who had picked cotton near Phoenix, melons in the Imperial Valley, grapes around Fresno. On one side of the street I counted thirteen cars, most of them battered Fords, and every car carried a California license. Loaded in the cars, upon the running boards, on racks behind, on bumpers in front, and even on the tops, was a motley and ill-arranged display of every conceivable thing which a family might collect as part of housekeeping equipment. There were beds, bedsprings, mattresses, washtubs, cooking utensils, washboards, trunks, cots, tents, tent poles, bedding; and atop one of the loads was a crate of live chickens. Up at the customs house, the very courteous little Mexican stenographer with whom I chatted told me all about the chickens. "Yes, they bring their animals!" she exclaimed, throwing up her hands in a gesture of despair. "They bring their dogs and their cats and their chickens, and yesterday a man brought a live goat. I ask them why they bring their chickens, and they say it is so they will have something to eat by the road!"

Vicente has acquired an automobile in the United States. It may not be much of a car, but it will run, and he has set his heart upon driving it over the trail that leads at last to the little town where

From "Goodbye, Vicente," by Robert N. McLean. *The Survey,* 66 (May 1, 1931).

he was born. No inconsiderable part of the movement back to Mexico is being propelled by gasoline.

It has been a long time since I heard the song, "I've reached the land of corn and wine!" But I heard it sung in Spanish in Juárez; heard it from laughing, brown-eyed children sitting upon rolls of bedding; heard it from patient wives and mothers, waiting in the cars for their husbands to conclude the tedious details of emigration; heard it from the men themselves as they tarried in their work of reloading to tell me why they were going home. And as I talked with them, while I was pretty sure about the wine, there grew up in my mind serious doubts about the corn. But you can say this for Vicente. He hasn't had a real job for months. His children have eaten the bread of charity. He hardly knows where he is going, and he has forgotten what Mexico is like. But his heart is singing, and he is sure that everything is going to be all right. . . .

Up at the customs house, there is a large corral, where early in January more than two thousand *repatriados* camped and starved, huddled together, waiting for a kind government to provide them with transportation so that they could move on. Upon their little charcoal burners they cooked their tortillas and boiled their beans. Through the chilly nights they shivered because of insufficient clothing. The little Mexican stenographer told me that when it rained the big examination rooms of the customs house were opened to them. Juárez citizens organized as best they could to provide food, but there was much suffering. Women swarmed about the warehouses picking up one by one the beans which spilled through holes in the sacks. Then, late in the month, the government sent a train of thirty-three boxcars—and then a second train—to take them south and scatter them over the country. Twenty-seven hundred people were thus removed from the "Tortilla Line" in Juárez. Now one or two cars are attached daily to the regular southbound train by the Mexican government, and there is a normal daily movement of from thirty to fifty *repatriados* who pay their own way.

Sometimes families with automobiles camp for days in Juárez awaiting the customs-house examination. The Mexican officials seem to be doing all they can to avoid congestion, as nobody wants a repetition of what happened in January and early

February. However, both personnel and equipment are adequate to handle the crowd.

Up at the station they wait also; always for the "tomorrow" when there will be room for them on the train. At the edge of the platform, I saw the tortillas cooking on the hot charcoal stoves, the crowd all the while milling around. Little children scampered about, as happy as though picking flowers in green meadows. And against the wall, propped up with a roll of bedding, a great hulk of a man slept noisily, oblivious to the flies crawling over his face.

If you are out for exact figures, you can find almost anything you are looking for. If you want to prove that all of the million and three quarter Mexicans in this country are going home, you can see and hear plenty of things to back your theory. In 1930, 30,298 Mexican nationals moved southward through Laredo alone, while 2,144 went through this port last January. But if you are convinced that the excess Mexican labor is flowing over the edge of the "melting pot," you can find facts and figures to substantiate your view. The Mexican school enrollment in Los Angeles is just about what it was last year—around thirty-five thousand. In the Ramona school of San Bernardino, which is 100 percent Mexican, there are eleven hundred children as against a thousand last year.

But before having much to say about figures, we must clarify our discussion by dividing the Mexicans who constitute the return labor movement to their own country into four groups.

First come the deported Mexicans. This is by far the smallest group. Thousands of Mexicans are in this country illegally. Formerly it was impossible to deport many because of insufficient funds at the disposal of the immigration service. Then came the economic depression, with the resulting demand for a Mexican quota. Increased funds were provided, the Border Patrol was strengthened, and things began to happen. According to the estimate of the Mexican consul, between thirty and forty Mexicans a month are deported from the thirty-first district with headquarters at Los Angeles. The El Paso office handles about two hundred a month. The estimate for the whole country set by the Department of Labor for the fiscal year ending June 30 next is 18,500, and it is probable that the proportion of Mexicans will be somewhat more than half.

Much larger, however, is the group made up of those called

"voluntary returns." These are people who are liable to deportation but whom the immigration service for humanitarian or other reasons gives a chance to act for themselves. There are thousands of Mexicans who are being told to go or they will be deported. It is a case of "What's your hurry, here's your hat!"

Still larger is the group made up of those who are either here legally, or whose status has never come under the scrutiny of the immigration service. Among them are many of the better-class Mexicans, and they are going by sea, by train, and by automobile. Because of the new law making it a felony to come into the United States illegally, many have been living in fear for months lest some day a uniformed man call at the door or they be stopped on the street. For them the strain has become unbearable. As one border official has said, "The new law has put the fear of God in their hearts."

It is difficult to say how many people belong to this group. From January 1 to April 6, the Juárez customs house checked through a total of 1,169 families. Counting an average of five persons to the family, this would give us an approximate total of nearly six thousand persons in a little more than three months. We have already seen that the movement through Laredo is a little larger. More Mexicans go through these two points than through any others, but we must remember that there are at least a dozen ways by which Mexicans can go home. It is interesting to note that practically all those who are going through El Paso by train are demanding "check-outs." These establish proof of their residence in this country and permit them to return if they so desire. Evidently Vicente is not entirely sure that Mexico will prove to be the promised land.

The fourth class is made up of indigent Mexicans whose hearts are singing the songs of Morelos, Jalisco, and Michoacán, but who do not have the money to return. When in January the burden of relief became particularly heavy in Los Angeles, the Mexican consul went to the Associated Charities and made the point that it would be better to pay the way of indigent Mexicans to El Paso than to continue supporting them all winter in Los Angeles. The Southern Pacific Company offered to cooperate in the movement by fixing very low "charity Mexican fares." The plan had three things in its favor. It helped satisfy the ambitions of Mexico for the repatriation of its citizens, it removed human misery from the city of the angels, and it was cheap. Late in March a trainload of 260 Mexicans thus had their way paid to El Paso.

Counting the movement represented by deportations, "voluntary returns," ordinary returns, and charity cases, it is estimated that about forty-two thousand people have returned to Mexico in the last nine months. The monthly average may be checked somewhat by the call of the crops for workers, but the movement has been going on at the rate of from fifty to sixty thousand persons a year. . . .

And what will Vicente do when he gets there? A man cannot live in a country thirteen years, share in its social and economic life, beget his children under its flag, and send them to its schools without something happening to him. Will that something fit Chihuahua?

As you cross the bridge into Juárez you see a great new sign, ¡BIENVENIDOS TODOS!—Mexico's welcome to its returning sons who have seen their muscle changed by the alchemy of trade into gold and have then been turned out. As the cycle of business swings upward in this country, the time will come when we shall want to hang that sign on the north end of the other bridge. And I cannot help feeling that there will be a day when Vicente's eyes will see it and his heart will be glad.

GETTING RID
OF THE MEXICAN

No one knows how many Mexicans were "repatriated" during the 1930's. Many city, county, and state agencies instituted programs to send welfare

From "Getting Rid of the Mexican," by Carey McWilliams. *The American Mercury*, 28 (March 1933). Copyright © 1933, The American Mercury, Inc., P.O. Box 1306, Torrance, California 90505. Reprinted by permission.

recipients of Mexican origin back to Mexico, irrespective of citizenship or
desire. Los Angeles's rationale for "repatriating the Mexican" is described
by Carey McWilliams.

In 1930 a fact-finding committee reported to the governor of
California that, as a result of the passage of the immigration acts
of 1921 and 1924, Mexicans were being used on a large scale in
the Southwest to replace the supply of cheap labor that had been
formerly recruited in southeastern Europe. The report revealed a
concentration of this new immigration in Texas, Arizona, and
California, with an ever-increasing number of Mexicans giving
California as the state of their "intended future permanent
residence." It was also discovered that, within the state, this new
population was concentrated in ten southern counties.

For a long time Mexicans had regarded Southern California,
more particularly Los Angeles, with favor, and during the decade
from 1919 to 1929, the facts justified this view. At that time there
was a scarcity of cheap labor in the region and Mexicans were
made welcome. When cautious observers pointed out some of the
consequences that might reasonably be expected to follow from a
rash encouragement of this immigration, they were shouted down
by the wise men of the Chamber of Commerce. Mexican labor
was eulogized as cheap, plentiful, and docile. Even so late as 1930,
little effort had been made to unionize it. The Los Angeles
shopkeepers joined with the industrialists in denouncing, as a
union-labor conspiracy, the agitation to place Mexican immigration on a quota basis. Dr. Paul S. Taylor quotes this typical
utterance from a merchant:

> Mexican business is for cash. They don't criticize prices. You can sell
> them higher priced articles than they intended to purchase when they
> came in. They spend every cent they make. Nothing is too good for a
> Mexican if he has the money. They spend their entire paycheck. If they
> come into your store first, you get it. If they go to the other fellow's
> store first, he gets it.

During this period, academic circles in Southern California
exuded a wondrous solicitude for the Mexican immigrant. Teachers of sociology, social-service workers, and other subsidized

sympathizers were deeply concerned about his welfare. Was he capable of assimilating American idealism? What antisocial traits did he possess? Wasn't he made morose by his native diet? What could be done to make him relish spinach and Brussels sprouts? What was the percentage of this and that disease, or this and that crime, in the Mexican population of Los Angeles? How many Mexican mothers fed their youngsters according to the diet schedules promulgated by manufacturers of American infant foods? In short, the do-gooders subjected the Mexican population to a relentless barrage of surveys, investigations, and clinical conferences.

But a marked change has occurred since 1930. When it became apparent last year that the program for the relief of the unemployed would assume huge proportions in the Mexican quarter, the community swung to a determination to oust the Mexican. Thanks to the rapacity of his overlords, he had not been able to accumulate any savings. He was in default in his rent. He was a burden to the taxpayer. At this juncture, an ingenious social worker suggested the desirability of a wholesale deportation. But when the federal authorities were consulted, they could promise but slight assistance, since many of the younger Mexicans in Southern California were American citizens, being the American-born children of immigrants. Moreover, the federal officials insisted on, in cases of illegal entry, a public hearing and a formal order of deportation. This procedure involved delay and expense, and, moreover, it could not be used to advantage in ousting any large number.

A better scheme was soon devised. Social workers reported that many of the Mexicans who were receiving charity had signified their "willingness" to return to Mexico. Negotiations were at once opened with the social-minded officials of the Southern Pacific Railroad. It was discovered that, in wholesale lots, the Mexicans could be shipped to Mexico City for $14.70 *per capita*. This sum represented less than the cost of a week's board and lodging. And so, about February 1931, the first trainload was dispatched, and shipments at the rate of about one a month have continued ever since. A shipment consisting of three special trains left Los Angeles on December 8. The loading commenced at about six o'clock in the morning and continued for hours. More than twenty-five such special trains had left the Southern Pacific station before last April.

No one seems to know precisely how many Mexicans have been "repatriated" in this manner to date. The Los Angeles *Times* of November 18 gave an estimate of eleven thousand for the year 1932. The monthly shipments of late have ranged from thirteen hundred to six thousand. The *Times* reported last April that altogether more than 200,000 *repatriados* had left the United States in the twelve months immediately preceding, of which it estimated that from fifty to seventy-five thousand were from California, and over thirty-five thousand from Los Angeles County. Of those from Los Angeles County, a large number were charity deportations.

The repatriation program is regarded locally as a piece of consummate statescraft. The average per family cost of executing it is $71.14, including food and transportation. It cost Los Angeles County $77,249.29 to repatriate one shipment of 6,024. It would have cost $424,933.70 to provide this number with such charitable assistance as they would have been entitled to had they remained —a saving of $347,684.41.

One wonders what has happened to all the Americanization programs of yesteryear. The Chamber of Commerce has been forced to issue a statement assuring the Mexican authorities that the community is in no sense unfriendly to Mexican labor and that repatriation is a policy designed solely for the relief of the destitute—even, presumably, in cases where invalids are removed from the County Hospital in Los Angeles and carted across the line. But those who once agitated for Mexican exclusion are no longer regarded as the puppets of union labor.

What of the Mexican himself? The repatriation program, apparently, is a matter of indifference to this amiable ex-American. He never objected to exploitation while he was welcome, and now he acquiesces in repatriation. He doubtless enjoys the free train ride home. Probably he has had his fill of bootleg liquor and of the mirage created by paychecks that never seemed to buy as much as they should. Considering the antisocial character commonly attributed to him by the sociological myth-makers, he has cooperated nicely with the authorities. Thousands have departed of their own volition. In battered Fords, carrying two and three families and all their worldly possessions, they are drifting back to *el terrenaso*—the big land. They have been shunted back and forth across the border for so many years by war, revolution, and the law of supply and demand that it would seem that neither expatriation nor repatriation held any more terror for them.

The Los Angeles industrialists confidently predict that the Mexican can be lured back, "whenever we need him." But I am not so sure of this. He may be placed on a quota basis in the meantime, or possibly he will no longer look north to Los Angeles as the goal of his dreams. At present he is probably delighted to abandon an empty paradise. But it is difficult for his children. A friend of mine, who was recently in Mazatlán, found a young Mexican girl on one of the southbound trains crying because she had had to leave Belmont High School. Such an abrupt severance of the Americanization program is a contingency that the professors of sociology did not anticipate.

THE MEXICAN IN THE NORTHERN URBAN AREA

Widespread belief that Mexicans were alien provided the rationale for deportation during the 1930's. Urban as well as rural Mexican workers were adversely affected by this attitude. Norman S. Goldner documents the problems of unemployment, relief, and repatriation for Mexicans and Mexican Americans in St. Paul, Minnesota.

From "The Mexicans in the Northern Urban Area," by Norman S. Goldner. Minneapolis: M.A. thesis, University of Minnesota, 1959. Reprinted, with deletions, by permission of the author.

Nineteen twenty-nine is generally regarded as an important year in the formation of the Mexican colony [in St. Paul, Minnesota]. At this time, the Depression began and immigration from "south of the border" reached its peak. Employment became a serious problem. The three packing plants where most of the Mexicans were employed furnished only seasonal work. In the beet fields, the workers had no supplementary work between August 15 and September 25 (between the hoeing and topping process). Some women from the beet fields were employed in the canning factory at Le Sueur while the men harvested the corn which was to be sent there. A few women found work in the packing plants at this time, for they were apparently unemployable as domestics because of prejudice and their unfamiliarity with the demands of the Anglo household.

The packing plants averaged about twenty-five Mexican workers during the summer or slack seasons, and about eighty during the busiest months of October and November. This apparent scarcity of employment occurred even though the beet acreage planted was double in 1929 what it was in 1928. The beet company was experiencing great difficulty in obtaining enough workers from the Minnesota population. The beet company then sent a representative to the St. Paul colony in the spring. He established headquarters in a Mexican store for the purpose of recruiting people for beet work. At this time, jobs were secured by applying directly to the company.

The need for field workers increased during the Depression, and more workers were imported, forming a pool for the growing urban Mexican population. By examining federal census figures and the estimates of observers, it seems the population increased from 70 Mexicans in 1920 to 400 in 1924, to 350 in 1925, to 628 in 1930, to 1,500 in 1936.

On March 4, 1929, legislation was evolved which provided for imprisonment and deportation of any Mexican who, after that date, obtained entry to the United States by a false or misleading statement about his potential as a public charge. The exclusion law also required moral, social, and intellectual competency. Moreover, in 1931, the American Sugar Beet Company abandoned many of its welfare practices, increasing the influx of

Mexicans to the urban areas where they eventually became known to practically all of the social agencies.

The Mexican relief requirements began to overburden the available community resources. A movement to deport or repatriate the unemployed gathered nationwide momentum. St. Paul was among the first to institute this measure. In 1934, relief authorities deported 328 Mexicans, including children who were born in this country and legally citizens. Thereafter, families underwent extreme hardship rather than request relief and risk deportation.

A movement to recruit voluntary repatriates was started. Families which had legally established residence in Ramsey County were advised to return to their former residence; or they would be denied relief. These attempts to rid the county of dependents were singularly unsuccessful. The effect was to create suspicion of the welfare agencies, an attitude which, to some extent, still exists in the colony today.

By 1935, the employment situation had become more serious because of the increased size of the colony and the unavailability of jobs. The three packing plants were a source of employment from early fall until February for from eighty to one hundred persons. During the summer, the employees dwindled to twenty-five. The Burlington Railroad employed from twenty-three to thirty Mexicans the year round. This represented the only steady employment available, but the type of unskilled labor it involved was poor preparation for the urban skills that the worker must develop if he were to be occupationally mobile in an industrial setting. The Street Railway Company employed a maximum of thirty Mexicans.

A few women continued to be employed in the packing plants. The International Institute believed the young women would make good domestics and planned to train a small group in this capacity as an experiment.

In 1935, the major source of employment for the Mexican was still the beet field. Two hundred and eight schedules believed to tap the entire population of 1,083 St. Paul Mexicans revealed that 136 family heads were regularly employed in the beet fields. They preferred to work in industries in the winter, but only sixteen had found work in the packing plants that winter. These were in addition to those who considered work in the packing plants as their regular employment and did not go to the beet fields. Nine heads of families who did not migrate were employed by railroads, and thirteen claimed other miscellaneous employment, including three who described their occupations as "living off the city dump." One professional man, a chemist, appeared in the survey. Several young, unmarried (not family heads) men were doing clerical work, and a tailor, carpenter, shoemaker, and baker were listed. At this time, the institute considered race prejudice a threat to the employment future of the Mexican young people. It, along with education, was one of the outstanding problems among the Mexicans.

With urban employment scarce and unsteady, the agencies turned their attention to guiding Mexicans back to the beet fields so that they might relieve some of the drain placed on county relief sources.

In 1936, there were 3,123 Mexican beet workers who made this state their home. The beet workers constituted 96 percent of the Mexican population of Minnesota. A large number of these workers applied for and received relief. In 1936, 1,791 beet workers resided in Ramsey County, and 1,761 of these were on relief. . . .

The belief that the beet workers were an "alien population" provided the rationale for a deportation policy. A study in 1936, however, indicated that of 2,961 persons questioned 72 percent were citizens of the United States. Less than 5 percent who had citizenship had acquired it through naturalization (suggesting that the adults were not prone to actively seek citizenship). Observers in the community point out that the Mexican migrant in the United States considered his stay only temporary. However, when faced with the reality of resuming a migratory life, many chose to remain. At least as early as 1936, welfare officials realized the inadvisability and untenability of deportations and repatriations.

In April 1936, the Board of Public Welfare policy was to extend relief to those families which had been coming to St. Paul for several years even though not legally residents, while families which were residents of other counties or states were to return to those places for relief after the year's beet season.

The WPA program was, by 1936, expected to provide employment for many who formerly had to leave in May for the fields. At this time complaints were made to county officials to the effect that out-of-state migrants were getting all of the beet contracts, because the company official failed to appear in St. Paul for the annual recruitment. After several appearances by the representative that year, contracts were finally signed, but complaints were made in December to the effect that the promises of transportation to the fields had not been kept.

Nineteen thirty-seven saw a tightening of relief policy in regard to non-residents. To have established residency, a family must have lived in Ramsey County for twelve months continuously without having received help of any kind from the Public Welfare Agency. Families known to have come to the state for the first time were informed that they would not be eligible for relief in Minnesota. Neither were single men or employable families without children under sixteen years of age. Offers of transportation to Mexico were continued.

The employment situation continued to be poor in July 1938. WPA had provided only slight relief. Packing-plant wages dropped from 42½ cents per hour to about 30 cents, which meant that a laborer would receive more aid from relief than if he worked. About 3,637 Mexicans were in the state, 3,123 of whom were beet workers. This situation was essentially identical to that of 1936. About 2,782 beet workers were on relief.

A survey in Ramsey County in March 1938, involving 259 family groups and 1,505 individuals, revealed that 168 of the 259 families were on relief, and 25 worked for the WPA. A tabulation of the heads of families demonstrated that urban skills were not quickly acquired. Forty people were employed or had been employed at some time in the packing industry; twenty-one were either employed or had been at times on railroad-section or street-railway work; and five were or had been employed in foundry work. Thus, a total of only sixty-six had ever had other than beet work, except for a small group of skilled people, which involved such occupations as houseworker, one stenographer, one translator on WPA, one chemical engineer, two carpenters, one cobbler, one baker, and one machine operator. . . .

Such was the situation during the years of the Depression. The Mexicans had sampled some of the advantages of the city and chose to remain. The Depression and their lack of occupational skills were their main problems. The advent of World War II changed the picture. . . .

THE MEXICANS
WHO WENT HOME

Lack of concern for Mexicans caught in the web of repatriation permeated the 1930's. On their return to Mexico, an inevitably painful process of readjustment awaited many repatriates, who received little help from either the Mexican or American government. Reporter Jack Starr-Hunt concerns himself with various aspects of this problem.

It started out to be a semirelief project, it has become one of the most important and significant movements in the history of two nations.

They were poor here. The competitive conditions which have within the last three years assailed every human activity made their existence difficult. So they went home—to Mexico. Three hundred thousand of them, from all the border states; thousands from Texas and California, many thousands—about half of the 300,000—from Los Angeles and Southern California.

Today, in Mexico, however, those repatriates who were poor here bid fair to become an important factor in the progress of the southern republic. They are already introducing into sections which once were untouched by anything American the latest in American educational, agricultural, and industrial ideas. And

From "The Mexicans Who Went Home," by Jack Starr-Hunt. Los Angeles *Times*, Sunday Magazine, 52 (March 26, 1933).

they've seized upon the opportunities supplied them by the Mexican government with all the avidity of pioneers discovering a new country.

Mexico offers great opportunities for trained men.

More important than any recent diplomatic stroke will be the effect upon the relations of the two republics of the return of the 300,000. Virtually, they become unofficial agents of the United States in the neighboring republic. Many of them had been in this country for years. They absorbed American atmosphere, American ideas of organization, American methods. There are now Mexicans in Mexico who "understand Americans"—an important factor in the relations of the two countries.

The Mexican government is distributing the repatriates on federal lands, some in newly irrigated districts, others in more remote territories.

President [Abelardo] Rodríguez, himself once a resident of Nogales and a student in Arizona, a man who understands peculiarly the advantages his people acquired in this country, was quick to see the value to Mexico of the American-trained repatriates.

"The purpose of the government," he said in Mexico City recently to a *Times* writer, "is not to confine repatriates to determined colonies, but to scatter them throughout the country in order to take advantage of their experience and knowledge.

"Experienced farmers will produce immediate benefits in various parts of the country. Industrial workers will undoubtedly be employed in our industrial centers."

Observers in both countries believe that still-further migrations may be expected as the influence of these original groups is felt. Many areas of the country will be developed, which will create opportunities for more who will return to join in the new pioneering.

Those who have already gone did so of their own volition. No "pressure" whatsoever was applied in either country. The opportunity was created, through the joint accord of both nations; the Mexicans responded en masse, whole trainloads leaving week after week. Only recently, twelve thousand arrived in Mexico from Los Angeles. About $500,000 was expended in this country to foster the movement. Rodríguez himself contributed the first 5,000 pesos toward a 500,000-peso fund in Mexico for the bringing back and distribution of the repatriates. A drive for funds is still on in Mexico. On the whole, the nation has responded patriotically to the call for aid.

Distribution, allocation, and segregation of the hundreds of thousands are carried on by a National Committee of Repatriates, a government-supported and -aided organization.

"The Federal government, through the National Irrigation Commission, is constructing various irrigation systems, and the lands deriving benefit from these systems are at the disposal of all Mexican farmers, not repatriates only, providing they comply with the necessary regulations," President Rodríguez explained.

Projects being worked are numbered and called "systems." The Irrigation Commission has concluded Systems 1, 2, 3, and 6, respectively in Pabellón, state of Aguascalientes, Villa Juárez, in Tamaulipas; Tula, in Hidalgo, and San Carlos, in Coahuila. These lands are already occupied and cannot now be considered in the repatriation movement.

Projects being completed are: System 4—Don Martín Dam, in the states of Nuevo León and Coahuila. There are actually seventy-five thousand acres colonized here. Fifty-five thousand acres are yet to be colonized, and colonization is proceeding at the rate of 3,750 acres per month. System 5, the Boquilla Dam, state of Chihuahua, impounds waters of the Conchos River. Five thousand acres of this project have already been colonized, and 125,000 more are available to be settled at the rate of 3,750 each month.

Lastly, under government direction, is the Rodríguez Dam, northern district of Baja California, to impound waters of the Tijuana River, a project which will cover five thousand acres.

In addition, the National Committee of Repatriates has a program.

"The principal program of our committee," said Frederico T. de Lachica, Mexican industrialist and chairman, "is the establishment of five centers of population, fundamentally farming in nature, in the states of Oaxaca, Guerrero, Chiapas, Michoacán, and another yet to be decided upon.

"The repatriates, being superior in scientific methods, are of distinct value in these projects. It is well known that our national life is distinctly unequal in level, there being districts where both the most ancient and the most modern of methods are used.

"It is to be expected that the psychological knowledge obtained by men who sought to engage in a more intense field of struggle will show an influence within the more limited confines of labor. Agriculture is the foundation of the country's enormously unexplored wealth, and the greatest immediate and future benefit will undoubtedly be seen in this field."

In addition to the government-sponsored projects, several projects of more local nature are under way. A notable one is that in Lower California in the delta of the Colorado River. Here nine hundred Mexican families have joined in a vast cooperative farming scheme, made possible by the vision of Governor Olachea and the cooperation of American landowners, who provided land and some of the equipment. More than 150,000 acres here were planted to cotton last season. A peso a day is paid the colonists in provisions and clothing, and many went through the season without so much as a centavo in their pockets, yet were comfortable and happy.

Cooperating were the Colorado River Land Company, the Pacific Oil Mills, and the Globe Mills.

Another project sponsored locally was the placing of sixty Santa Monica Mexican families on land in Valle de Las Palmas, Baja California. This was done by Dr. C. N. Thomas, a retired minister, long a friend of the Mexican people. The site of this colony is thirty-five miles southeast of Tijuana.

Dr. Thomas, unique among humanitarians, raised as an orphan, once a classmate of King George of England at Heidelberg University, Germany, states the case of Americans who aid Mexicans to return to their homeland: "By helping Mexicans return to their own country, we relieve conditions in this country. These Mexicans are practically doomed here economically unless there is a remarkable revival of economic manufacture. That means they may become charges on the public; furthermore, it means deterioration, while, placed in Mexico and aided in getting a start, they will become self-sustaining and useful factors.

Moreover, they will be friends of this country. As they become better established, they will use American machinery and equipment.

"Personal gain? I get mine in satisfaction only. It is pleasant to have a part in helping to develop a beautiful valley like Valle de Las Palmas, which, throughout the ages, has been lying idle and untilled.

"I find the Mexicans most appreciative and grateful when they are helped. They respond with remarkable enthusiasm to opportunity—and they never forget a kindness.

THE SAN JOAQUIN
COTTON STRIKE

Low wages and inhumane conditions led to a series of farm-labor strikes in California between 1930 and 1935. The 1933 San Joaquin Valley cotton strike with its center at Corcoran, California, stands out as an example of early farm-labor organization. The report of State Labor Commissioner Frank C. McDonald to Governor James Rolf, Jr., describes the events leading to mediation of the dispute.

November 3, 1933

Honorable James Rolf, Jr.
Governor of California, State Capitol
Sacramento, California
My Dear Governor: On or about Sunday, September 17, 1933, representatives of the cotton pickers in the San Joaquin Valley announced that the cotton pickers had decided that they would pick cotton for $1 per hundred pounds.

From Hearings before a Subcommittee of the Committee on Education and Labor, U.S. Senate, 76th Cong., 3rd sess. Washington: U.S. Government Printing Office, 1940.

On September 19, 1933, a meeting of officers and members of the San Joaquin Valley Agricultural Labor Bureau was held in Fresno. At that meeting it was decided that cotton growers would pay 60 cents per hundred pounds for the picking of cotton. The decision of the Labor Bureau Association was given publicity.

On Wednesday, October 4, 1933, an extensive strike in which some ten thousand cotton pickers were involved was declared. This strike affected the California cotton-growing area of Kern, Kings, Tulare, Fresno, Madera, and Merced Counties. The effect of the strike was most pronounced in Kings, Tulare, and Kern Counties. . . .

On Saturday, October 7, 1933, a brief physical encounter took place between the cotton growers and the strikers in Woodville, Tulare County.

Mr. Guy W. Lowe, leader of the cotton growers, made the following statement to Deputy Labor Commissioner Herbert J. Williamson concerning the Woodville episode—

"Growers in Woodville District organized on Saturday, October 7, 1933, and elected G. W. Lowe speaker, then proceeded to the open-air lot next to the service station and store around which the strikers of the district were gathered. The growers notified the strikers that they would not permit any further public meetings.

"Then the growers went in automobiles throughout the surrounding highway and took away from the pickets their banners and signs and notified the strikers to leave the district within twenty-four hours. . . .

"On October 9, 1933, the following paid advertisement was published in the issue of the Tulare Daily Advance Register:

[PAID ADVERTISEMENT]

NOTICE TO THE CITIZENS OF TULARE

WE, THE FARMERS OF YOUR COMMUNITY, WHOM YOU DEPEND UPON FOR SUPPORT, FEEL THAT YOU HAVE NURSED TOO LONG THE VIPER THAT IS AT OUR DOOR.

THESE COMMUNIST AGITATORS MUST BE DRIVEN FROM TOWN BY YOU, AND YOUR HARBORING THEM FURTHER WILL PROVE TO US YOUR NON-COOPERATION WITH US, AND MAKE IT NECESSARY FOR US TO

GIVE OUR SUPPORT AND TRADE TO ANOTHER TOWN THAT WILL
SUPPORT AND COOPERATE WITH US.

FARMER'S PROTECTIVE ASSOCIATION

On the evening of October 10, 1933, press dispatches stated
that two strikers had been killed and eight wounded in front of
the cotton pickers' strike headquarters in Pixley, Tulare County.
Subsequently, eight cotton growers were indicted by the Tulare
County Grand Jury for the murder of the two striking cotton
pickers. Press dispatches of the same date also stated that one
striker had been killed and a number of strikers and cotton
growers had been injured during a fight at the E. O. Mitchell
Ranch in Kern County. As a result of this fight, seven strikers were
arrested on a charge of rioting. The next day, October 11, 1933,
pursuant to your instructions that I give the strike situation my
undivided personal attention, I hurried to Visalia, Tulare County.
I there conferred with public officials, prominent cotton growers,
and responsible leaders of the district and urged the wisdom and
necessity of mediation or arbitration as a settlement of the
strike. . . .

Owing to the tense, dangerous situation maintaining in the
strike area, the deputy labor commissioners in the district and I,
assisted by Mexican consuls E. Bravo and L. D. Acosta, redoubled
our efforts to bring about the termination of the strike. We were
informed by a large number of strikers and also by a number of
cotton growers of their willingness to settle the strike by
mediation or arbitration. I thereupon phoned to San Francisco to
Mr. Edward Fitzgerald, Conciliator of the United States Department of Labor, and advised him of the danger of the situation,
urging him to come immediately to Visalia to assist in bringing
about a settlement of the strike. Commissioner Fitzgerald arrived
in Visalia on Friday, October 13, 1933, and after we had conferred
upon the situation, Commissioner Fitzgerald, Mexican consuls
E. Bravo, L. D. Acosta, Deputy Labor Commissioners Huss,
Williamson, and myself met with a committee representing the
cotton growers, the cotton-gin owners, representatives of financial
interests, and others, in the Farm Bureau headquarters in Visalia.
During the meeting Mexican consul Bravo stated that the

Mexican strikers had informed him that they had four hundred guns and were prepared to die defending their rights.

Commissioner Fitzgerald earnestly urged the wisdom and advisability of the growers agreeing to arbitration of the controversy. He informed the members of the committee present that after conference with Mr. George Creel, Chairman, California Divison, NRA, you had appointed an arbitration commission. . . .

A fact-finding commission composed of the Most Reverend Edward J. Hanna, Catholic Archbishop of San Francisco; Dr. Tully Knoles, University of the Pacific; and Dr. Ira B. Cross, University of California (Dr. Cross having been substituted for Professor Orrin K. McMurray, Dean of School of Jurisprudence, University of California, who was unable to serve) held public hearings in the Municipal Auditorium in Tulare on October 19, 1933, and October 20, 1933. At these meetings all interested parties, striking cotton pickers and cotton growers and their representatives were accorded full opportunity to present all their evidence to the commission.

During the strike, the strikers had continuously used what is known as "mass-picketing tactics." On October 23, 1933, a large number of striking pickets, principally Mexican men and women, proceeded along the highway until they came to the Guiberson Ranch near Corcoran, where they found strikebreakers at work, picking cotton. The strikers invaded the ranch, and in the fight which ensued between the strikers and strikebreakers, a number of persons were struck with clubs and fists. It is also reported that the sacks containing cotton were slashed and ripped open.

On that same day, October 23, 1933, your Fact Finding Commission announced the following decision:

> Your Fact Finding Commission appointed to investigate strike conditions in cotton areas in San Joaquin Valley after two day session at which both sides had full and ample opportunity under leadership of attorneys and other representatives to present their cases, begs leave to report as follows: It is judgment of Commission that upon evidence presented growers can pay for picking at rate of seventy-five cents per hundred pounds and your Commission begs leave, therefore, to advise this rate of payment be established. Without question civil rights of strikers have been violated. We appeal to constituted authorities to see

that strikers are protected in rights conferred upon them by laws of State and by Federal and State Constitutions.

Signed: E. J. HANNA, Chairman
IRA B. CROSS
TULLY C. KNOLES

Immediately following the announcement of this decision, Deputy Labor Commissioners Fred C. Huss, John S. Kilsby, Charles Crook, E. B. Daniel, and L. A. Barnes, and I, waited upon cotton growers and their representatives, striking cotton pickers, their leaders and representatives, and urged them to accept the decision of your Fact Finding Commission. The leaders of the striking cotton pickers refused to accept the 75 cents per hundred decision of the Fact Finding Commission and issued a demand for 80 cents per hundred, a copy of which demand is attached hereto. Leaders of the cotton growers also declined at that time to accept the 75 cents per hundred rate decision of the Fact Finding Commission.

Thereafter, on October 25, 1933, representatives of the cotton growers of Kern, Kings, Tulare, Fresno, Madera, and Merced Counties assembled in Fresno and accepted the findings of your Fact Finding Commission and served public notice of their willingness to pay 75 cents per hundred pounds for the picking of cotton. . . .

Late that evening, October 25, 1933, I received information to the effect that the strikers would not declare off the strike and that they would not pick cotton for 75 cents per hundred pounds. The next morning, accompanied by Deputy Labor Commissioners Huss and Kilsby and by the Mexican consular representative L. D. Acosta, we proceeded to the strike headquarters in Tulare and to the Central Strike Encampment at Corcoran. We informed strike leaders and strikers that they were not acting in good faith; that they had previously given us assurance on numerous occasions that they would accept the Fact Finding Commission's report, would declare off the strike, and would pick cotton for 75 cents per hundred pounds.

At about eleven o'clock a.m., October 26, 1933, W. V. Buckner, Sheriff of Tulare County, addressed the strikers at their camp in Corcoran and served notice that the strikers must evacuate the camp by three o'clock p.m. that day. Prior to addressing the strikers, a cordon of some thirty California state traffic officers, accompanied by a corps of deputy sheriffs, formed a line in front of the sheriff, armed with revolvers and, I am informed, with gas bombs, ready to meet the dangerous emergency of riot and bloodshed which threatened.

The notification served by Sheriff W. V. Buckner that the camp must be evacuated by three o'clock p.m. was met with angry hoots and jeers and cries of "We won't leave" by the assembled mass of strikers. A most critical and dangerous situation threatened.

The least overt act by any person would undoubtedly have precipitated a bloody battle. Shortly after the serving of the ultimatum by Sheriff Buckner, strike leaders, who our deputy labor commissioners were urging to terminate the strike, protested that the sheriff's ultimatum was illegal, that the strikers were legally occupying the campsite, that the state health authorities had not condemned the camp, and that therefore they had a lawful right to resist any attempt of the sheriff to evict them. They insisted that the sheriff had no lawful right to serve an evacuation notice until the matter had been passed upon by the courts and that any attempt upon his part to enforce his ultimatum by force would be resisted. . . .

During the afternoon the strikers massed their men at the entrance to their camp and informed the deputy labor commissioners that they would resist any attempt to force them and their women and children, which it was estimated at that time to be some twenty-five hundred persons, to leave the camp.

A large number of cotton growers and their sympathizers also assembled at the camp, and angry threats were made by persons thus assembled to the effect that they would force the strikers to leave the camp. Unquestionably, had such an effort been made at that time, an entirely unnecessary and unjustifiable bloody battle would have been precipitated. The lives of many would have been taken, and numerous men, women, and children would have been injured, for it must be remembered that not only were the authorities armed but the Mexican strikers had significantly notified Mexican consul Bravo that they had four hundred guns. The situation was gravely tense and dangerous. At a quarter to three o'clock, I caused an automobile truck to be driven to a point immediately in front of the striking cotton pickers, who were massed at the entrance to their camp. Standing on the platform of the truck, I then addressed the strikers and advised them of the request that had been made by the Central Strike Committee for an extension of time of evacuation of the camp and also of the assurance that had been given by the strike committee that they would that day vote upon the question of accepting the 75 cents per hundred pounds for picking cotton. I urged the strikers as far as I could consistently so do, without derogation to the honor and dignity of the state of California, which I was privileged to represent, to accept the 75-cents decision of the Fact Finding Commission and to declare the strike off. Mexican consular representative L. D. Acosta then addressed the strikers and translated my remarks into Spanish to the assembled strikers, the great majority of whom were Mexicans. Thereafter, at 3:30 p.m. on that day, October 26, 1933, the Central Strike Committee accepted the 75 cents per hundred pounds rate for cotton picking, subject to conditions that were not requested or agreed to at the time of their appearing before your Fact Finding Commission. . . .

LET THE MEXICANS ORGANIZE!

Not all employers of migrant Mexican workers were unfeeling exploiters of cheap labor. Some were sympathetic toward Mexican American efforts to organize in order to improve their economic conditions. Frank Stokes, a citrus grower, explains his views of the Orange County citrus strike of 1936, led by Guillermo Velarde against the California Fruit Growers' Exchange.

From "Let the Mexicans Organize," by Frank Stokes. *The Nation*, 143 (December 19, 1936).

California citrus-fruit growers have joined the legions of the exploiters of labor. They have taken over at the same time the whole vicious machinery of vigilantes, strikebreakers, night riders, tear gas, and prejudiced newspapers. This appears strange considering that there was a time when these citrus-fruit growers themselves were so sorely oppressed that they were driven to create one of the first, and certainly one of the greatest, cooperative organizations ever formed by tillers of the soil. Because they were being exploited and robbed by brokers and shippers, the California citrus farmers were forced to organize or perish. Their object was to obtain a greater return for their sweat and labor. Yet now they are determined that others shall not be permitted to organize for the same purpose.

Oppression was the father and desperation the mother of the California Fruit Growers' Exchange. It has become a mighty organization with 13,500 grower members. There are in California approximately 309,000 citrus-growing acres valued at close to $618,000,000, and more than 75 percent of this acreage and value are represented in the exchange. Its headquarters are in the new Sunkist building, which it owns, in the city of Los Angeles. All this is the result of the banding together of an exploited group of citrus-fruit growers. It is this group which recently crushed ruthlessly an attempt by Mexican workers to organize a union of citrus-fruit pickers.

The Mexican is to agricultural California what the Negro is to the medieval South. His treatment by the vegetable growers of the Imperial Valley is well known. What has happened to him in the San Joaquin has likewise been told. But for a time at least it appeared that the "citrus belt" was different. Then came the strike of the Mexican fruit pickers in Orange County. In its wake came the vigilantes, the night riders, the strikebreakers, the reporters whose job it was to "slant" all stories in favor of packers and grove owners. There followed the State Motor Patrol, which for the first time in the history of strike disorders in California set up a portable radio broadcasting station "in a secret place" in the strike area "to direct law-and-order activities." And special deputy badges blossomed as thick as Roosevelt buttons in the recent campaign.

Sheriff Jackson declared bravely: "It was the strikers themselves who drew first blood so from now on we will meet them on that basis. This is no fight," said he, "between orchardists and pickers. It is a fight between the entire population of Orange County and a bunch of Communists." However, dozens and dozens of non-Communist Mexican fruit pickers were jailed; 116 were arrested en masse while traveling in automobiles along the highway. They were charged with riot and placed under bail of $500 each. Twice their preliminary hearing was delayed on motion of the district attorney. After they had spent fifteen days in jail, the hearing was finally held—and the state's witnesses were able to identify only one person as having taken part in trouble occurring on the Charles Wagner ranch. Judge Ames of the Superior Court ordered the release of all but the one identified prisoner and severely criticized the authorities for holding the Mexicans in jail for so long a time when they must have known it would not be possible to identify even a small proportion of the prisoners.

For weeks during the strike, newspaper stories described the brave stand taken by "law-abiding citizens." These stories were adorned with such headlines as "Vigilantes Battle Citrus Strikers in War on Reds." During all this time, so far as I know, only one paper—the Los Angeles *Evening News*—defended the fruit pickers. In an editorial the *News* said:

> Be it known that the "heroic band of vigilantes," twenty-eight in number, who last Friday with clubs and tear-gas bombs stole up on a peaceful meeting of 150 Mexican fruit pickers in Placentia, fell upon the dumbfounded workers without warning, smashed jaws and cracked heads, dispersed the group save for one striker smashed into unconsciousness and left lying on the ground, were exactly this:
>
> Twenty-eight Los Angeles bums, recruited from streets and beer-halls through a detective agency and paid eight dollars a day by the citrus growers to foment violence and terrorize the striking Mexican pickers.

I have not mentioned all the iniquities perpetrated upon these humble, exploited Mexicans by citrus-grove owners and packing-house operators along with their various aides-de-camp. I have mentioned only enough to show that in this respect the strike was exactly like all other strikes. What differentiates it is the fact that the strike was directed against an employing group that knows what it is to be exploited, against an employing group that has carried cooperation to the highest degree of perfection.

These Mexicans were asking for a well-deserved wage increase and free transportation to and from the widely scattered groves; they also asked that tools be furnished by the employers. Finally they asked recognition of their newly formed union. Recognition of the Mexican laboring man's union, his cooperative organization formed in order that he might obtain a little more for his commodity, which is labor—here was the crucial point. The growers and packers agreed to furnish tools; they agreed to furnish transportation to and from the groves. They even agreed to a slight wage increase, which still left the workers underpaid. But recognition of the Mexican workers' union? Never!

I have been an orange grower and a member of the California Fruit Growers' Exchange for twenty years. I have also had connections with other types of ranching less efficiently organized or not organized at all. Only in the citrus business is the producer free of all selling worries. My job is merely to grow the fruit. The exchange picks it, packs it, pools it, according to grade, with the fruit of other members, ships it, sells it, and sends me the proceeds. I have often borrowed money from my packing house, secured by my crop, thereby saving interest at the bank. Through the Fruit Growers' Supply Company (owned and operated by the associations within the exchange system) I can buy automobile tires or radios, shotguns or fertilizer, generally at a very substantial discount. I can pay for them at the end of the season.

The Fruit Growers' Supply Company provides other benefits. Because the company owns vast acres of timber and its lumber mill at Susanville, my fruit is shipped in containers furnished at cost. More than 100 million feet of lumber are required each year for the making of exchange box stock. Cooperation even extends to the maintenance of a group of pest-control experts whose services are free to exchange members. In many other ways the citrus-fruit growers of California have profited by cooperation. I irrigate my orchard with water delivered by a non-profit combination of growers. My trees are sprayed or fumigated by a non-profit partnership. Because of cooperation I can sleep through the winter nights or until a voice on the telephone informs me that my thermometers have dropped to the danger point.

One would think that California citrus people, at least those belonging to the exchange, would not be adverse to organization by others, especially since the directors of the Fruit Exchange at a meeting held on December 4, 1935 (only a few months before the strike), voted substantial salary increases in the higher brackets. The general manager's salary was increased from $18,000 to $22,000 yearly; the general sales manager's wages were raised from $16,200 to $18,000; and the advertising manager's pay envelope contained an additional thousand, or a total of $10,000.

It has been said in defense of the exchange that it should not be blamed for the trouble in Orange County, for, as Sheriff Jackson stated, "the entire population of Orange County" was opposed to the Mexican fruit pickers. Nevertheless, more than three fourths of all citrus growers are steadfast cooperators. If these cooperators had raised their voices to protest against the unjust treatment of the Mexicans, the affair might have ended with honor to us all.

The fact is, however, that Jack Prizer, manager of an exchange packing house in Orange County and a member of the exchange board of directors (the very same board that voted substantial increases in salaries at the top), was one of those most active in crushing the strike. The entire population of Orange County did seem to oppose the strikers, with the exception of Judge H. C. Ames, who dared to go against intense public opinion.

During the strike I made several excursions into Orange County. I found scab pickers, often high-school boys, "gloming" the "golden fruit" in the beautiful California sunshine, while mockingbirds sang on the housetops, snow-covered Mount Baldy glistened in the distance—and armed guards patrolled the groves behind long rows of NO TRESPASSING signs. Trucks came to the groves with empty boxes and went away with full ones—trucks with rifle barrels protruding from their cabs. Men in uniforms,

mounted on motorcycles, dashed back and forth. Sirens scream-
ing, everybody jittery, everybody damning the Reds—and the
Mexicans!

One day I decided to have a look at the record of the Covina
(Los Angeles County) packing house through which my fruit is
shipped. I learned that during the boom period of 1928–9, from
the middle of December to the ninth of the following October,
Francisco López, our top picker, was called to labor 225 days. He
missed only two possible working days in those eleven months.
For that period he earned $830.41. And this man is with his
clippers what Kreisler is with a violin.

During the season of 1934–5, Francisco López, still a "top
hand," earned only $637.44. The yearly income of the other
pickers ranged from this figure down to starvation wages. And
most of these men have families. Also, it must be remembered that
conditions in the San Gabriel Valley are far better than in many
other places.

I have said that the Mexicans are to agricultural California what
the Negro is to the medieval South, exploited and despised. Before
the day of the CCC camps, Spanish was the language most
frequently heard on every mountain fire line; and those Spanish-
speaking people were taken to the fires by force, even though the
burning mountains, with their high peaks stopping rain clouds and
their dense brush storing water, were vastly more important to
white men than to Mexicans. Towns and cities, farms and
orchards, valley springs and deep sunk wells all depend upon
those mountains.

Not only in the fields are the Mexican people exploited. Not
only as earners but as buyers, they are looked upon as legitimate
prey—for old washing machines that will not clean clothes, for old
automobiles that wheeze and let down, for woolen blankets made
of cotton, for last season's shopworn wearing apparel. Gathered in
villages composed of rough board shanties, or drifting with the
seasons from the vegetable fields of the Imperial Valley to the
grape vineyards of the San Joaquin, wherever they go, it is
the same old pathetic story. Cheap labor!

Usually these people are patient and yielding. But occasionally a leader appears—he is always said to be a Communist—and then they rise up in their righteous wrath and strike. They struck in the Imperial Valley—and they lost. They struck in that glorious land north of the Tehachapi—and again they lost. They lost because of tear-gas bombs, special deputies, and unfriendly newspapers. Lastly, they struck in Orange County. And once more they have lost.

THE PRE-WORLD WAR II MEXICAN AMERICAN

Mexicans have always occupied a unique position among immigrants to the United States, unaided by their precursors, relegated to the lowest-paying jobs, and forced to live in rural squalor and degrading urban slums. Professor Manuel Servín, concerned with the history and education of Mexican Americans, synthesizes Anglo-Mexican American relations before the war and cites lack of educational attainment as the greatest failure of Mexican Americans in this period.

The Mexican American resident in the United States constitutes this nation's most unique, if not mystifying, minority group.

From "The Pre-World War II Mexican American," by Manuel P. Servín. *California Historical Society Quarterly,* 45, 4 (December 1966). Reprinted, with deletions, by permission of the author and the publisher. The *California Historical Society Quarterly* is published four times a year by the California Historical Society in spring, summer, fall, and winter. Contents copyright © 1966 by the California Historical Society. Editorial offices at 2090 Jackson Street, San Francisco, California 94109; office of publication at 1120 Old Mill Road, San Marino, California 91108.

Descendant of the aboriginal American inhabitants and of the first European settlers in the New World, the Mexican American, despite the fact that he preponderantly lived and still lives in areas that were wrested from him, has until the recent war years been considered not an American but a foreigner. This fact has been so evident that even European immigrants, whose accents patently reveal their very recent arrival in the United States, did not hesitate to regard the Mexican American not as an American but as a Mexican whom they considered less American than themselves.

That such an attitude should prevail is clearly understandable to those possessing a historical insight into early North American-Mexican relations. Incredible as it may seem, the Mexicans became a minority group—a despised minority—not when they immigrated to the North American republic but rather when the North Americans migrated to Mexican Texas and California, finding on the whole a poor class of Hispanic settler. Consequently, despite his residence on his own national soil, it was the Mexican who became the backward, somewhat unassimilable foreigner. . . .

The panoramic picture presented of the early twentieth-century Mexican, who was born before 1926 and who did not enjoy the social and economic opportunities resulting from World War II, is interesting and, compared to that of the post-World War I Mexican American, a more respectable one. Arriving in poverty, unable to speak English, and inheriting the anti-Mexican prejudice engendered decades before, the Mexican was definitely at a disadvantage and greatly in need of help. Unfortunately, such help was not given, particularly by the groups from which the Mexican expected aid. The Spanish-speaking aristocracy—old Mexicans who disguised their heritage under such euphemisms as Californios, Spanish-Americans, and Hispanos—generally not only ignored but apparently despised the immigrant. The Roman Catholic Church, aside from building churches and stationing refugee Mexican priests in Spanish-speaking parishes, did little to aid materially or socially. Paradoxically, it was certain Protestant churches, especially the Methodist, that appeared to be most cognizant of the plight of the immigrant. It is, therefore, not strange that bitterness toward the Spanish-speaking aristocracy and some antipathy toward the Church should have developed—a bitterness characterizing the aristocracy in a most unprintable manner and an antipathy resulting in the conversion of many Mexicans to Protestantism.

Unaided by their own groups and unable to obtain work in their previous occupations, the Mexicans were forced to take the lowest-paying jobs as well as the most difficult work. In the agricultural areas of Texas, Colorado, and California they became the neglected, underpaid, exploited, migratory farm workers. In the north central areas of the nation they performed various forms of low-paid, unskilled labor. In Chicago and the Calumet area, for example, they worked in the railroad sections and in the meat-packing plants. In Minnesota they worked in the sugar-beet industry. And in the area of Bethlehem, Pennsylvania, they became unskilled steel workers. Thus, the Mexicans were consciously relegated to the lowest working positions. Perhaps the classical example of this policy was best expressed to Dr. [Paul S.] Taylor by an executive in the Chicago and the Calumet area who bluntly stated the hiring policy found in the area: "We use no Mexicans. We have more refined work and have not had to resort to the greasers. They use them for rough work and around blast furnaces."

But regardless of the demeaning work which they were assigned, the Mexicans, despite conflicting testimony, appear to have been good but not excellent workers. Preferred in California and Texas as farm laborers, the Mexicans did not merit this preference and achievement because they were built closer to the ground and possessed a physical advantage. The preference was simply economic: they were unorganized, apparently docile, and did not demand decent wages and living conditions. In the industrial areas, their record, as in the farming areas, was also respectable. They compared both favorably and unfavorably with the Slovaks, Wends, Negroes, and Irish. Perhaps the most favorable report on the Mexicans' work occurred in Bethlehem when Dr. Taylor interviewed a number of executives, one of whom stated that he

> rated the Mexicans as equals or possibly the superior of the two important groups of Europeans available for the same work: "The Mexicans are a good class of men as a whole; the majority are good

steady workers. As a class their intelligence is above the Slavish [Slovaks] and Wendish. They are a bright, keen race, and good workers."

Notwithstanding the Mexican's at least average work record, he, along with the Negro, was the lowest paid of the workers, both on the farms and in the plants. Unlike the Japanese, who was disliked by his fellow workers because of his industriousness and efficiency, the Mexican was unacceptable to his co-workers for a number of reasons. The reasons generally cited were that he lowered wages and weakened union organization. But the racial difference, the dark skin, unhygienic appearance, and quaint dress habits appear to be, at least to me, the more basic reasons. Following an almost identical pattern of the well-known segregation that existed in Arizona, California, and Texas, the Mexican had difficulty renting in better neighborhoods. The litany of such forced segregation in the Midwest makes interesting but sad reading:

> The principal colony of Mexicans near the stockyards is located on the west side. The fact that its development was checked on the east side, where the Mexicans appeared first, and subsequently stimulated on the west side was attributed by local residents chiefly to the resistance of the Irish (including the second generation) living on the east side. . . .
>
> The movement of Mexicans west of the yards was also opposed. There they encountered violent attacks of the Poles. . . . The Poles and Lithuanians . . . decline to rent to Mexicans in their well established neighborhood. . . .
>
> In South Chicago a good deal of hostility was manifested toward Mexican neighbors, especially when they sought to move out from the more restricted and poorer locality which they occupied, largely among Negroes. An old resident, a German found the Mexicans satisfactory neighbors: . . . But others, particularly young Poles, probably American born, expressed vigorous complaints: . . .

The low wages received by the Mexicans, regardless of area, plus their own cultural and racial drawbacks, of course, had an essential influence upon their living conditions. While Texas has always possessed among both Mexicans and dogmatic liberals the worst reputation for oppressing Mexicans and for retaining them in the lowest substandard living conditions, it is my judgment—as a person who has traveled in Texas, attended school in New Mexico, journeyed extensively through Arizona, and was reared in California—that the living conditions, with some very few exceptions in New Mexico, were equally as poor in utopian California as in Texas, Arizona, and other areas.

Southern California, whose record for indiscriminate, hypocritical discrimination is difficult to excel, possessed perhaps the Southwest's most blatant opposing living conditions between the white North American and the Indian-Spanish Mexican. Few Mexican barrios could compete in poverty with that of Maravilla Park in Los Angeles County, where two and sometimes three shacks built of scrap lumber, old boxes, and other salvage were erected in one small lot; where there were forty houses to a city block; where the average family income in 1928 was $795; where almost all workers were unskilled laborers; and where out of 317 houses only ten had cesspools connected with flush toilets.

But in reality Maravilla Park was not an exception in California. Similar living conditions could be found in El Centro, San Fernando, and the outskirts of Montebello, Whittier, and El Monte—and, incidentally, in various cities of the San Joaquin Valley, even today.

Actually, such poverty was not unknown to the Mexican in his home country and would not be a great source of unhappiness. What did strike the Mexican was the irrational prejudice and disdain that he encountered. In many areas he could not eat in the same restaurant with the North American, nor could he swim in the same pools. In other areas he could not attend the same theaters, or if allowed to do so, he would have to sit in a segregated section; but this segregation, similar to his living among his own people, did not seem to bother him—perhaps he inwardly considered himself equal or even superior to the Americans in some areas. . . .

Possessing a rather good work record and not a bad adult and juvenile crime rate, the Mexican also possessed fairly good records in marital relations and relief. Insofar as married life was concerned, there is little doubt that his divorce rate was less than that of either the Negroes or whites. His public relief record, based upon statistics of California—the nation's most magnanimous or perhaps most foolish state—was not quite as good, but it was apparently below his proportional maximum. Despite unfavorable relief records in Los Angeles, Orange, and Riverside Counties, and despite the low and seasonal wages he was paid, it is evident from Governor C. C. Young's Report that the Mexican in California was not only not a burden on the state but that he did receive only a slight amount above his just proportion of relief funds. That such a case seems to have been true throughout the nation appears most plausible from the Report of the governor's Interracial Commission in Minnesota and from the Mexicans' practice of organizing societies such as the Cruz Azul for helping each other financially and otherwise.

Undoubtedly the Mexican's area of least success and greatest failure was in obtaining an education. Coming from a culture failing to prize mass education, finding it necessary to put even his elementary-age children to work, and perhaps feeling frustrated that an education would not help him overcome the prejudices and disdainful treatment he received throughout the Southwest, the Mexican failed drastically to take advantage of the educational opportunities opened to him. Of all the groups listed in the census of 1930, he had the lowest percentage of school attendance—a factor, of course, that in the long run militated and still militates against him and his future advancement.

Yet despite the prewar Mexican's lack of educational interest, language barrier, and racial and cultural prejudice, he made some formidable breakthroughs in addition to gradually changing his portrait in the areas of work, crime, family life, and relief. Unlike some other persecuted minorities, he established a very good cultural press, as exemplified by the Los Angeles *La Opinión*. He broke into the motion pictures and produced respectable and respected stars such as Ramon Novarro, Dolores Del Rio, and Gilbert Roland. In the East he gave such distinguished professional men as conquistador-descended Harold Medina, the jurist; Alonso E. Escalante, American Maryknoll missionary bishop for Mexico; and American-trained dancer-choreographer, José Limón. In crime, he at least showed some ability to think "big," as exemplified in the case of the fugitive Los Angeles police lieutenant, Peter Del Gado. In music he developed popular crooners such as Andy Russell and more serious singers as José Mojica and Tito Guízar. And, in higher education, in addition to the colonial-descended and highly distinguished Espinoza family, he came forth with such academic limelights as Carlos Eduardo Castañeda and George Isidore Sánchez, both from the University of Texas. . . .

The period of the pre-World War II Mexican in the United States came to an end with the opening of hostilities late in 1941 and early in 1942. The post-World War II young Mexican, who was either in secondary or elementary school, that is, the young Mexican-descended person who was born after 1925 or 1926, encountered entirely different social and economic conditions than did his predecessors. He now became an American, even though he was hyphenated. Jobs, previously denied to his racial group, were open to him. Positions of authority, previously unattainable, were much more within his grasp. He could also swim in the same pools and eat in the same restaurants with North Americans. Furthermore, the war made it possible, at least for the older Mexican Americans, to obtain a college education as the result of the GI Bill of Rights.

Unfortunately, a minority of the wartime Mexican American youths, the pachucos or zoot-suiters, reacted in a most un-Mexican-like manner. Dressed outlandishly, as they followed the styles of less acceptable minorities, they quickly undid the hard-earned reputation of the prewar Mexican. Rejecting their own culture, the bizarrely attired pachucos attacked the United States servicemen in a rat-pack manner and, regardless of justification or guilt, gave the Mexican community—which incidentally seemed to condemn the pachucos as much as did the North American—an undeserved reputation for lawlessness, cowardice, and disloyalty. As a result, the heroic service of the Mexican Americans in the Philippines as well as the outstanding bravery of the numerous Congressional Medal of Honor winners in World War II were ignored by the North Americans.

Thus the period of the pre-World War II Mexican came to an

end. Instead of being acknowledged for his behavior, his hard working habits, and his bravery, he was mistakenly identified with the pachuco and deprived of a well-deserved recognition.

IV
HEROES AND VILLAINS

In 1939, World War II broke out in Europe, and a few days after Japan attacked Pearl Harbor, the United States entered this major conflict. As in World War I, manpower needs rapidly increased to enormous proportions, and once again economic opportunities began to improve for many Mexican Americans. Thousands moved to Midwestern industrial centers and to West Coast metropolitan areas; Los Angeles soon became an area with the largest concentration of Mexicans outside of Mexico City. However, although Mexican Americans served valiantly in the armed forces and worked hard on the home front, they continued to suffer from discrimination and exploitation.

Two incidents that took place in Los Angeles during the war years contradicted the four basic freedoms that the war was ostensibly being fought for. In early August 1942 the first of these incidents occurred. Labeled the Sleepy Lagoon case by newspapermen and quickly becoming a *cause célèbre*, it created a climate of racial tensions. In this controversial case José Díaz, a Chicano youth, died from a severe beating at the hands of persons unknown. However, twenty-three Chicano youths and one Anglo were soon indicted for his murder. After a much-publicized trial replete with anti-Mexican bias, seventeen Chicano youths were found guilty on circumstantial evidence. This astonishing verdict resulted in the organization of a Sleepy Lagoon Defense Committee headed by Carey McWilliams, whose concern for justice led him to a lifetime interest in Mexican American civil rights. This committee successfully appealed the convictions to a higher court, which two years later reversed the lower court's ruling.

The Sleepy Lagoon case became a focal point for anti-Mexican prejudice during this period and also generated asinine theories using race as an explanation for violence and crime. Contributing to an already inflamed situation, Los Angeles newspapers emphasized crime attributed to Mexican Americans, which in turn provided the police with justification for initiating repressive surveillance of Mexican American teenagers. Complaints to federal agencies by Mexican government officials in Washington soon led to pressure being applied to newspaper reporters to avoid the word "Mexican" in connection with crime reporting. Very quickly, as a result, the word "Mexican" was replaced by the terms "pachuco" and "zoot-suiter." The latter term was widely used during the forties when referring to individuals sporting a distinctive dress style, consisting of a broad-brimmed hat, a long draped coat, and high-waisted, pegged trousers. Because of their inconformity and distinct life style, many members of pachuco gangs adopted zoot-suit dress as a sartorial badge.

Following the Sleepy Lagoon affair, there developed early in 1943 skirmishes between pachuco gangs and navy personnel in Los Angeles. During June more serious clashes took place as groups of sailors and soldiers began roaming the streets looking for zoot-suiters on whom to vent their anger and frustration. Indiscriminately, Chicanos were brutally attacked and beaten as this new wave of violence ran its course. What began as a series of street brawls quickly turned into a race war. Only after several days of rioting did military and civil police move to restore order. Before this riot ended, it had become an international incident embarrassing the war effort as a shameful example of latent racism in American society.

Mexican Americans in the armed forces, on the other hand, were finding a greater degree of acceptance, though they too encountered discrimination. About one third of a million Mexican Americans served in various branches of the military and were especially numerous in combat divisions and in more dangerous branches of the service such as the paratroopers and marines. Beginning with Bataan in the Philippines and extending from

Africa to the Aleutian theater of operations, they made their reputations as courageous and tenacious fighters. By the war's end, seventeen had earned Congressional Medals of Honor for extraordinary bravery and many more were granted Silver Stars, Distinguished Service Crosses, Purple Hearts, and other awards for valor.

Experience gained during World War II proved to be a valuable asset to returning Chicano veterans. Many came back home with new attitudes and widened horizons based on a heightened sense of self-confidence and personal worth. Aware of possibilities for improving their economic status, many pursued new ambitions, set fresh goals, and sought better jobs.

This new-found awareness also led to the establishing of a number of important Mexican American organizations with political and community-service orientation. Among the most important were the American G.I. Forum, CSO (Community Service Organization), MAPA (Mexican American Political Association), and PASO (Political Association of Spanish-Speaking Organizations), all of which served as vehicles for improving the lot of La Raza in American society.

World War II also saw the formalizing of a program to bring to the United States Mexican contract workers known as braceros. Wartime needs in Western agriculture had caused California beet and citrus growers to request Mexican workers early in 1942. After Mexico entered the war in May of that same year, it agreed to supply laborers for farm and railroad work as part of its contribution to the war effort. Details of the bracero agreement were worked out by a commission of Mexican and American representatives, and in September the first trainload of fifteen hundred braceros arrived at Stockton, California. Five years later this program was officially terminated; during its existence it supplied the United States war effort with more than 200,000 braceros.

PACHUCOS IN THE MAKING

Blatant discrimination against Mexican Americans in the early 1940's led to widespread racial outbreaks in many urban centers. The Los Angeles "zoot-suit riots" of June 1943 stand out as an extreme example of this violence. George I. Sánchez describes the factors leading to racial hostilities between pachucos, military, and the police.

The seed for the pachucos was sown a decade or more ago by unintelligent educational measures, by discriminatory social and economic practices, by provincial smugness and self-assigned "racial" superiority. Today we reap the whirlwind in youth whose greatest crime was to be born into an environment which, through various kinds and degrees of social ostracism and prejudicial economic subjugation, made them a caste apart, fair prey to the cancer of gangsterism. The crimes of these youths should be appropriately punished, yes. But what of the society which is an accessory before and after the fact?

Almost ten years ago, I raised this issue in an article in the *Journal of Applied Psychology:* "The frequent prostitution of democratic ideals to the cause of expediency, politics, vested interests, ignorance, class and 'race' prejudice, and to indifference and inefficiency is a sad commentary on the intelligence and justice of a society that makes claims to those very progressive democratic ideals. The dual system of education presented in 'Mexican' and 'white' schools, the family system of contract labor, social and economic discrimination, educational negligence on the part of local and state authorities, 'homogeneous grouping' to mask professional inefficiency—all point to the need for greater insight into a problem which is inherent in a 'melting pot' society.

From "Pachucos in the Making," by George I. Sánchez. *Common Ground,* 4, 1 (Autumn 1943).

The progress of our country is dependent upon the most efficient utilization of the heterogeneous masses which constitute its population—the degree to which the 2 million or more Spanish-speaking people, and their increment, are permitted to develop is the extent to which the nation should expect returns from that section of its public."

When the pachuco "crime wave" broke last year, I communicated with the Office of War Information: "I understand that a grand jury is looking into the 'Mexican' problem in Los Angeles and that there seems to be considerable misunderstanding as to the causes of the gang activities of Mexican youth in that area. I hear also that much ado is being made about 'Aztec forebears,' 'blood lust,' and similar claptrap in interpreting the behavior of these citizens. It would be indeed unfortunate if this grand-jury investigation were to go off on a tangent, witchhunting in anthropological antecedents for causes which, in reality, lie right under the noses of the public service agencies in Los Angeles County."

Subsequent developments have borne out the fears implied above. And still, in June of this year, the Los Angeles City Council could think of no better answer to the deep-rooted negligence of public-service agencies than to deliberate over an ordinance outlawing zoot suits! The segregatory attitudes and practices, and the vicious economic exploitation directed against the "Mexican" in California in the past—not zoot suits—are responsible for the pachucos of today.

The pseudo-science of the Los Angeles official who is quoted as reporting to the grand jury on the Sleepy Lagoon murder case that "Mexican" youths are motivated to crime by certain biological or "racial" characteristics would be laughable if it were not so tragic, so dangerous, and, worse still, so typical of the biased attitudes and misguided thinking which are reflected in the practices, not only in California communities, but also elsewhere in this country.

The genesis of pachuquismo is an open book to those who care to look into the situations facing Spanish-speaking people in many parts of the Southwest. Arizona, Colorado, Texas, and, to a much lesser degree, even New Mexico have conditions analogous to those which have nurtured the California riots. In some communities in each of these states, "Mexican" is a term of opprobrium applied to anyone with a Spanish name—citizen and alien alike, of mestizo blood or of "pure white" Spanish colonial antecedents. In many places these people are denied service in restaurants, barber shops, and stores. Public parks and swimming pools, some of which were built by federal funds, are often closed to them. Some churches, courthouses, and public hospitals have been known to segregate them from "whites." Separate, and usually shockingly inferior, segregated "Mexican" schools have been set up for their children. Discriminatory employment practices and wage scales, even in war industries (the President's Executive Order 8802 and his Committee on Fair Employment Practices to the contrary notwithstanding), are still used to "keep the 'Mexican' in his place." . . .

A pathetic letter from a descendant of the colonial settlers of Texas states: "Do you think there is any hope of getting our problems solved? We wish you would do something to help us. We are being mistreated here every time we turn around. We are not allowed in cafés, movies, restaurants. Even Latin Americans in United States Army uniforms are sometimes told they can't see a show because the Mexican side is full. In the public schools our children are segregated. They are given only half a day's school because of the teacher shortage, while the others have full-time classes. There is no teacher shortage for them. Please tell us if there is anything to do about it. We wrote a letter to the Office of Civilian Defense, Washington, D.C. But we haven't heard from them. We don't know if that is the right place to write to or not. . . ."

Many communities provide a separate school for children of Spanish name. These "Mexican schools" are established ostensibly for "pedagogical reasons," thinly veiled excuses which do not conform with either the science of education or the facts in the case. Judging from current practice, these pseudo-pedagogical reasons call for short school terms, ramshackle school buildings, poorly paid and untrained teachers, and all varieties of prejudicial discrimination. The "language handicap" reason, so glibly advanced as the chief pedagogical excuse for the segregation of these schoolchildren, is extended to apply to all Spanish-name youngsters, regardless of the fact that some of them know more English and more about other school subjects than the children from whom they are segregated. In addition, some of these Spanish-name children know no Spanish whatsoever, coming from homes where only English has been spoken for two generations or more. . . .

On July 12, 1941, before the pachuco question had become a matter of general interest, a Spanish-American from California summarized the situation this way: "The so-called 'Mexican Problem' is not in fact a Mexican problem. It is a problem foisted by American mercenary interests upon the American people. It is an American problem made in the U.S.A." He was protesting the movement then on foot to permit the indiscriminate and whole-sale importation of laborers from Mexico. In response to such protests, steps were taken by the governments of the United States and of Mexico to protect both the imported alien and the residents of this area from the evils inherent in such letting down of the bars, evils of which ample evidence was furnished during World War I under similar circumstances. Today, however, the pressure of vested interests is finding loopholes in that enlightened policy and, again, the bars are rapidly being let down. . . .

The establishment of segregated schools for "Mexicans" lays the foundation for most of the prejudice and discrimination. Local and state educational authorities have the power to institute satisfactory remedies. There is no legal requirement in any state calling for the organization of such schools. There are all sorts of legal mandates to the contrary. Forthright action by school authorities could remove these blots on American education in a very brief period of time. As an illustration of how this may be done in Texas, consider this provision adopted by the state legislature in 1943: "The State Board of Education with the approval of the State Superintendent of Public Instruction shall have the authority to withhold the per capita apportionment to any school district at any time that a discrimination between groups of white scholastics exists."

The exclusion of "Mexicans" from public places, solely on the basis of "race" (legally they are "white"), can be stopped through the enforcement of such provisions as that embodied in the legislative Concurrent Resolution adopted in Texas a few months ago: "(1) All persons of the Caucasian Race within the jurisdiction of this State are entitled to the full and equal accommodations, advantages, facilities, and privileges of all public places of business or amusement, subject only to the conditions and limitations established by law, and rules and regulations applicable alike to all persons of the Caucasian Race. (2) Whoever denies to any person the full advantages, facilities, and privileges enumerated in the preceding paragraph or who aids or incites such denial or whoever makes any discrimination, distinction, or restriction except for good cause applicable alike to all persons of the Caucasian Race, respecting accommodations, advantages, facilities, and privileges of all public places of business, or whoever aids or incites such discrimination, distinction, or restriction shall be considered as violating the good neighbor policy of our State." Vigorous action by public officials in enforcing this mandate in Texas, and similar legal provisions in other states, would go far in solving this fundamental phase of the whole "Mexican" question.

These illustrations of specific remedial action could be multiplied by reference to legal mandates as to suffrage, jury service, practices in war industries, etc. Public officials—local, state, and federal—have in their hands the power to correct the discriminatory practices which lie at the root of prejudicial attitudes and actions on the part of some sectors of the public. I have the fullest confidence that the great majority of Americans would applaud the enforcement of those legal mandates.

The Spanish-speaking people of the United States need to be incorporated into, and made fully participating members of, the American way of life. The "Mexican" needs education, he needs vocational training and placement in American industry on an American basis, he needs active encouragement to participate in civic affairs and to discharge his civic obligations, and he needs constant protection by public officials from the pitfalls into which his cultural differences may lead him or into which he may be forced by unthinking sectors of the public. . . .

EDWARD DURAN AYRES REPORT

As part of the testimony in the Sleepy Lagoon case, Los Angeles Lieutenant Edward Duran Ayres testified before the 1942 grand jury regarding criminal tendencies among Mexican American youths. Attitudes based on genetic factors were advanced by Lieutenant Ayres and endorsed by Los Angeles Sheriff E. W. Biscailuz as explanation for a juvenile crime wave. These views were widely accepted by the public.

There are a number of factors contributing to the great proportion of crime by a certain element of the Mexican population. Among the contributing factors are those of economics, lack of employment, and small wages that cause certain ones to commit theft and robbery for the purpose of obtaining the means to own and drive automobiles and to have money to spend on their girl friends, liquor, clothes, etc., also to obtain the wherewithal to live.

Mexicans as a whole in this country are restricted in the main to only certain kinds of labor—and that being the lowest paid. It must be admitted that they are discriminated against and have been heretofore practically barred from learning trades, etc. This has been very much in evidence in our defense plants, in spite of President Roosevelt's instructions to the contrary, and in the great majority of the occupations and trades which are unionized, the Mexicans are automatically barred, as they are not allowed to belong to the union, thus keeping them from remunerative employment.

Economic conditions in their home life are of course not conducive to a higher standard of living, and consequently a lower perspective of responsibility and citizenship is the result. Lack of recreation centers is another factor.

From "Statistics," by Edward Duran Ayres. Sleepy Lagoon Commission Papers, Collection 107, Box 5, Los Angeles: University of California, 1942.

Discrimination and segregation as evidenced by public signs and rules such as appear in certain restaurants, public swimming plunges, public parks, theaters, and even in schools, causes resentment among the Mexican people. There are certain parks in this state in which a Mexican may not appear, or else only on a certain day of the week. There are certain plunges where they are not allowed to swim, or else only on one day of the week, and this is made evident by signs reading to that effect; for instance "Tuesdays reserved for Negroes and Mexicans."

Certain theaters in certain towns either do not allow the Mexicans to enter or else segregate them in a certain section. Some restaurants absolutely refuse to serve them a meal and so state by public signs. The Mexicans take the attitude that they pay taxes for the maintenence of the public institutions the same as anyone else. Certain court actions have been brought by them to force the admittance of their children into certain public schools. All this applies to both the foreign- and American-born Mexican. Broken homes, liquor, loose morals are also contributing factors. All of these, and other factors, are the causes of the Mexican youth remaining within their own racial groups, resulting in what is now practically gang warfare—not only among themselves, but also between them and the Anglo-Saxons.

But to get a true perspective of this condition, we must look for a cause that is even more fundamental than the factors already mentioned, no matter how basic they may appear. Let us view it from the biological basis—in fact, as the main basis to work from. Although a wild cat and a domestic cat are of the same family, they have certain biological characteristics so different that while one may be domesticated, the other would have to be caged to be kept in captivity, and there is practically as much difference between the races of man as so aptly recognized by Rudyard Kipling when he said when writing of the Oriental: "East is East and West is West, and never the twain shall meet," which gives us an insight into the present problem, because the Indian, from Alaska to Patagonia, is evidently Oriental in background—at least he shows many of the Oriental characteristics, especially so in his utter disregard for the value of life.

When the Spaniards conquered Mexico, they found an organized society composed of many tribes of Indians ruled by the Aztecs, who were given over to human sacrifice. Historians record that as many as thirty thousand Indians were sacrificed on their heathen altars in one day, their bodies being opened by stone knives and their hearts being torn out while still beating. This total disregard for human life has always been universal throughout the Americas among the Indian population, which of course is well known to everyone.

Now, to have a true perspective of the problem, we must realize that it would be a mistake to classify the Mexican nation in this category, as being Indian, just as it would not be right for us to classify the United States as being Indian, because, as we well know, all Indians in our country are Americans but all Americans are not Indians. In Mexico, all Indians are Mexicans but all Mexicans are not Indians. The percentage, of course, is greater in that country. Mexico has a population of approximately 20 million people, of which less than 20 percent are pure Caucasians or white. The remaining population is Indian and mestizo, or a mixture of the Caucasian and Indian.

For four hundred years the Mexican people, including their forefathers from Spain, have been confronted with the same problem that we are confronted with today, and they have given just as much study and thought to the problem as we have. In fact, the revolution that started in Mexico under Madero in 1910 had as its objective the freeing and betterment of the Indian, and also much of the mestizo element, from peonage. Many social experiments were tried out, some of them running to the extreme in their good intentions, but all ending in apparent failure. Mexican authorities state that in spite of every well-meant social reform and leniency shown to a certain element under the program of rehabilitation, the said element has not responded to their hopes, and that even from the economic standpoint, when higher wages are given and an opportunity for a higher standard of life is opened to them, instead of availing themselves of that opportunity, they prefer to work half a week instead of a whole week, and we find that same condition here in a great many instances among this same element.

Beginning in 1910, there has been a great influx of Mexican

labor into our country that had as its inception the demand for it by agricultural, mining, railway, and other interests. However, the Mexicans did not remain in their fields of activity, but in ever-increasing numbers they settled in the cities and towns where they are now living in colonies, many of them much as they did in Mexico, speaking their own language, clinging to their own customs, etc. In Mexico the authorities have always adopted a firm hand in dealing with criminals, or those given over to forms of violence. They have stated that which we are now learning the hard way, the Mexican Indian is mostly Indian—and that is the element which migrated to the United States in such large numbers and looks upon leniency by authorities as an evidence of weakness or fear, or else he considers that he was able to outsmart the authorities. Whenever this element is shown leniency in our courts, by our probation officers and other authorities, and is released from custody without serving a sentence, being put on probation, etc., he becomes a hero among his own gang members and boasts that the law was afraid to do anything to him or else that the authorities were dumb and that he put it over on them. However, whenever this Mexican element receives swift and sure punishment, such as proper incarceration, he then, and then only, respects authority. It is just as essential to incarcerate every member of a particular gang, whether there be ten or fifty, as it is to incarcerate one or two of the ringleaders. In other words—take them out of circulation until they realize that the authorities will not tolerate gangsterism.

In Mexico far more severe measures are adopted in dealing with them. All those eighteen years of age and over should be found a place in the armed forces of our country at this time. All those under eighteen who will not attend school should work, and even if they do work, if they resort to such criminal acts as evidenced lately by these gangs, then they should be incarcerated where they must work under supervision and discipline. Many of these young gangsters have comparatively good jobs, so economics is not a determining factor in their case. In fact, as mentioned above, economics as well as some of the other features are contributing factors, but basically it is biological—one cannot change the spots of a leopard.

The Caucasian, especially the Anglo-Saxon, when engaged in fighting, particularly among youths, resorts to fisticuffs and may at times kick one another, which is considered unsporting, but this Mexican element considers all that to be a sign of weakness, and all he knows and feels is a desire to use a knife or some lethal weapon. In other words, his desire is to kill, or at least let blood.

That is why it is difficult for the Anglo-Saxon to understand the psychology of the Indian or even the Latin, and it is just as difficult for the Indian or the Latin to understand the psychology of the Anglo-Saxon or those from northern Europe. When there is added to this inborn characteristic that has come down through the ages the use of liquor, then we certainly have crimes of violence. Ofttimes the element of jealousy enters into it.

There is a feeling among the Mexican population that they do not have even the control over their children that they would have in Mexico, because if they try to restrain their children and punish them for going out nights, a complaint is made against them and they are then haled into court for punishing their children. Therefore, the youth is allowed to run wild—both boys and girls. There is also a notable lack of cooperation on the part of the parents with the authorities. Certainly the curfew laws should be strictly enforced, and if they are not broad enough, then other laws should be passed in order that the youth might be kept off the streets at night, unless properly chaperoned and supervised.

Certainly the legality of fingerprinting everyone taken into custody, whether for prosecution or merely for investigation, should be clarified, and if it is not legal to do so, then it should be made legal to do so, as it has been found a splendid deterrent to crime. We all have to sign our signatures whenever occasion demands it, such as in banks, registrations, and many other ways. In fact, we cannot vote without signing our signature, and one's fingerprints are nature's best and most natural signature. . . .

Again, let us repeat, the hoodlum element as a whole must be indicted as a whole. The time to rehabilitate them is both before and after the crime has been committed, as well as during incarceration, but it appears useless to turn the hoodlum loose without having served a sentence. As stated above, he considers it an act of fear or weakness on the part of the authorities, and due to his exaggerated ego, he believes that he has outsmarted everyone. We also recognize the fact that the great majority of the Mexican people here are law-abiding and are just as anxious as we are to prevent crime among this element, as they rightly consider that it is a reflection on the Mexican population as a whole. They state they are most anxious to cooperate with the authorities to end this intolerable condition. They state that it is a shame and a crime that a certain small percentage of the entire Mexican population should jeopardize the friendly relations and goodwill that so long have prevailed. They consider, and rightly so, that they are an integral part of American society.

Representatives of the Mexican colony may claim that the contributing factors mentioned, and others, are the sole causes of this crime wave by this particular Mexican element, and they will be loath to admit that it is in any way biological—for reasons one can quite understand, pride of race, nationality, etc., but the fact remains that the same factors, discrimination, lack of recreation facilities, economics, etc., have also always applied to the Chinese and Japanese in California, yet they have always been law-abiding and have never given our authorities trouble except in that of opium among the Chinese and that of gambling among both the Chinese and Japanese, but such acts of violence as now are in evidence among the young Mexicans have been entirely unknown among these two Oriental peoples. . . .

August 20, 1942

Dear Mr. Oliver [Foreman, 1942 Grand Jury]:

In appreciation of the courteous reception accorded Chief of Police Horrall and myself on August 11th, the date of our appearance before your honorable body, I wish to take this opportunity of acknowledging the splendid cooperation of the 1942 Grand Jury in endeavoring to find a solution to the present juvenile problem.

The statistics and data embodied in the report read before your body by Lt. Edward Duran Ayres of my Foreign Relations Bureau, and the report of Clem Peoples, Chief of the Criminal Division, together with the statements submitted by the Los Angeles Police Department, I believe fully cover the situation.

I feel that the continued coordinated efforts of the several departments to meet the problem would be furthered if the recommendations submitted for your respectful consideration were adopted.

Assuring you of our full cooperation, I am

Yours very truly,

[Signed] E. W. Biscailuz

E. W. BISCAILUZ, SHERIFF

THE ZOOT-SUIT RIOTS

The "zoot-suit riots" of 1943 represented a culmination of both deeply buried Chicano resentments and long-held Anglo racial attitudes put into action. Carey McWilliams gives a contemporary account of the events and suggests some possible consequences.

On the evening of Thursday, June 3, the Alpine Club—a group made up of youngsters of Mexican descent—held a meeting in a police substation in Los Angeles. They met in the police station, at the invitation of an officer, because of the circumstance that the nearby public school happened to be closed. With a police officer present, they met to discuss their problems, foremost of which, at this meeting, was the urgent question of how best to preserve the peace in their locality. At the conclusion of the meeting, they were taken in squad cars to the street corner nearest the neighborhood in which most of them lived. The squad cars were scarcely out of sight when the boys were assaulted. Thus began the recent weekend race riots in Los Angeles.

On the following nights of June 4, 5, and 6, various attacks were made upon so-called "zoot-suiters" in Los Angeles. These attacks reached a fine frenzy on Monday evening, June 7, when a mob of

From "The Zoot-Suit Riots," by Carey McWilliams. *The New Republic*, 108, 25 (June 21, 1943).

a thousand or more soldiers and sailors, with some civilians, set out to round up all zoot-suiters within reach. The mob pushed its way into every important downtown motion-picture theater, ranged up and down the aisles, and grabbed Mexicans out of their seats. Mexicans and a few Negroes were taken into the streets, beaten, kicked around, their clothing torn. Mobs ranged the length of Main Street in downtown Los Angeles (a distance of some ten or twelve blocks), got as far into the Negro section as Twelfth and Central (just on the edge of the district), and then turned back through the Mexican sections on the east side. Zoot-suiters, so-called, were attacked in the streets, in the theaters, in the bars; streetcars were stopped and searched for Mexicans; and boys as young as twelve and thirteen years of age were beaten. Perhaps not more than half the victims were actually wearing zoot suits. In several cases on Main Street, in downtown Los Angeles, Mexicans were stripped of their clothes and left lying naked on the pavements (front-page pictures of these victims were gleefully displayed in such sedate sheets as the Los Angeles *Times*). During all of this uproar, both regular and special police were observed in the streets, outside the theaters, and, in some cases, they were even noted going ahead of the mob. That there was going to be trouble on Main Street on Monday night was known throughout the community for at least twenty-four hours in advance. Crowds collected there, in fact, in anticipation of the fracas. On the following nights the same type of rioting occurred on a smaller scale in Los Angeles, with similar disturbances in Pasadena, Long Beach, and San Diego.

Immediate responsibility for the outbreak of the riots must be placed upon the Los Angeles press and the Los Angeles police. For more than a year now, the press (and particularly the Hearst press) has been building up anti-Mexican sentiment in Los Angeles. Using the familiar Harlem crime-wave technique, the press has headlined every case in which a Mexican has been arrested, featured photographs of Mexicans dressed in zoot suits, checked back over the criminal records to "prove" that there has been an increase in Mexican "crime," and constantly needled the police to make more arrests. This campaign reached such a pitch, during the Sleepy Lagoon case in August 1942, that the OWI

[Office of War Information] sent a representative to Los Angeles to reason with the publishers. The press was most obliging: it dropped the word "Mexican" and began to feature "zoot suit." The constant repetition of the phrase "zoot suit," coupled with Mexican names and pictures of Mexicans, had the effect of convincing the public that all Mexicans were zoot-suiters and all zoot-suiters were criminals; ergo, all Mexicans were criminals. On Sunday night and Monday morning (June 6 and 7), stories appeared in the press warning that an armed mob of five hundred zoot-suiters was going to engage in acts of retaliation Monday night (thus ensuring a good turnout for the show that evening).

At the time of the Sleepy Lagoon case last year, the police launched a campaign, which coincided perfectly with the newspaper campaign, against "Mexican crime." Almost on the eve of a speech by Vice President Wallace in Los Angeles on the good-neighbor policy, police arrested more than three hundred Mexican youngsters in what the Los Angeles *Times* referred to as "the biggest roundup since prohibition days." At about this time, Captain Ayres of the sheriff's office submitted a report to the grand jury in which he characterized the Mexican as being "biologically" predisposed toward criminal behavior. For more than a year this campaign of police terrorization has continued. Prowl cars have been cruising through the Mexican section constantly, youngsters have been ordered off the streets and "frisked" whenever two or more have been found together, and persistent complaints of police brutality have issued from both the Mexican and the Negro communities. There are, of course, some fine officers on the force—men who know and understand the problem. To some extent, also, the police have been goaded into the use of repressive measures by the press and by the race-baiting of some local officials. The manner in which the problem of the Japanese *évacués* has been kept before the public, for example, has had a tendency to make people race-conscious. Nor have some local officials yet changed their attitudes. "Mayor Pledges Two-Fisted Action. No Wrist Slap," read a headline in the Los Angeles *Examiner* (June 10). At the same time, the attitude of certain military officials has also been rather shocking.

The "official version" of the riots, adopted by all the major newspapers, is now as follows: the soldiers and sailors acted in self-defense, and most emphatically, there was no element of race prejudice involved ("Zoot-Suit Gangsters Plan War on Navy"— headline, the Los Angeles *Daily News*, June 8, 1943). This theory is desperately repeated, despite the fact that *only Mexicans and Negroes* were singled out for attack. As for prejudice against *Mexicans*—from whom we acquired so many elements of our "culture"—why, the very suggestion of such a thought would seem to be abhorrent to the post-riot conscience of every publisher in Los Angeles. In fact, the fanciest journalistic double talk that I have seen in the Los Angeles press during a residence of twenty-one years appeared in the editorials of June 11.

Several facts need to be rather dogmatically asserted:

1. There are no "zoot-suit" gangs in Los Angeles in the criminal sense of the word "gang." The pachuco "gangs" are loosely organized neighborhood or geographical groups; they are not tied together into an "organization." Many of them are, in effect, nothing more than boys' clubs without a clubhouse.

2. Juvenile delinquency has increased in Los Angeles since the war, but while delinquency among Mexican youth has risen as part of this general situation, it has actually increased less than that of other ethnic groups and less than the citywide average for all groups.

3. Much of the miscellaneous crime that the newspapers have been shouting about has been committed, not by youngsters, but by men.

4. While individual Mexicans may, in a few cases, have attacked soldiers and sailors (and, incidentally, the reverse of this proposition is true), it is merely the craziest nonsense to suggest that the soldiers and sailors were driven to mob violence in self-defense.

5. It should be kept in mind that about 98 percent of Mexican youth in Los Angeles is American-raised, American-edu-cated. Like most second-generation immigrant groups, they have their special problems. But their actual record for law observance is, all things considered, exceptionally good.

While the riots have now subsided (business has been complaining about the cancellation of military leaves), the situation itself has not been corrected. In the absence of a full and open investigation, the public has been left with the general impression (a) that the soldiers and sailors acted in self-defense; and (b) that, all things considered, the riots were "wholesome" and had a "good effect." Resentment of the riots in the Mexican and Negro communities has reached an intensity and bitterness that could not be exaggerated. While Governor Warren promptly appointed an investigating committee, it is painfully apparent that the committee intends to "report" and not to investigate.

Not only should there be a full federal investigation, particularly of the charges made by the Mexican consul and other individuals and groups, but there are additional avenues of inquiry that should be explored. What role the local *Sinarquistas*, Mexican Catholic-fascist organizations, have played in the entire situation during the last year I do not know. But I do know that the Special War Policies Unit of the Department of Justice completed an elaborate investigation of the local *Sinarquistas* months ago. I am told that nothing has been done to put the recommendations of this report into effect because of objections raised by the State Department. Since there can be no doubt whatever that the *Sinarquistas* are a fascist group, why not make the report public? And why not prod the Los Angeles office of the Coordinator of Inter-American Affairs into at least the semblance of activity?

After months of persuasion, the coordinator finally opened an office in Los Angeles some months ago. One of his first acts was to appoint a committee of twenty-five citizens to administer a fund which has been granted them for the ostensible purpose of "doing something about the local Mexican problem." The coordinator was so anxious that only the "right people" serve on the committee that he appointed a former president of the Los Angeles Chamber of Commerce as its chairman, virtually permitted this gentleman to hand-pick the committee, and neglected to appoint a single Latin American. During the events of the last week, the committee has maintained a silence in keeping with the theory of the local representative of Mr. [Nelson] Rockefeller's office that the riots were not "race riots" at all but merely disputes between two groups of American citizens (one group being white, one group being dark)—see the Los Angeles *Examiner*, June 10, 1943, Part 1, page 9. I am reliably informed that the coordinator has worked out an arrangement with the State Department as follows: the State Department will make no objections to a program in aid of local Latin American groups, provided (a) that these programs are kept on a "cultural" level (no social-action programs will be approved); and (b) that the coordinator will turn these projects over to the Cultural Division of the State Department as rapidly as possible. In furtherance of this arrangement, I am also informed that Mr. Rockefeller has given his valuable support to the request of the Cultural Division of the State Department for a greatly increased budget.

It requires no imagination to appreciate the consequences of these riots. According to the United Press (June 11), "Radio Tokyo yesterday seized upon the Los Angeles disorders." The exploitation of the riots by Axis propagandists, however, is only part of the story. One township alone, on the east side of Los Angeles, has provided twenty-seven hundred men of Mexican descent who are now serving in the armed forces. These men have families living on the east side. If space permitted, I should like to quote what a young army sergeant—of Mexican descent—said to me recently about the riots. It would make excellent copy.

REPORT OF THE
CITIZENS COMMITTEE

Governor Earl Warren immediately appointed a citizens committee to investigate the zoot-suit disturbances and to recommend a course of action. Headed by Reverend Joseph T. McGucken, the committee found

From "Report and Recommendations of the Citizens Committee," by Joseph T. McGucken et al. Los Angeles, Calif.: June 12, 1943.

that these riots developed as a result of violent racial prejudice long existing in the Los Angeles community. The report and recommendations of the committee follow.

Under Governor Warren's call for an investigation for the purpose of curative action, the Citizens Committee has carefully investigated the outbreaks of violence in Los Angeles during the week of June 6, 1943.

One of the most important facts the committee has found is that the problems have been aggravated by misconceptions of the nature and extent of the outbreaks. It is of the utmost importance, not simply as a matter of community education, but for the purpose of helping solve the difficulties involved that the public, as well as responsible authorities, should view the situation from its proper perspective.

Immediate curative action, which was called for by the governor in creating this committee, demands that crimes of violence must be brought to justice, and the guilty must be punished regardless of what clothes they wear—whether they be zoot suits, police, army, or navy uniforms. The streets of Los Angeles must be made safe for servicemen as well as civilians, regardless of national origins. The community as well as its visitors must learn that no group has the right to take the law into its own hands.

Curative action must, however, be thorough, and this means that the causes must be reached in order to prevent recurrences. One of the causes has been the failure properly to present the facts.

The committee has found:

I

That the problem is one of American youth, not confined to any racial group. The wearers of zoot suits are not necessarily persons of Mexican descent, criminals, or juveniles. Many young people today wear zoot suits.

II

It is a mistake in fact and an aggravating practice to link the phrase "zoot suit" with the report of a crime. Repeated reports of this character tend to inflame public opinion on false premises and excite further outbreaks.

All juvenile delinquency has increased recently in Los Angeles. This includes crimes committed by youths of Mexican origin. But the fact is that the increase of delinquency in the case of youths of Mexican families has been less than in the case of other national or racial groups and less than the average increase for the community.

Between 1914 and 1929, all of California—and Los Angeles County in particular—had a rapid increase in Mexican population. The tremendous difficulties experienced by immigrants in making adjustments to their new surroundings are well known. We have learned that the problem is especially acute in the case of the second generation. The foreign-born parent loses authority over his American-born child; families tend to be broken up; and if the children are not completely accepted by their neighbors, they are often without responsible guidance.

These facts shed light on the youths of Mexican descent in Los Angeles. Many of them are second-generation. About 98 percent of them are American-born.

III

Of the serious crimes committed by persons of Mexican descent, only 25 percent are committed by minors. Most of the so-called zoot-suit crime amounting to felony has been committed by persons who are fully and legally responsible for their acts.

IV

There are approximately 240,000 persons of Mexican descent in Los Angeles County. Living conditions among the majority of these people are far below the general level of the community. Housing is inadequate; sanitation is bad and is made worse by congestion. Recreational facilities for children are very poor; and there is insufficient supervision of the playgrounds, swimming pools, and other youth centers. Such conditions are breeding places for juvenile delinquency.

V

This committee has found that there are approximately thirty-five neighborhood gangs in Los Angeles, many of whose members have criminal records. In addition to these well-defined gangs, there are many small, unorganized neighborhood gangs. Some of the members of these gangs wear zoot suits; some do not. Some are Mexican, some Negro, and some are so-called Anglo-American, that is, they include all types or classifications of youth. Only a small percentage of these neighborhood groups have been involved in the recent outbreaks. Many of them are wholesome social groups, meeting in public schools, in subpolice stations, and under the supervision of responsible officials.

VI

Mass arrests, dragnet raids, and other wholesale classifications of groups of people are based on false premises and tend merely to aggravate the situation. Any American citizen suspected of crime is entitled to be treated as an individual, to be indicted as such, and to be tried, both at law and in the forum of public opinion, on his merits or errors, regardless of race, color, creed, or the kind of clothes he wears.

Group accusations foster race prejudice; the entire group accused want revenge and vindication. The public is led to believe that every person in the accused group is guilty of crime.

VII

It is significant that most of the persons mistreated during the recent incidents in Los Angeles were either persons of Mexican descent or Negroes. In undertaking to deal with the cause of these outbreaks, the existence of race prejudice cannot be ignored.

Youth is peculiarly sensitive; to be rejected by the community may throw the youth upon evil companions.

Any solution of the problems involves, among other things, an educational program throughout the community designed to combat race prejudice in all its forms.

This committee has had the advantage of many excellent studies already perfected by various groups and committees. We have taken the liberty of coordinating and applying these studies evolved by the patient research of the following groups, to whom we acknowledge our indebtedness: Conference on Childhood and Youth in Wartime; Judge Robert Scott's Special Committee on Older Youth Gang Activities; Los Angeles County Schools Workshop in Education of Mexican and Spanish Speaking Students; Los Angeles County Grand Jury of 1942; Citizens Committee appointed by the Los Angeles County Board of Supervisors; Citizens Committee for Latin-American Youth.

RECOMMENDATIONS

Based on their findings and on the studies referred to, we make the following recommendations:

DELINQUENCY

1. Arrests for criminal or gang activity should be made without undue emphasis on members of minority groups.
2. The cooperation of the press should be solicited in minimizing the publication of the names or pictures of youthful delinquents.
3. The Central Juvenile File, covering Los Angeles County, now being established, should be properly financed and staffed.
4. Law-enforcement agencies should provide special training for officers dealing with minority groups.
5. Law-enforcement officers should be provided who speak Spanish and who understand the psychology of the Spanish-speaking groups in Los Angeles.

6. Additional detention facilities should be provided for the care and study of delinquent youth.

7. A Juvenile Forestry Camp should be established by the Probation Department to care for delinquent youth under the age of sixteen.

8. The Youth Authority of California should at once provide additional facilities to aid all counties of the state in caring for the more seriously delinquent youth.

9. All law-enforcement agencies should be provided with Spanish-speaking personnel.

10. Lawyers' associations should continue to enlist panels of attorneys to protect the rights of youth arrested for participation in gang activity. . . .

RECREATION

1. Additional recreational and group work facilities should be provided in all neighborhoods in a quantity sufficient to meet the needs of the community.

2. Churches in Los Angeles County should increase their program for youth.

GENERAL RECOMMENDATIONS

1. Discrimination against any race in the provision or use of public facilities should be abolished.

2. Additional public-housing projects should be set up to meet the needs of minority groups.

3. A program of education should be undertaken to make the entire community understand the problems and background of the minority groups.

4. The leadership of minority groups should assume their responsibilities in meeting these community problems.

CONTINUATION OF WORK

1. The governor's Citizens Committee should be regarded as

remaining in session. As additional problems arise, the committee will convene and will be able to utilize the results of this investigation and the studies that have been made.

2. The chairman of the committee should call upon the leaders of all groups, majority as well as minority, to mobilize public opinion and other citizens committees behind the recommendations which have been made.

Dated: June 12, 1943.

> *Respectfully submitted,*
> JOSEPH T. MCGUCKEN, Chairman,
> Auxiliary Bishop of Los Angeles
> DR. WILLSIE MARTIN, Wilshire
> Methodist Church
> KARL HOLTON, Member of the
> Youth Correction Authority

WAR!

Within industry and the armed forces, World War II provided Mexican Americans with new opportunities for improving their economic and social conditions. However, despite some effort to end discrimination, not all Americans were willing to accept the returning Chicano veteran for what he now saw himself to be—equal to any American. Harold J. Alford describes both individual contributions and an incident of continuing Texas racism.

From *The Proud Peoples: The Heritage and Culture of Spanish-Speaking Peoples in the U.S.*, by Harold J. Alford. New York: David McKay, Inc., 1972. Copyright © 1972 by Harold J. Alford. Reprinted, with deletions, by permission of the publisher.

In landlocked New Mexico, the National Guard had two Coast Artillery battalions, the 200th and the 515th. As the United States tooled up for coming conflict in 1940, these two National Guard units were activated and dispatched to the Philippine Islands. Their selection was one of the more logical moves in the military, in that these New Mexico National Guard units were made up largely of Spanish-speaking personnel, both officers and enlisted men.

When the Japanese invaded and conquered the Philippines, more than a quarter of the men captured or killed in the last-ditch fighting on Bataan Peninsula were United States soldiers whose native language was Spanish, although their native land was New Mexico.

On October 29, 1941, President Franklin Delano Roosevelt pulled a capsule containing a slip of paper with a number on it from a great bin of capsules and initiated the United States Selective Service. In Los Angeles, Pedro Aguilar Despart looked at the number of his draft card. The number on the slip of paper President Roosevelt removed from the capsule and the number of Pedro Aguilar's card were identical: 158. Pedro Aguilar was No. 1 in the draft for what was to be World War II.

At mushrooming army camps across the country, post commanders were faced with groups of wiry, eager young draftees who had been born on ranchos and raised on the move as part of migrant farm-working families. Following the furrows from planting to harvest, and never pausing in one place long enough to learn any language except that of their parents and their parents' friends, many of these draftees could speak no English and could understand little. Yet, organized into special platoons led by officers who had a smattering of Spanish, they emerged from the thirteen-week training cycle with both a knowledge of the fundamentals of soldiering and an operational knowledge of conversational English. Moved into predominantly Anglo units, they performed not only adequately but often brilliantly.

In addition to the expansion of the armed forces, part of the United States's tooling up for war involved the expansion of defense industries.

Trucks, tanks, clothing, construction, munitions, and the manufacture of massive quantities of the essentials for millions of men on the move required the recruiting, not only of skilled labor, but also of men and women who could effectively man the proliferating production lines. There the quickly learned task of adding a single piece to gradually growing identical structures moving at a regular pace in an endless procession—self-propelled or pushed—required no knowledge of the English language, of mathematics, or of other academic skills but rather demanded manual dexterity and a tolerance for monotony, repetition, and tedium—occupational aptitudes that the residents of the barrios, the *colonias*, and the migrant-worker camps had, out of necessity, developed to a high level of efficiency over the years.

Responding to government pressure for speed and volume production, manufacturers were able to negotiate contracts based on cost plus a fixed profit percentage, so that keeping wages down was not necessary to fiscal survival. As a result, unskilled laborers were able to move from the field to the factory and earn more in a week than they had earned previously in a month. And with production lines running around the clock—three shifts in twenty-four hours—the whole family was employable, individuals sometimes holding down more than one job.

Moreover, the accelerating assembly line did not discriminate among Anglo housewife, Spanish-American field hand, off-reservation Indian, northern-migrating Negro, newly arrived Puerto Rican, Filipino, Chinese, or individuals with any other ethnic backgrounds. . . .

Also in 1942–3, while the bracero program was tooling up and the zoot-suit fuse was sputtering to an explosion, Mexican Americans were contributing to the war effort overseas.

Taoseño Joe Martínez had left the warm hills of New Mexico to work in the sugar-beet fields of Colorado. When the war came along, he enlisted and was shipped to Alaska, where, in the only battle of World War II in what is now part of the United States—the Battle of Attu, in the frigid, foggy Aleutians—he was killed. But in the Battle of Attu, Joe Martínez so distinguished himself that he was posthumously awarded the Congressional Medal of Honor.

Private First Class Manuel Pérez, of Oklahoma City, killed in the Battle of Luzon, was also posthumously awarded the Congressional Medal of Honor.

Sylvester Herreras, of Phoenix, Arizona, survived to accept his Medal of Honor in person, but the presentation was made to him while he was sitting in a wheelchair, for he had lost both his legs in the heroic action which led to his award.

Sergeant José Mendoza López, of Brownsville, Texas, one of five Texans of Mexican descent to be awarded the Congressional Medal of Honor, had just returned from a goodwill tour of Mexico arranged by the United States Army, when he entered a restaurant in a small town in the Lower Rio Grande Valley.

"No Mexies in here," the paunchy man behind the counter said, as he turned from the grill, wiping his greasy hands on his already dirty apron. "This joint's for white folks only. Get out."

Sergeant Mendoza left, but only because he did not want any food prepared by the "chef" in that restaurant. His protest through army channels, however, took some of the complacency from some of the Anglos in the area.

Sergeant Macario García, another Texas Medal of Honor winner, was visiting his parents, who were working in the beet fields at a place called Sugarland in his home state. He dropped into the Oasis Café for a cup of coffee and was greeted by the "We don't serve no Mexies in here," so familiar to members of La Raza wherever they went in the United States.

"You'll serve me," Sergeant García said. "If I'm good enough to fight your war for you, I'm good enough for you to serve a cup of coffee to."

"Listen, you dirty greaser," the proprietor said, coming around the end of the counter toward García, "you disgrace that uniform just by wearing it. Now get out of here before I throw you out."

At a table by the window, two sailors were finishing their roast-beef hot plates. "Hey, come on, give the sarge a cup of coffee," one sailor called.

"You keep out of this, sailor boy," the proprietor said. "This punk thinks just because he's got some stripes on his arms and ribbons on his chest he's as good as a white man."

He grabbed Sergeant García by the collar and by the seat of the pants and was trying to swing him from the counter stool and head him toward the door.

The two sailors were on their feet and coming over to try to stop the action. Three other customers were on their feet, too, coming from various directions toward the spot where the proprietor was still trying to unseat Sergeant García.

But before any of them could get there, the sergeant's combat-trained reflexes took over, and his left elbow dug into the proprietor's stomach. As García spun on the stool, the side of his right hand caught the proprietor on the point of the chin as he doubled forward from the punch to his stomach. A split second sooner and García's hand would have smashed into the proprietor's throat, above the Adam's apple; as it was, the force of the chop sent the proprietor sprawling back into the arms of the two sailors.

By that time, the other customers had arrived where the action was, and García found himself struggling against the pinioning arms of two of them. Still another customer had grabbed the phone at the end of the counter and was busy dialing. For a brief time, the Oasis sounded more like a herd of stampeding Texas longhorns than a quiet café, and then the door burst open and a deputy sheriff charged in.

"Cut it out or I'll arrest the lot of you!" he shouted. And he had to shout, "Shut up, all of you!" several times before he got an idea of what had happened.

"Look at that ribbon," one of the sailors told him. "It's the Congressional Medal of Honor. That's the highest decoration a guy can get, and anybody who's wearing it ought to be able to eat anywhere."

The deputy shook his head. "I don't know nothing about that," he said, "but I do know this place is a mess. I'm closing it up for the night. All you guys go on home, and you," pointing to the proprietor, "lock this door and clean up the mess. The best thing to do is for everybody to forget the whole thing."

So the fracas seemingly ended.

But that was not the end of the incident.

Everybody involved talked about it, and diplomatic channels from Mexico City to Washington, D.C., burned hot over the issue.

Then Walter Winchell, with his "Good evening, Mr. and Mrs. America, let's go to press," told the national radio audience about the insult to hero Sergeant Macario García in the Oasis Café in Sugarland, Texas. As a result, the sheriff, in order to "uphold the honor of the county," arrested Sergeant Macario García and charged him with "aggravated assault." . . .

POLITICIZATION
OF MEXICAN AMERICANS

The post-World War II period saw the development of a more aggressive approach toward achieving full social and political rights for the Chicano. Returning Mexican American veterans refused to accept second-class citizenship and spoke out for their rights. Alfredo Cuéllar describes this rapidly accelerating political activity.

The politicization of Mexican American communities in the Southwest dates only from the years following World War II. For the most part politicization was prefaced by deep social changes among the Mexican American population. . . . In sum, they brought Mexicans into new and partly unforeseen contact with American society, particularly in urban areas. The word "urbanization" hardly conveys their impact. A demand for labor brought hundreds of thousands of Mexicans into cities from rural areas, and at the same time many hundreds of thousands of young Mexican American men found themselves in uniform—and racially invisible to Anglos from other areas of the United States and

From "Perspectives on Politics," by Alfredo Cuéllar. In Joan W. Moore with Alfredo Cuéllar, *Mexican Americans,* Englewood Cliffs, N.J., 1970. Copyright © 1970. Reprinted, with deletions, by permission of Prentice-Hall, Inc., Englewood Cliffs, N.J.

to other peoples in foreign lands. At the same time, however, their families began to find that the urban areas of the Southwest, like rural ones, were highly discriminatory (this was the time of the zoot-suit riots in Los Angeles and San Diego, California). In the rural areas, however, the social fabric that supported and justified discrimination was hardly changed.

In the cities the urban migrants could find only poor housing, the lowest unskilled employment, and restricted access to schools and other public facilities. As before, few Mexican Americans took part in political activity, although the tradition of political accommodation now seemed outmoded. So did the political organizations built to formalize this relationship to the larger community. A middle class had begun to increase rather rapidly as a result of wartime prosperity, and it was increasingly dissatisfied. Against this background, a group of articulate former servicemen (helped substantially by the educational and training benefits of the GI Bill of Rights) began to press for changes in the community. In Los Angeles a more open environment facilitated a new alliance with labor elements, Anglo civil leaders, and religious leaders.

One outcome of this alliance was the California-based Community Service Organization (CSO). In Los Angeles the CSO tried to develop indigenous leaders to organize community activity around local issues, using the techniques of larger-scale grassroots community organization. In this manner the Community Service Organization mobilized large segments of the Mexican American community into activities directed against restricted housing, police brutality, segregated schools, inequitable justice, and discriminatory employment, all problems endemic in the Mexican American areas of Southern California as much as in other parts of the Southwest. In this process CSO became an important and meaningful post-World War II political phenomenon in the Mexican American community.

In general CSO pressed for full and equal rights for Mexican Americans. The new emphasis was the extra appeal for active and increased participation by as many elements of the community as possible. Therefore, in contrast to previous organizations, CSO tended to be more egalitarian. Under the influence of an outside catalyst (Saul Alinsky's Industrial Areas Foundation), it became a group that no longer served as the vehicle of a relatively few and successful Mexican Americans. Although the leadership tended to be new middle class, on the whole it made an effort to recruit members of the working class and other lower-class elements, including new arrivals from Mexico. CSO also had some non-Mexican members, although they were comparatively few.

This idea of an alliance of equals from various strata of Mexican American society became important. In contrast to the paternalism of previous organizations such as LULAC, there was little concern with the assimilation of lower-class elements into the mainstream of American life. Nor, for that matter, did CSO show any interest in "Mexican culture." The guiding idea of CSO was to cope with concrete and immediate social, economic, and political problems.

The founders of CSO assumed that American institutions were basically responsive to the needs and demands of the Mexican American population. There were no questions about the legitimacy of these institutions; it was always assumed that proper community organization and action would force Anglo institutions to respond to the needs of Mexican Americans. Accordingly, getting Mexicans to exercise the right to vote became a prime CSO objective. Members organized large-scale nonpartisan community drives to register voters. In Los Angeles these registration drives rather significantly increased the number of Spanish-surname voters. The immediate results were electoral victories by Mexican American candidates, there and in nearby communities. Furthermore, CSO pressure on public-housing authorities, on the Fair Employment Practices Commission (FEPC), and against police brutality also yielded results. Housing authorities eased discriminatory practices, Mexican American representation was included in the FEPC, and the police department agreed "to go easy on Mexicans" on the Los Angeles east side.

At the time members considered CSO tactics radical and militant, and throughout the 1950's the CSO remained a politically powerful organization that emphasized direct grassroots community action. Numerous CSO chapters were organized throughout the state of California, each duplicating the Alinsky approach to community organization.

In recent years CSO has declined as a potent community organization, in part because of the withdrawal of financial support from the Industrial Areas Foundation, and in part because it lost some of its most energetic members. For example, the single most well-known former member of CSO, César Chávez, split with the urban-centered CSO to organize a union of farm workers. Also contributing to the decline of CSO was the rise of competing organizations of Mexican Americans.

Other organizations in the Southwest reflect the aggressive political style growing after World War II. In Texas, there is the important American G.I. Forum. The G.I. Forum was founded by a south Texas physician, Dr. Hector García; the immediate cause of its formation was the refusal of a funeral home in Three Rivers, Texas, to bury a Mexican American war veteran in 1948. The incident attracted national attention, and the idea of the G.I. Forum spread rapidly, not only in Texas, but also throughout the Southwest, to several Midwestern states and to Washington, D.C. Although the Forum is concerned with nonpartisan civic action, it has moved increasingly toward more direct and aggressive political activities. In Texas, where its main strength lies, the G.I. Forum launched intensive "Get out the vote" and "Pay your poll tax" drives in the 1950's. Subsequently, it has continued voter-registration drives since the repeal of the Texas poll tax. On a number of other issues, the Forum continues to act as a spokesman against the problems that beset the Mexican American community in Texas.

If the CSO and the American G.I. Forum reflect the goals of the immediate postwar years, two political groups founded in the late 1950's show a shift in both the political goals and the resources available in the community. In California the Mexican American Political Association (MAPA), founded in 1958, and in Texas the Political Association of Spanish-Speaking Organizations (PASSO) were organized essentially as groups pressuring the political system at the party level. These were not primarily attempts to organize the Mexican American poor to register and vote; they were efforts to use growing middle-class strength to win concessions for Mexican Americans from the Anglo-dominated political parties. Essentially the goal of both associations was simply to get Mexican Americans into political office, either as nominees for elective office in the regular parties or as appointees of elected Anglo officials. Thus the best-publicized effort of either group was the successful deposition of the Anglo political structure in Crystal City, Texas, in the early 1960's. In this venture, PASSO joined with some non-Mexican groups, notably the Teamsters and the Catholic Bishops' Committee for the Spanish-Speaking. (Although the victory in Crystal City was short-lived, it was as significant to Texas Mexicans as the more recent victory of a Negro mayor in Mississippi was to the black community.)

Both MAPA and PASSO gain strength by virtue of their statewide connections, which are particularly important in the outlying rural areas where repression has been a norm. Statewide ties give courage and support to local efforts. (At this writing one of the strongest MAPA chapters in California is the chapter in the Coachella Valley, a citrus- and date-growing area not far from Palm Springs. The local chairman, a vociferous spokesman for Mexican American laborers, is constantly subject to harassment. He is also constantly in demand outside the immediate area. The intervention of outside elements in a local and rather repressive situation has reduced isolation and repression. As in Crystal City, one of MAPA's victories has been the election of Mexican American officials in the grower-dominated town of Coachella.)

Although both MAPA and PASSO are still largely confined to California and Texas, respectively, there are branches and organizational efforts in other states. The two associations once considered amalgamation into a regional group, but incredibly, the effort failed because the two groups could not agree on a common name. Texas Mexicans could not afford the then-too-overt ethnic pride suggested by "Mexican American," and the California group would not accept the euphemism "Spanish-speaking." At these discussions, one disgusted delegate finally proposed CACA (a Spanish equivalent of the English "doo-doo") to represent the "Confederated Alliance of Chicano Associations." Interestingly, only in such an intensely in-group situation could the name "Chicano" be suggested. At the time this word could not be used for a serious political discussion. . . .

THE 1942 BRACERO AGREEMENT

Although thousands of Mexican workers had entered the United States since 1900, a formal agreement had never been reached concerning the status of these laborers. However, as a result of wartime exigencies and Mexican insistence, the World War II bracero program was instituted. Nelson G. Copp describes details of the 1942 agreement.

The first legal importation of Mexican labor during the emergency of World War II was pursuant to the Executive Agreement of August 4, 1942. In its "general principles" this agreement provided that Mexicans contracting to work in the United States would not be subject to military service; that no discrimination would be shown in the use of Mexicans so imported; that these Mexicans would enjoy guarantees of transportation, living expenses, and repatriation in accordance with Mexican Labor Law; and that such labor would not be used to displace other workers in the United States or reduce rates of pay in a locality where such rates had previously been established.

This 1942 agreement provided that the two governments would be the contracting parties. Mexico insisted on this as a means of placing responsibility for execution of the provisions of the agreement. The "employer" as used in these contracts meant the Farm Security Administration of the Department of Agriculture of the United States of America. The "sub-employer" was the

From "Wetbacks and Braceros," by Nelson G. Copp. Boston: Ph.D. diss., Boston University, 1963. Reprinted by permission of the author's estate.

operator of the farm where the workers were to be used. The contracts between the employer and the Mexican workers were made under the supervision of the Mexican government and had to be written in Spanish. The employer must then enter into contracts with the sub-employer, who would guarantee the observance of the provisions of the agreement.

The employer would meet all transportation and living expenses from the place of origin to the destination of the worker in the United States, as well as necessary incidental expenses. The worker would carry with him about seventy-two pounds (thirty-five kilos) of baggage. The United States tried in vain to persuade Mexico to let the worker's family accompany him. Not being able to be with his family was one reason why a worker often became dissatisfied, left his employment, and asked to be repatriated. The sub-employer was then required to reimburse the United States government for the transportation expense. The transportation issue became more serious a few years later when a large cotton crop was ready for harvest in the northern part of Mexico, and, therefore, it insisted that all labor recruitment be from the interior. No doubt Mexico also realized that workers from the interior would not be as likely to attempt to re-enter the United States at a later date as those nearer the border. After 1946, the regulations on transportation were unnecessarily burdensome, according to American employers.

The "Wages and Employment" provisions of the agreement provided that the wages would be the same as those paid to other agricultural laborers in the same region. In no case was the wage to be less than 30 cents an hour, and piece rates were to be such as to enable a worker of average ability to earn the "prevailing wage." However, the agreement did not exactly define the meaning of the term "prevailing wage." No clarification occurred until the report of the President's Commission on Migratory Labor in 1951, which included the following explanation, though not a definition, of "prevailing wage" as it applied to all the preceding agreements:

> The president of the New Mexico Farm and Livestock Bureau candidly described the method of setting the "prevailing wage" as follows:

The prevailing wage is really set by the farmers for the various types of jobs on the farm, and it will vary, depending upon the type of work the man does . . . We have a meeting at the beginning of the season; the farmers have a meeting and they determine, roughly, what they are going to pay. It doesn't mean that they will hold to it; it will vary, as a matter of fact.

This wage, as decided upon by farm employers, usually weeks in advance of the work period, is accepted by the public employment services as the going wage until the season opens and employment actually gets under way.

No government agency determined or fixed the wages. Neither government agencies, nor employers, nor workers could give the President's commission an accurate idea of the meaning of prevailing wage. There was evidence that "occasionally" Mexican workers under contract were paid less than domestic workers for the same type of employment. The term "prevailing wage" was in reality practically meaningless. Since the employers setting the wage did not consider whether the amount agreed upon was sufficient to attract the necessary labor, it could not "very well serve as the price to equate the supply of and demand for labor." The vagueness of the term becomes all the more evident when foreign workers are brought into a locality, a situation which in itself tends to set a wage pattern. Certainly this method of setting wages is a far cry from the ideal of establishing a wage by negotiation of workers and employers on an equal footing.

As early as 1936, some thought had been given to a minimum prevailing wage for industry in the Walsh-Healy Act. In the employment of Mexican contract labor for agricultural use, however, the phrase has a different meaning. Rates of pay are usually set by collective bargaining, not by action of the employers alone. The wage considered in this act was for actual employment, to attract employees, not for work to be performed later as in contract employment. Also, under the Walsh-Healy Act, the prevailing wage is determined officially and formally for a particular job under consideration. In agriculture there is no such official determination available as a guide for workers or employers.

The President's Commission on Migratory Labor in 1951 noted

that in some localities, not specified in the report, there was a
falling wage rate and also a shortage of labor, a combination
which seemed incongruous. The reason undoubtedly was that the
arbitrary wage agreed upon was not sufficient to attract the
number of laborers needed and had a direct relation to the desire
to import alien labor. The associations of farm employers had set
one-sided wage rates, thus creating their own "labor shortage."

Other important phases besides wages were also covered by the
agreement of 1942 in great detail. Mexico provided that members
of a worker's family could be employed at less than the rates set in
the agreement when, because of age or sex, they could not do a
full day's work. Minors under fourteen years of age were strictly
prohibited from work, and all minors were to have the same
opportunities to attend school as other agricultural laborers'
children.

Workers under contract were to be used in agriculture only,
and any change in type of employment required the approval of
the worker and the Mexican government. No collections or
assessments were to be made against the workers, and they might
purchase goods where they wished and not be compelled to trade
at a store owned by the employer.

Housing facilities for Mexicans had to be identical with those
enjoyed by other agricultural workers in the same locality.
Another provision stated that:

> Workers admitted under this understanding shall enjoy as regards
> occupational diseases and accidents the same guarantees enjoyed by
> other agricultural workers under United States legislation.

This was a meaningless stipulation at that time since there was no
workmen's compensation or anything comparable for agricultural
workers under existing laws, but was necessary in the light of its
future application to the possible recruitment of industrial labor.
Mexicans had the right to elect their own representatives to deal
with employers, but such representatives had to be working
members of their groups. The braceros would be paid $3 a day for
subsistence in periods of unemployment, exclusive of Sundays.
One would think that this provision would ensure their regular
and continuous employment. A rise in the cost of living would

naturally require reconsideration of a contract. At the expiration of his contract, the continued stay of a Mexican in the United States would be illegal "from an immigration point of view." The exception provided was "physical impossibility," a term not more clearly defined.

The 1942 agreement covered security for the earnings of the Mexican workers. They would place their money in a Rural Savings Fund, and it would be transferred to the *Banco de Crédito Agrícola*. If workers wished to purchase agricultural equipment in the United States, the money was transferred to this bank for the payment of such implements. The Farm Security Administration agreed to recommend priority on these items.

The number of laborers required was not known at the time the agreement was made, but the United States Department of Agriculture would furnish the information to the government of Mexico from requests made by prospective employers as to their probable needs.

The Mexican government required advance notice of the number of workers in order to determine the number which might be allowed to leave Mexico without detriment to its national economy.

The same provisions were intended to apply to non-agricultural workers. The agreement could be renounced by either government after ninety days' advance notice. It was drawn up in Mexico City and signed there on July 23, 1942. By an exchange of notes, it became effective on August 4, 1942.

It should be remembered that this agreement was signed when the United States was at war with powerful enemies. There had been private contracting of Mexican labor before World War II, but the war had complicated entry and other matters which then required mutual governmental action by Mexico and the United States.

Recruitment in Mexico began under the supervisory control of the War Food Administration of the United States Department of Agriculture with the purpose of preventing the abuses which had accompanied private recruitment by American employers. The workers were examined in Mexico, given an identification card, and sent to employment centers in the United States. These workers, being only temporarily admitted, were exempt from the head tax and literacy test required under the United States immigration laws.

The agreement of 1942, though revised many times, has become the basis for a more comfortable relationship between the United States and Mexico and serves today as the foundation of the bracero program. . . .

V

THE SLAVES WE RENT

Mojados, or illegal wetbacks, were without doubt the most ill treated of all workers in the Southwest during the postwar period. Entering the United States clandestinely, they were forced to accept the lowest wages, live in the poorest housing, and exist at a subhuman level. Moreover, they became objects of discrimination and racketeering from Mexicans, Chicanos, and Anglos. This serious problem of mistreatment and the equally serious problem of rapidly increasing numbers of mojados were never successfully dealt with by either the United States or Mexico.

Concern for the plight of mojados by Mexico and American worries about their increasing numbers led to the development of a "drying out" process in the late 1940's. By this technique thousands of illegal Mexican immigrants were given identification slips, sent back across the border, and then allowed to re-enter legally as braceros. While this scheme provided minimal guarantees for these Mexican workers, it did not attack the problem of controlling illegal entrants.

Mexico, unhappy with the treatment of her nationals for some time, informed the United States at the outbreak of fighting in Korea in 1950 that a return to government-to-government arrangements was basic to any expanded use of Mexican labor in American agriculture. This attitude was instrumental in passage by Congress of Public Law 78, outlining a new bracero program of administered migration under the Department of Labor. As a result, in August 1951, Mexico and the United States signed an agreement on migrant labor.

In the Southwest, Chicanos, for the most part, reacted ambivalently to mojados inasmuch as they were of la raza but also clearly had a depressant effect on the economics of Chicano communities. On the national level as early as 1948 a congressional committee began investigating the rapidly rising tide of these illegal immigrants. However, nothing was really done until the Attorney General's office undertook a massive deportation effort, known as "Operation Wetback," in 1954.

Illegal Mexican laborers and postwar braceros rapidly increased in numbers until they peaked at about 1½ million in the mid-1950's. This massive influx of Mexican workers quickly led to a sizable migration of Chicanos from such labor-reservoir areas as Los Angeles, El Paso, and San Antonio, as labor surpluses developed, especially in low-skill job categories.

In many cases Southwestern employers deliberately discouraged local labor in order to use braceros or mojados maximally. This widespread practice in the 1950's resulted in underemployment and unemployment of domestic workers and held down agricultural wages to bracero levels. Texas became both the largest importer of Mexican nationals and largest exporter of Chicano workers to other states as the subsequent depressing effect on wages caused thousands of local workers and their families to hit the migrant trails.

Since the 1920's, efforts to organize Western agricultural workers had been undertaken, especially in California. The enormity of this task and the concerted and vigorous opposition of agricultural interests—small growers, large growers, and agribusiness—doomed these efforts to failure.

In the early 1960's César Chávez, who had extensive organizational experience in the Community Service Organization, began to organize farm workers in the great central valley of California. Then in 1965 the Delano grape strike took place. This movement, based on non-violence and the use of outside support, pitted Chávez and his followers against overwhelming odds to obtain humane conditions of employment for farm workers. Aided by a number of factors, including the end of the bracero program in December 1964 and Church, civil rights, and labor support, Chávez's United Farm Workers' Organizing Committee in mid-1970 finally succeeded in signing up a majority of California grape growers.

During this organizational period, grower use of scab labor became the major problem for the UFWOC. Growers recruited these strikebreakers mostly from commuter traffic, which increased in volume when the bracero program terminated. Legal commuters are usually Mexican nationals who live in Mexico but work in the United States, although many are American citizens who choose to live in Mexico. Commuters are permitted to cross the border under various permits allowing them to work in the United States.

This commuter pattern has existed for many years, and though its volume is not known, estimates run into tens of thousands annually. In recent years commuters and increasing numbers of illegal entrants have supplied much of the labor formerly done by braceros. Given the differences in economic conditions that exist between the United States and Mexico, commuters and illegal entrants will continue to be a factor in American labor organization.

WETBACKS AND
THE BORDER PATROL

American postwar needs led to expanded demand for Mexican workers throughout the Midwest and Southwest. Great increases in the number of illegal aliens entering the country caused rising concern in both govern-

From "Wetbacks and Braceros," by Nelson G. Copp. Boston: Ph.D. diss., Boston University, 1963. Reprinted by permission of the author's estate.

ment and labor sectors. Nelson G. Copp describes the problem and efforts to solve it.

Postwar prosperity in the United States created even greater needs for Mexican labor which were not provided for in the agreements with Mexico. This inadequacy was revealed in 1949, when American employers contracted for only thirty-five thousand workers, but the Commissioner of Immigration and Naturalization estimated that several times that number of wetbacks were coming over the boundary for indefinite periods. A new arrangement was negotiated on August 1, 1949, in which both governments consented to take all measures to suppress "radically" the illegal traffic in Mexican workers.

Nonetheless, the wetback problem grew from year to year, and, in 1950, the Commissioner of Immigration and Naturalization reported:

> From Texas, California, and the cotton areas of Arkansas, Mississippi and Tennessee, west and north as far as Alaska, come reports of Mexican nationals in agricultural work who are here illegally. So great was the influx that almost 500,000 deportable aliens were apprehended by Border Patrol in 1950 and were granted voluntary departure in lieu of deportation—since immigration officer personnel was totally inadequate to hold deportation proceedings in any but the most aggravated cases.

The District Director of the Immigration and Naturalization Service in San Antonio, Texas, saw the only solution to the wetback problem as additional legislation making it an offense to hire an alien obviously in the country unlawfully. Also, in 1950, the district director at Los Angeles reported:

> The increasing number of our apprehensions demonstrates the growth of the army of Mexicans who throng the towns on the Mexican side of the border—penniless, hungry and desperately anxious to obtain employment on this side of the line to obtain some money to send their families in Mexico.

A new approach to the riddle of the wetbacks in 1950 attempted to place those already in the United States under legal contract. In effect, 96,239 wetbacks were legalized in this way in 1950 alone. Certainly this move did nothing to discourage the flow of wetbacks but rather encouraged it.

Public Law 78, enacted on July 12, 1951, provided for a new program to establish reception centers near the border and to provide housing, subsistence, and transportation for legally contracted braceros in accordance with the Migrant Labor Agreement with Mexico in 1951. This law was a real effort to discourage illegal migrants. Recruitment and management of the program were under the United States Department of Labor, and entry and departure procedures were under the Immigration and Naturalization Service. In 1952, 219,074 braceros, legally contracted laborers, were admitted from Mexico. The one remaining deficiency was in apprehending and deporting those Mexicans who were already in the United States without benefit of documents.

By 1953, however, it was apparent that even this program of contracting for Mexican workers was not a success insofar as its impact on the continued mass invasion of illegal entrants from Mexico. Especially bothersome, the Commissioner of Immigration and Naturalization noted, was a change in attitude of the wetbacks themselves:

> The report of the Border Patrol reflected an increasing belligerence on the part of the Mexican aliens apprehended. This same attitude has made the job of security officers increasingly difficult. The number of aliens who escaped from custody increased during the past year, particularly along the Mexican border. In one instance recently nine detainees went over an 11-foot fence enclosing the Chula Vista Camp in accordance with a well thought out plan. In the past Mexicans have been a fairly docile group of individuals requiring only minimum safe-guards and limited detention personnel. However, aggravated economic conditions in Mexico, plus tougher Border Patrol enforcement during the past three years, have had a cumulative effect upon the Mexican illegal entrant, especially the teen-ager. He now frequently resents apprehension, detention, and efforts to deport him, is abusive and displays little respect for authority. This situation, which is general along the border, has compelled the Service to adopt stricter security measures in detention facilities.

Despite the stiffening surveillance of the Border Patrol, despite the swelling numbers of Mexican nationals legally admitted to the United States as temporary agricultural workers, despite the competition from other laborers admitted on a temporary basis from Canada, the British West Indies, British Honduras, and British Guiana, the wetbacks surged across the border. Evidently the desire of Mexicans to journey "stateside" increased after their compatriots had returned home to relate the wonders and economic attractions encountered during their brief stay. The money and goods which they brought were proof enough to induce thousands of other villagers to take the same path.

What preventive measures could the United States enforce? Border Patrolmen watched more vigilantly. In 1953, apprehensions of Mexicans exceeded 875,000. Of these, thirty thousand were working in trade or industry at the time of their arrest. Many others escaped arrest and went inland by freight trains. One officer's report included this incident:

> One night at Yuma, Arizona, local law enforcement officers joined with the Border Patrol to clear the railroad yards there of a group of illegal aliens who had missed outgoing trains. There were an estimated fifteeen hundred illegal aliens in the railroad yards at one time, at Yuma that night.

During 1953, twelve light planes were assigned to border patrolling. Groups crossing late in the evening or early in the morning were spotted, and officers informed by radio could proceed by horse or jeep to apprehend or deter the offending aliens. Air lift and train lift were used to transport Mexicans back to points in the interior of their country near their homes but away from the border. Because of drought in 1953 and the preceding years, the lower Rio Grande near McAllen, Texas, was nearly empty of water. In this area alone 333,079 aliens were arrested. They were taken to a detention camp in McAllen and shipped by bus back to Mexico.

Despite its exertions, the Border Patrol could not establish "effective control" over the line between Mexico and the United States after 1949. The Commissioner of the Immigration Service admitted that the personnel under his command could not prevent "all illegal crossings of the border at the international line. Nothing short of an impassable barrier could do that." Especially elusive and troublesome were the smugglers who loaded Mexicans into airplanes and darted across the border. Airplanes used more and more as efficient tools for trafficking in aliens were difficult to police.

Although the task of patrolling the border had always been difficult at best, it became very serious after 1949. Nevertheless, the Commissioner of the Immigration and Naturalization Service confidently predicted that his officers could keep the border effectively policed if the governments of the United States and Mexico would resolutely agree to permit traffic only in the case of temporary laborers *under contract.* In short, he contended that a bracero program, properly administered, would eliminate wet-backs from the scene. He disagreed sharply with legislators and those in the executive branch of the government who felt that effective control could not be maintained regardless of the number of personnel and the amount of equipment. He proved his point in 1954, after the initiation of "Operation Wetback," when his agency conducted a nationwide roundup of Mexican aliens and returned more than a million of them to Mexico. The Mexican government supported the bracero program and was glad to regain control over her nationals. At the same time, she benefited from the foreign exchange that the wetbacks brought home. There was, therefore, no disapproval of this forced repatriation. Undoubtedly, many who had entered illegally from Mexico did manage to elude the law and continued to live as permanent residents in the United States.

The substantial increase of Mexican population in the Southwest during the last twenty-five years has been due in some degree to the success of illegal migrants in escaping detection. Especially noteworthy has been the concentration of Mexican stock in Texas. In 1930, the Latin-American population of Texas was 683,688, of whom 266,046 were born in Mexico. In 1949, a socio-economic survey made under a Rockefeller grant placed the number at 1,121,639, based on a scholastic population count. The "Spanish-name" count, made subsequent to the 1950 census, resulted in a figure of 1,028,790. Authorities agree that these counts are probably too low. A 1955 estimate placed the number of Latin-Americans in Texas at 1,500,000. The gain in Latin-American population has been more rapid than the increase of the state's population as a whole.

In summary, therefore, the political and economic realities finally overwhelmed the wetback and permitted the bracero to perform his true role, freed of the competition of wetbacks. While no attempt has been made to distinguish the problems of the wetback, bracero, permanent resident, or citizen of Mexican descent, all met the same political and economic hazards, except that the latter two groups of Mexicans had no fear of being returned to Mexico. As the Mexican was viewed only as a source of inexpensive labor, fine distinctions of immigration status were of little importance to the Mexicans or Americans.

BRACERO'S JOURNEY

Bracerismo expanded enormously after World War II, and thousands of Mexicans endured the hardships of a long trip—prelude to what was to come in the United States. By working there temporarily, they hoped to realize their plans for a better future in Mexico. S. W. Coombs, a photo-journalist, accompanied braceros on their two-thousand-mile journey.

The covered shoebox resting in the crook of the state deputy's arm contained forty-one marbles, six white and thirty-five colored. One marble for each of the forty-one men of the hamlet of Rancho Astillero, in the northwestern part of Zacatecas State in

From "Bracero's Journey," by S. W. Coombs. *AMERICAS,* 5 (December 1963). Reprinted from *AMERICAS* monthly magazine published by the Pan American Union in English, Spanish, and Portuguese.

Mexico. Before noon the next day, six men would be on their way to join the ranks of braceros working across the U.S. border, and the other thirty-five would return to their dusty fields. Although the odds in this drawing were nearly seven to one against each man, one of them—Asunción Renéndez Cruz—had a feeling that one white marble was for him.

Asunción, forty-four-year-old father of eleven children, owner of one cow and two burros, a half-dozen chickens, and ten rocky acres, is not a man to spend his time daydreaming. But today was different; one white marble could change so much. It could make him the owner of a pair of sturdy young mules and a new factory-made steel plow. María, his wife, would have a treadle sewing machine and there would be clothes for the children.

A similar marble drawing took place later that same afternoon at nearby Rancho Tejones. Every adult male under age fifty was there, including a young man named Mauricio Realsola Caredel. His thoughts were wandering. Mauricio could think only of the shiny new grinding mill that he dreamed of purchasing.

Mauricio and his wife Amavilla have only one child, a fifteen-month-old daughter. The mother is eighteen years old, Mauricio is twenty-four. Like many of Mexico's younger generation, they hope for a better future and have a "special" plan for making those hopes come true. Mauricio's going to the United States to work as a bracero is a vital part of that plan. . . .

Except for the few ranchers with herds, average cash income at Rancho Astillero and Rancho Tejones is less than three thousand pesos a year ($280 U.S.). That explains why so many men are anxious to get seasonal employment on farms in the United States.

By evening the marble drawings were over in Zacatecas; a total of 140 men were selected from nineteen ranchos, and among them were Asunción and Mauricio. Not all the men showed up at the local bracero office as instructed, because some were unable to raise the 150-peso bus fare to Empalme, Mexico's West Coast Workers Immigration Station. In hopes of filling the twenty or so resulting vacancies, losers in the day's drawings crowded the office to plead their cases. Due to a new ruling by the governor, their trip to town was in vain. Now only the men who actually draw the white marbles are eligible. This ruling as well as the new system of drawing marbles is only a part of the overall reform program inaugurated by the newly elected young governor of Zacatecas, José Rodríguez Elias.

Asunción was one of the men who had a problem in raising the bus fare. Thirty-eight pesos was all the money he had. A merchant offered him the necessary money at 10 percent per month interest, but Asunción refused, remembering the plight of a fellow *campesino* who borrowed his expense money at high interest only to be turned down by the examining doctor at the Empalme Immigration Station. Upon his return this man faced the almost hopeless task of repaying the loan as the interest compounded. Asunción's caution was wise, for at the last moment a fellow *campesino* lent him 125 pesos at no interest. As he waited in line for his papers to be stamped, Asunción reflected that he would have only 13 pesos for food and personal expenses for a trip that would last a week and maybe longer.

At eight o'clock the next morning, two second-class buses lumbered down Valparaíso's cobbled streets, each loaded with sixty excited passengers and two drivers. The bus carrying Mauricio and Asunción broke down eighty miles later with a fractured front end, which is not surprising considering the rutted path they were following. The passengers spent the next four hours resting on the shady side of the bus until the acetylene torch was snuffed and the front end was again part of the bus. It was thirty-five more hours of steel bouncing on steel, the hard straight-back seats providing little cushion between bodies and highway, before the unlighted outskirts of Empalme were sighted.

Empalme, founded in 1905, is an important rail center. Since the Workers Immigration Station opened in 1955, the town has enjoyed a second important source of income—the feeding and housing of the hordes of prospective braceros. The facilities for this feeding and housing are rustic by any standard. Hundreds of residents rent out garages, lean-tos, and front porches at one peso per night per sleeping space.

As the dawn slowly broke up the night sky, the men who had curled under porches and sheds or hunched against buildings and in doorways struggled to their feet and numbly made their way to the station compound. By seven, more than five thousand were crowded around the calling area under the watchful eyes of the soldiers garrisoned nearby. In every mind there was a single thought. The burning hope that today they would hear their names called over the station's loudspeaker. Between two hundred and one thousand men are processed each day, depending upon the orders received from the U.S. Department of Labor in El Centro, California.

It was five long days and six longer nights of fighting hunger, cold, and boredom before Asunción and Mauricio boarded the train for Mexicali. Asunción, always slender, had turned into a gaunt skeleton. The usual sparkle in his eyes had faded and the ready smile disappeared. It was difficult for him to remember why he was here or to think of what lay ahead. When the Valparaíso men boarded the train, Asunción refused to enter into the jubilant mood of his fellow *campesinos*.

It was another day and night before the train reached Mexicali. A day and a night on wood-slatted benches, looking through dirty windows that would not open, twisting water spigots that long ago had stopped working. But the physical discomforts of the accommodations failed to dull the partylike atmosphere.

The border procedures were brief. Papers were checked, baggage inspected and sprayed with DDT, then the men boarded the waiting buses for the short trip to El Centro and the first hot meal in several days.

Asunción sat mechanically chewing, oblivious to the happy din of the mess hall. Mauricio bolted his food, anxious for the processing to begin. He knew available contracts would be announced immediately after the results of the physical examination were determined. He would look for a chance to go to the Salinas area to work in the lettuce fields. Last fall he had talked with a bracero who had worked five months in that area. Since hearing of this beautiful green country beside a turquoise sea, Mauricio had dreamed of one day going there himself.

The physical examination at El Centro is more thorough than the one at Empalme. About 7 percent of the men never get farther into the United States than El Centro because of positive readings on the X rays, or other health conditions. Each man is checked, head to toe, and inside out. Processing up to two thousand men a day, the center is a model of efficiency. But to the men from rural Mexico, it is a frightening and bewildering introduction to the United States. At last the chest thumping, fingerprinting, picture taking, and interviewing are over, and the men go to a large hall where contracts are read in Spanish. . . .

In the hall the men from Valparaíso heard farm-association representatives explain the various contracts available that day. The last contract was for work in Salinas on the Bud Antle Ranch, the world's largest lettuce grower. Mauricio, Asunción, and the entire Valparaíso group signed up for the $1.17 hourly guarantee there, which is seventeen cents above the minimum set up by the Department of Labor for the state. The length of the contract, piece rates, cost of board, the benefits and cost of hospital and disability insurance were explained in detail.

Soon the men were heading north on the last lap of their long trip. It was close to midnight when the bus crested the last of the San Bernardino hills and they saw the lights of Los Angeles.

Arriving at the ranch on a Saturday morning was a stroke of fortunate timing, for it meant a two-day rest before beginning work.

Abruptly it was Monday. At 6 a.m. the mess-hall bell announced breakfast. While the braceros gulped down their scrambled eggs, sausages, and Mexican-style beans, the field buses waited outside, motors idling.

The first day in the fields was a trying one for all concerned. Many of the men had never seen a head of lettuce. The mass-production methods of the Antle Ranch were confusing and unfamiliar.

By the end of the first week the newly arrived braceros had caught on to the work procedures and had gradually adapted themselves to the semiregimented life of the ranch; the days passed with no unusual happenings to disrupt the system—every day was the same, only the fields changed. Up at six, line up to wash, line up for breakfast, a bouncy ride in the field buses to the inexhaustible lettuce, eight to twelve hours of hot sweaty work, back to the bunkhouse, line up to wash, and one last line of the day for supper. If the men were not too exhausted from the day's labor, there might be an impromptu baseball game after supper, always a bunkhouse card game. . . .

The weeks became months, thousands of carloads of lettuce were shipped, money was sent home to Mexico: sewing machines, portable radios, and toys accumulated in the storeroom. Mauricio has made many visits to the farm-machinery dealer to look at "his" corn-grinding mill. Skipping the cards and baseball, he now spends his evenings curled up on his bunk with notebook and pencil stub figuring, planning, and dreaming. The price of $1,480, or as Mauricio counts, the staggering sum of 18,500 pesos, is the cause of much frustration and sadness. Over and over he estimates the wages he will earn, the amount he must send home, and the amount he can save. The notebook pages fill up but the answer is always the same, no matter how many times he adds and subtracts. He will not have enough money to buy the mill by the end of his contract. There is only one solution. Mauricio must return to Mexico and wait another year, or perhaps several, and draw another white marble before the mill will be his. . . .

TEXAS MIGRANTS

Migrant patterns, appearing first in Texas, resulted from seasonal demands in commercial agriculture for large numbers of farm laborers. Mexican and Mexican American workers supplied most of this demand in Western agriculture. Lowell L. Tubbs describes the development of migrancy from Texas centers and the patterns of migrant trails.

Nearly every state in the United States has some Spanish-name

From "A Survey of the Problems of the Migratory Mexicans," by Lowell L. Tubbs. Austin, Texas: M.A. thesis, University of Texas, 1952. Reprinted, with deletions, by permission of the author.

residents; however, most of them are found in five Southwestern states: California, New Mexico, Colorado, Texas, and Arizona. It is within these states that the Mexican population reaches a sizable percentage of the entire population. In 1948 it was estimated that there were from 2 million to 3,500,000 Spanish-name people in the United States. This is not a large number when compared with the total United States population, but nevertheless these people constitute a significant group in five Southwestern states. The percentage of the Spanish-name population within the above-mentioned five states ranges from 50 percent in New Mexico to 10 percent in Colorado. The steady increase of the Mexican population within these states and the bordering states cannot be ignored.

The Mexican population has been centered in the Southwestern United States with a growing tendency to move west and north as a result of the push-and-pull system created by conditions in Mexico and the opportunity for the wetback to temporarily better his economic situation in the United States. The entry of the wetback into the United States has gradually forced the American-born and naturalized citizens of Mexican descent to push on into border states and, in many instances, to join the migratory farm-worker procession in an attempt to obtain relief from economic pressure caused by the low wage scale generally existing in areas where illegal alien labor is accepted.

Texas has more Spanish-name people than any other single state. In many instances, Texas has been the greatest contributor of Spanish-speaking people to other states. It has been the hub on which the wheel of Mexican population in the United States has revolved. One authority has stated that it is virtually impossible to obtain a satisfactory estimate of the number of Mexicans in Texas at any given time. What has been said about the actual count of Mexicans in Texas can perhaps be applied to the other Southwestern states.

In 1949 the Spanish-name population of Texas was estimated to be somewhere between 1 million and 1,500,000. This statement was made by Lyle Saunders:

   It is probably safe to say that the Spanish-speaking population of Texas numbers somewhere between 1,100,000 and 1,300,000. It should be remembered, however, that no allowance is made in these figures for the wetback population, which has been estimated between 100,000 and 500,000.

In Texas, as in the United States, the Spanish-name population is not distributed evenly throughout the state. A few of the counties have a heavy concentration while others have relatively few. . . .

Some of the Spanish-name people have been able to adapt themselves to American ways and have engaged in trades, the professions, businesses, and government work. Others have become large landowners and successful commercial farmers and ranchers. For the larger mass of the Mexican population, the picture has been different. Gradually the ownership of land passed from their hands. They learned to look for wage-paying jobs to lighten their burdens. They had no alternative since it became impossible for them to make a living in one location. Thus a migrant group was formed, and the past twenty years have witnessed an alarming growth of this group.

The reasons for migrancy have been stated in the report of the President's Commission on Migratory Labor. Perhaps the most important single reason for migrancy is that people find it impossible to make a living in one location. Technological displacement, business recession and consequent unemployment in industry, crop failure, changes in the sharecropper system, lack of vocational training and education are other reasons listed as factors responsible for migrancy.

An accurate count of migratory farm workers in the United States has been hard to obtain. A migratory worker moves several times during the year and not always in the same mobility pattern. Some move only short distances if the crops have been good in that locality. At other times, crop failures or shortages cause the migrant to move more often and greater distances. . . .

Every year thousands of farm workers migrate from their homes to "follow the crops," often through many states. Usually they return to their homes when cold weather drives them from the fields. Some are unable to finance the return trip and consequently remain to become a public concern to the locality in which they are forced to reside. Others find employment opportunities on a more permanent basis and establish residence.

The farm laborers have formed intricate mobility patterns due to seasonal crops. They have obtained their work by bits and pieces here and there in an attempt to obtain a year's work. Minor mobility patterns have been formed by groups that require a month or two of seasonal labor to supplement their earnings at home. They usually make a swing through several counties before returning home. Employment opportunities determine the distance and time consumed on the trip.

Some groups of migratory farm laborers make a wide swing through their home state covering many miles and consuming from two to twelve months or longer. Other groups make a larger swing through several states. The migratory swings start at different times of the year and at different locations. Workers constantly leave the swing while at the same time others join the procession.

It has been generally accepted that there are two major mobility patterns relating to farm workers and the South and Southwest. One pattern follows the Atlantic coast from Florida to New England. Few Mexican migratory farm workers have been involved in this pattern. The mobility pattern of the "Texas-Mexican" migration begins in Texas and goes through Arkansas into the Great Lakes states. In describing migratory labor patterns, it has become the practice to list the amount of work which is supposed to be available along the route.

Comparably, the estimated employment potential of the Texas–Great Lakes States migratory pattern is said to include the following:
1. South Texas—vegetables, citrus—December to May—140 days.
2. Arkansas—strawberries—May—20 days.
3. Michigan—sugar beets—May, June, October—50 days and 30 days.
4. Michigan—cherries—June, July—50 days.
5. Wisconsin—cherries—July, August—20 days.
6. Michigan—peaches—August—20 days.
7. Indiana, Ohio—tomatoes—August, September, October—45 days.

8. Mississippi Delta—cotton—September, October, November—80 days.

9. Texas—cotton—July, August, September, November—120 days.

MEXICANS
TO MICHIGAN

Conditions that migrant workers had to accept and the helplessness of their "captivity" shamed modern America. Carey McWilliams, a long-time fighter for social justice for the Mexican American, details the insecurity, inhumane conditions, and disappointing financial results for migrants.

The Mexican barrio of San Antonio is an indolent and rather attractive quarter. Unpainted shacks, in a state of perpetual ill repair, rest on stilts and lean precariously in all directions; dogs bark, children yell, and radios blare in every hovel. But the windows are decorated with plants, feeble shrubs sprout in the dirt yards, and morning glories climb the fence posts. Every corner has its grocery store and beer hall (and above the beer hall the *bagnio*). Thousands of Mexicans, constituting perhaps 40 percent of the population of San Antonio, live in the quarter. It is the hunting ground of labor contractors; the capital of the Mexico that lies within the United States.

Here, on El Paso Street—the "skid row"—are the headquarters of Frank Cortez. A versatile citizen, Mr. Cortez is the principal emigrant agent or labor contractor in Texas, and also the operator of several stores, cafés, and a funeral parlor in the barrio. Young, snappily dressed, affable, Mr. Cortez was once a migrant worker himself. One year in the service of a Pennsylvania steel mill as a

From "Mexicans to Michigan," by Carey McWilliams. *Common Ground,* 2, 1 (Autumn 1941).

contract employee was enough, however, to convince him he should seek another vocation. He returned to San Antonio and opened a funeral parlor—a happy decision, for the death rate among the Mexican population is high, the Mexicans like ornate funerals, and most of them carry burial insurance.

A few years ago, Mr. Cortez became a licensed emigrant agent, authorized by the state of Texas to recruit labor for employment beyond its borders. From mid-March until May each year, he is busy signing up Mexican sugar-beet workers at the funeral parlor for his good friend Max Henderson of the Michigan Beet Growers' Employment Committee. Each year he recruits six thousand workers for the committee, for whom he is paid $1 a head.

"There isn't much expense, and I make $6,000 for about three weeks' work. It's a nice business," says Mr. Cortez.

Of the northern sugar-beet areas in the Midwest, Michigan imports, by a considerable margin, the most Mexican labor. The average planting, about 140,000 acres, necessitates the employment of nearly twenty thousand field workers. Ninety-five percent of this acreage is handled by contract labor (that is, labor performed not by the growers but by field labor under contract), and two thirds of it comes from Texas. At least ten thousand and perhaps fifteen thousand field workers make the trip to Michigan every season. . . .

They begin to arrive from all over Texas. The flow of traffic around the funeral parlor is so heavy special police squads have to be called in to maintain order. Trucks and jalopies, heavily loaded with women, youngsters, dogs, goats, chickens, and all the accoutrements of travel, are parked for blocks around. At four in the morning, the line begins to form outside the office. Thousands of Mexicans, shuffling in the morning half-light, are silhouetted against the walls of the buildings. They stand three abreast in a line that stretches down the block and around the corner for another block. There are camp followers, too: fancy girls, marijuana peddlers, sleight-of-hand artists. But Mr. Cortez, a member of the Rotary and the Order of Neptune, will have no truck with these "gypsies"; he endeavors, he says, to eliminate all "racketeering" elements.

As the line passes through the office, each applicant is interviewed. Has he ever worked in beets before? Where? How many in the family? The records grow, and it becomes possible to weed out the "undesirable" or "troublesome" individuals. The acceptable ones are given a physical examination. . . .

Once the examination is over, there is nothing for the Mexicans to do but wait for the order for departure. The growers do not want them to arrive until the precise moment they are needed. If they come too soon, they attract public attention, and advances have to be made to keep them alive. Nor, in San Antonio, does Mr. Cortez want to be caught short of workers when the signal is given. So, sometimes for a week or ten days, thousands of them, with their wives and children, often without a dime to their names, mill around the funeral parlor. They dare not stray far away; they keep reporting to the office day in, day out, waiting with extraordinary patience for the signal to depart. They live with friends or relatives in the barrio or camp on the outskirts of the town or sleep in their cars and trucks. . . .

The green signal flashes from Michigan. The army starts northward. . . .

Traveling from Texas to Michigan by truck is a nightmare. Most of the trucks are the open-stake kind, never intended for passenger transportation. Old models, seldom in a state of good repair, they are used during the season to haul sugar beets from field to factory. Before starting out, the driver is careful to substitute Michigan license plates (which have been forwarded to him) for his Texas plates, so he will not catch the eye of a wary highway patrolman in Michigan. Planks or benches are then placed on the truck, and it is loaded with passengers and equipment. Frequently sixty and sixty-five are huddled together. Although some companies have issued instructions that not more than twenty-five passengers be carried on a truck (quite a load in itself), the average carries about fifty people, their bedding and equipment and food for the trip. Once the Mexicans have crowded into the back, a heavy tarpaulin is thrown over them and fastened down around the edges so they are concealed. Outwardly the truck looks as though it were loaded with a cargo of potatoes. Before climbing into the driver's seat, the trucker tosses a couple of coffee cans into the back to be used as urinals during the journey. Then, usually around midnight, the truck rolls out of El Paso Street for the long trip north. . . .

Instead of traveling the main highways, however, they pursue a zigzag course, making many detours, zooming along country roads and minor highways to avoid patrolmen. As a rule they are as arrogant as captains on a slave galley. They pay little heed to their passengers, drink to stay awake, and drive against time. Notoriously bad drivers, and traveling under these circumstances, they have many accidents every season. On March 14, 1940, one such truck, with wooden sides and a tarpaulin covering forty-four workers, was struck by a train while crossing a railroad grading near McAllen, Texas; twenty-nine were killed, eleven of them children under sixteen.

Testimony by the Texas State Employment Service to the Tolan Committee investigating this truck traffic indicates its nightmare quality. One affidavit says that in a trip to Linwood, Michigan, not over two stops were made in twenty-four-hour intervals, that three days and nights were required to make the journey, that stops were never made even for bowel evacuations unless the passengers made so much noise the driver had to stop, that the truckers kept themselves awake with liquor or marijuana. . . .

Those who travel in their own cars have a somewhat easier trip. Most of them leave San Antonio, however, without a cent; advances frequently have to be made to enable them to buy their gasoline and oil. Their cars are old and broken-down: they often have to stop for repairs and wire ahead for further advances to get their cars out of hock. Fines for traffic violations are, of course, major calamities. . . .

Workers arrive in Michigan from April 15 to June 1. The first labor operation—blocking, thinning, and cultivating the beets— consumes about thirty days. After an interval of several weeks, there is a second hoeing and weeding operation which takes about fifteen days. Once this is concluded, there is nothing to be done until the harvest, which starts around October 15 and is usually over by December 1. Although workers may be in Michigan in fulfillment of their contracts for seven or eight months, they may actually be working in sugar beets for only seventy-five or eighty

days. During the period they are not working in beets, they can
pick up some non-contract work in such crops as pickles, string
beans, cherries, tomatoes, chicory, onions, and mint. But they
cannot migrate far from the beet fields, for, by the terms of their
contract, they are held to the crop. There is usually a provision in
the agreement that requires them to be constantly available. Also,
a hold-back payment of $2 an acre forces compliance with the
contract under penalty of forfeiting a major part of the compensation. . . .

At the going rate of $19 an acre, seasonal earnings are
necessarily low. The larger families can, however, handle allot-
ments on several different farms and, to some extent, supplement
their earnings by working in other crops during the slack period in
beets. The Department of Social Welfare in 1937 estimated
average seasonal earnings per worker as $216 (Saginaw County)
and $344 (Monroe and Lenawee Counties); with seasonal *family*
earnings $644 (Tuscola County). These estimates are quite
generous. Mr. Brown has said that "these people average about $8
a week and live on about $1 of foodstuffs a week per person,
which is the average credit extended to them by the company. As
a rule they work from 5 a.m. until sundown in the field." . . .

By the time the harvest is over in December, it is cold and rainy
in Michigan and the Mexicans are eager to get back to Texas. But
many have difficulty in getting out of the state. Since there are
two major labor operations in sugar beets, the companies (who
keep all the books) make payments on contracts twice during the
season, the first in August after the blocking, thinning, and
cultivating. Since Mexicans try to leave Michigan as soon as the
harvest is over, they cannot collect the final payment because the
companies have not, by that time, closed their books. The final
checks are given to field men of the companies, who mail them to
the workers in Texas. Generally, therefore, they have to get an
advance to leave Michigan, just as they had to get one to leave the
South. . . .

Mexicans arrive in Texas, as they left, with scarcely any money.
The report of the WPA in San Antonio for November 1939 states
that "Mexicans are returning in a much worse state than when
they left. Of all these people re-interviewed, not one has started

his children to school this term. They state that they barely manage to buy food enough to exist and can buy no clothes at all." While some families fare much better than others, it is debatable if the average family is able to accumulate as much as $200 for eight months' employment in Michigan; yet earnings there are higher than for field work in Texas, where the migratory labor problem is even greater and more complex—"the worst in the nation," in the words of the Farm Security Administration. . . .

The great march is over; the army is disbanded. But when spring rolls around again, they will be back in front of Mr. Cortez's funeral parlor on El Paso Street. They are a brave army, an army capable of almost incredible endurance. They are also an amazingly patient army: they make few complaints . . . which usually go unheard. . . .

THEY WORK
FOR PENNIES

Mexican American labor has always been adversely affected by use of Mexican nationals. Importation of braceros undercut the bargaining power of Mexican Americans for better working conditions and eventually led to their displacement. Ernesto Galarza, dean of Mexican Americanists, points out that the United States and Mexican governments showed little concern about this serious problem.

From July 1, 1951, to March 1, 1952, the U.S. Immigration Service reports, 343,700 illegal aliens from Mexico were apprehended and deported. Of this number, 17,300 were arrested while

From "They Work for Pennies," by Ernesto Galarza. *American Federationist* (April 1952). Reprinted, with deletions, by permission of the AFL-CIO *American Federationist*.

employed in trades, crafts, and industries other than agriculture.

A million wetbacks were successful in slipping past the Border Patrol. These wetbacks are now working as bootleg labor in the United States. From the Rio Grande Valley of Texas and the Imperial Valley of California—the two major reservoirs of this underground tide of cheap labor—the wetbacks from Mexico flow over the South and West and penetrate into the industrial centers of the Midwest and the East.

American agricultural workers know what the illegal alien can do to the wage structure. The Mexican wetback, a fugitive from the law, takes whatever he is offered—25 cents an hour for weeding and harvesting work, 50 cents an hour for truck or tractor driving. Wetbacks have been discovered working on non-union construction jobs, doing skilled work for a fraction of the established union rates of pay.

A.F. of L. unions in California have found that a wetback will do a job for $15 when the union scale for the same job calls for $40.

Throughout 1951, California labor contractors operated an immense labor pool of illegals from which the corporation farms drew freely. In the upper San Joaquin Valley, about 25 percent of the tomato crop was harvested by wetbacks—a fact openly acknowledged, with gratification, by corporation farm spokesmen. During the harvest there were no Immigration Service raids on the tomato crews. Today the food markets and grocery stores of the United States are stocked with cans of fruits and vegetables, including baby food, that were harvested by a million exploited illegals.

The wetback is the anvil on which American farm wages are being flattened out. The hammer is the Mexican "contract national."

Last year some 190,000 contractees were brought in under Public Law 78. Of these, thirty-eight thousand were hired in California. Public Law 78, a corporation farm measure, made federal funds available for the transportation of nationals to this country. Because of the discriminatory character of that law, President Truman signed it "with great reluctance," demanding that immediate steps be taken by Congress to suppress the traffic in illegals. In view of what happened between February and December of 1951, Public Law 78 may well be described as "the reluctant rape of 3 million American farm workers."

The nationals brought in last year became, in fact, the supplementary mobile task forces to freeze or batter down U.S. farm wages. It is estimated that twenty to twenty-five thousand contractees jumped their contracts once they entered the United States and thus automatically became illegals.

Thus, by ways that are strange and devices that are peculiar, American workers, through their taxes, are subsidizing an unlawful and wide-flung attack on hard-won U.S. standards of wages and employment conditions. . . .

In 1951, as on earlier occasions, the wages of the Mexican workers were determined by associations of corporation farmers and then given the stamp of approval by government officials in Washington and Mexico City. In 1951 these wages were from 25 to 40 percent below the wages that American agricultural workers find barely adequate for subsistence.

Slashing of wages already far too low is the main purpose of the Mexican farm-labor-recruitment program. Few sectors of the American economy have received a more generous handout from the federal government than the mass-production farms. Productivity on these farms has increased, but the gap between farm and industrial wages has widened to the point where it represents a difference of about 60 percent.

All the misleading claims that nationals are paid prevailing wages and that they are brought into the United States only because of dire scarcities of domestic manpower cannot conceal the fact that the wages of agricultural workers have been nailed fast to the floor while the cost of living has ballooned higher and higher.

Last year Mexican nationals were paid 60 cents an hour in California's Imperial Valley. This year's contracts fixed the hourly rate at 70 cents. In the Salinas Valley the nationals have been working for 72 and 82 cents an hour. The domestic workers must adjust themselves to these rates, like it or not. Farmers in the San Joaquin Valley who four and five years ago were paying 90 cents and $1 an hour to American farm workers have been able to obtain nationals at 75 and 80 cents.

Hourly rates have been frozen or cut back. But that's not all. Working time has been reduced. For example, domestic workers who formerly were able to put in five or six hours topping carrots are often through for the day after a couple of hours in the fields. Last fall and winter members of the National Farm Labor Union who worked in carrots, lettuce, broccoli, and onions were frequently reduced to work weeks of twelve, fifteen, and twenty hours. By coincidence, many Mexican nationals complained of limited work weeks of about the same earning time.

Less obvious is the fact that nationals are used to wipe out wage differentials for different types of operations in large-scale, mechanized farming. The national is classified as an agricultural worker; and Congress, under political pressure, has widened the definition of agricultural labor. This makes it possible for growers to pay a given wage—say 75 cents—for tasks as distinct as weeding, loading, sorting, harvesting, irrigating, tractor driving, and maintenance.

Last fall nationals working for 82½ cents an hour as lettuce cutters in the morning were regularly used as packers and sorters in the afternoon at the same wages. Onion sorters and sackers in the Imperial Valley worked a shift in the sheds at 60 cents an hour after finishing an earlier shift as pickers in the fields at the same wage.

The national is in fact a handyman who is hired at a flat rate to do whatever chores may be assigned to him "around the place." The "place" may be the state of California.

The displacement of the domestic worker is an equally direct result of the Mexican national recruitment program. In the Rio Grande and Imperial Valleys, displacement has reached a critical stage. Entire communities have withered or faded away into ghost towns. The men and women who are being forced out by low wages and short work seasons were the original braceros who grubbed out the brush and cut the canals through the deserts that today produce millions of dollars in wealth.

From Brownsville to San Diego stretches a two-thousand-mile

arc of adobe communities, shanty towns, and tent camps out of which old resident families silently and sullenly steal northward, and into which as silently and fearfully steal the Mexican illegals and nationals who have undercut their wages and living conditions. . . .

Not the least effect on domestic farm labor of the Mexican recruitment program is that this program has strengthened the hand of the private labor contractor, whose role as contact man for the corporation farmers is notorious.

It is generally the contractor who manipulates the mixed crews of illegals and nationals. It is he who clips the take-home pay of these mixed crews. It is the contractor who, with a surplus of nationals and illegals on hand, offers occasional work to the domestic workers on an "or else" basis. . . .

The brutal fact is that it is possible for a legitimate, legal, authorized strike of organized workers in the United States to be broken by government-sponsored strike breakers from Mexico.

The violation of the international agreement and the individual work contracts is notorious. Over a year ago, the Farm Labor Union filed charges against Frank O'Dwyer and Keith Mets, Imperial Valley growers, for violation of the agreement. O'Dwyer is the brother of Ambassador William O'Dwyer. These charges were never publicly aired.

Aware that a public hearing under judicial procedures is one of the bulwarks of an American citizen's constitutional rights, the NFLU has repeatedly asked for such hearings from the State, Labor, and Justice Departments. To date, no such hearings have been held. Not a single documented charge made by the union of wage cutting or displacement by the use of nationals has been properly investigated and reported.

To be sure, city unemployment, dramatized by industrial unions, has become the object of research and investigation by teams of federal officials. But the smear of farm-labor displacement, which blots the entire Pacific Coast, is either cautiously denied or discreetly ignored. . . .

The wetback law recently passed by both houses by no means fulfills the solemn promises made by Senator Ellender and Congressman Poage to the Mexican government in 1951. It was ramrodded through the Senate and House, taking the friends of labor by surprise. Congress has cut the appropriations of the Border Patrol, whose assignment is as vital as it is dangerous.

The policy of the Mexican government has been an effective backstop for the battery of the corporation farmers' teams, with Senator Ellender of Louisiana pitching and Congressman Poage of Texas catching. Repeated threats of the Mexican government to guard the border with troops to prevent line-jumping have never been carried out.

The Alemán Administration has also stated flatly that it would not permit more nationals to come to this country unless a stringent and effective wetback law was passed by Congress. But in the Senate debate on this bill, Southern Senators, including Ellender, lashed the Alemán government for its own failures to stop the illegals.

That is the situation that the American farm workers are up against. It reflects the weight that the corporation farmers and their helpers in Congress can throw around.

The growers' associations maintain a modest front of dirt farmers and overall homesteaders. Behind this front, they hire wetbacks in open defiance of the law. They hire their own contractors to play the role of "representatives" of the Mexican nationals. They indignantly refuse American agricultural workers a written contract, but they quickly sign one with an alien because they know they can violate it with impunity.

And behind this front, the dislodgment and disfranchisement of American farm workers, economically and politically, goes on. . . .

ILLEGAL ALIEN LABOR

Widespread use of illegal Mexican labor for seasonal farm work in the late 1940's finally aroused concern in both American and Mexican government circles. Complexities of this migratory phenomenon are traced in the following report.

Before 1944 the illegal traffic on the Mexican border, though always going on, was never overwhelming in numbers. Apprehensions by immigration officials leading to deportations or voluntary departures before 1944 were fairly stable and under ten thousand per year. Although the exact size of the wetback traffic is virtually impossible to determine, the number of apprehensions by immigration officers is a general indicator but far from a precise means of measurement. The same individual may be apprehended several times during the season and therefore would be duplicated in the apprehension count. On the other hand, large numbers enter and leave without being apprehended and hence would not be in the deportation or departure figures at all.

The magnitude of the wetback traffic has reached entirely new levels in the past seven years. The number of deportations and voluntary departures has continuously mounted each year, from twenty-nine thousand in 1944 to 565,000 in 1950. In its newly achieved proportions, it is virtually an invasion. It is estimated that at least 400,000 of our migratory farm labor force of 1 million in 1949 were wetbacks. . . .

To understand the wetback traffic, it is essential to know something of its foundations and the forces that produce it. Essentially, its foundations lie in a combination of factors that

From *Migratory Labor in American Agriculture*, Report of the President's Commission on Migratory Labor. Washington: U.S. Government Printing Office, 1951.

push the Mexican national northward within his own country and pull him across the border in violation of immigration law. . . .

Farmers in the northern areas of Mexico require seasonal labor for the cotton harvest just as do the farmers on our side of the Rio Grande. There is, accordingly, an internal northward migration for this employment. Mexican farm employers in need of seasonal labor encourage northward migratory movements within Mexico.

This rapid economic development in the areas immediately south of the border has accelerated the wetback traffic in several ways. An official in Matamoros estimates that twenty-five thousand transient cotton pickers were needed in the 1950 season, whereas the number coming from interior Mexico was estimated at sixty thousand. It is to be expected that many Mexican workers coming north with the anticipation of working in northern Mexico do not find employment there and ultimately spill over the border and become wetbacks. Additionally, the resident labor force at the border is expanding by leaps and bounds. . . .

Thus, large reservoirs of potential wetbacks are accumulating at the border. It is difficult for the farm employer in the north of Mexico to get the labor supply he needs without contributing to the wetback traffic. Active seasonal employment in the Mexican areas near the border is about the same as in the areas of the United States above the border. Consequently, laborers brought north to work for Mexican farmers discover that work is available at better wages on the other side of the border and they slip over.

This involves an ever-widening and self-accelerating cycle. Mexican farm employers close to the border have to recruit more workers than they need because it can be expected that many of their recruits will be lost to the wetback traffic. By recruiting on this basis, they aggravate the wetback traffic because they get too many workers. . . .

The intensity of the wetback traffic is not uniform along the border. Most intense in the lower Rio Grande Valley, it lessens to the north and the west of Texas. The traffic is much more intense in the Imperial Valley than in Arizona or New Mexico. Of all the states offering the kind of employment in which wetbacks are found, Arizona evidently has the least wetback traffic. This

unequal access to wetback labor causes resentment, as is well
expressed in the testimony of the manager of the Arizona
Cooperative Cotton Growers' Association:

> Our farmers for several years have had a continuous and loud
> complaint that their friends and acquaintances in other bordering
> States have a comparatively large supply of wetback labor, while in
> Arizona the border patrol very successfully and carefully enforces the
> law against illegal aliens on the ranches. We have never tried to exert
> pressure to have this enforcement relieved, but we do want to call the
> attention of high figures [officials] to the fact that the other States
> should be treated alike; that if enforcement is being relaxed in other
> States, it should be relaxed in Arizona; that if enforcement is going to
> be strict in Arizona, we want it strict in other States. . . .

The hub of the wetback traffic is in the plazas of the Mexican
towns and cities immediately below the border. Here, or in
sections around the railroad which serve the same purpose, the
wetback seeks information about jobs in the United States and
how to get them. It is here that he encounters the first of many
exploiters he will come to know well before he is once again in his
homeland. The principal topic of conversation in the plazas of the
Mexican border towns for several months of the year is how to get
into the United States and what crops and jobs promise employment once there. His urgent need of food and money makes him
an easy mark for the smuggler, the labor contractor, or the agent
of the farm employer. He is eager when any of these approach
him and whisper that there is a way to get out of the vast mob, all
looking for a job and a chance to get into the United States where
jobs seem plentiful and wages seem high.

Although smuggling of wetbacks is widespread, the majority of
wetbacks apparently enter alone or in small groups without a
smuggler's assistance. In a group moving without the aid of a
smuggler, there usually is one who has made the trip before and
who is willing to show the way. Not infrequently the same
individual knows the farm to which the group intends to go and
sometimes he has made advance arrangements with the farm
employer to return at an appointed date with his group. Such
wetbacks stream into the United States by the thousands through

the deserts near El Paso and Calexico or across the Rio Grande
between Rio Grande City and Brownsville. When employment on
the farms adjacent to the border is filled, the wetbacks push
northward into new areas following rumor or promise of employment.

Often the wetbacks entering alone or in small groups have
written to farm employers or friends in the United States and have
made arrangements to be met at some crossroad, gate, or other
well-known place within a night's walk of the border. Some make
two or three separate entries within a season, after having been
apprehended, and head for the place where they were formerly
employed.

If the wetback makes a deal to be guided or escorted across the
Rio Grande or some section of the land border, everything he is
able to pay is usually extracted in return for the service, which
may be no more than being guided around the fence or being
given a boat ride across the Rio Grande. Wetbacks who are
without funds to pay the smuggler for bringing them in or to pay
the trucker-contractor who furnishes transportation and direction
from the boundary to the farm are frequently "sold" from one
exploiter to the next. For example, the smuggler will offer to bring
a specified number of wetbacks across the river for such an
amount as $10 or $15 per man. The smuggler or boatman with his
party in tow will be met by the trucker-contractor who will then
"buy" the wetback party by paying off the smuggler. This
trucker-contractor, in turn, will have a deal to deliver workers to
farm employers at an agreed-upon price per head.

There are other well-known and well-established practices to
facilitate and encourage the entrance of wetbacks. They range
from spreading news of employment in the plazas and over the
radio to the withholding from wages of what is called a "deposit"
which is intended to urge, if not guarantee, the return to the same
farm as quickly as possible of a wetback employee who may be
apprehended and taken back to Mexico.

The term "deposit" requires some explanation. Members of this
commission personally interviewed wetback workers apprehended by immigration officers in the lower Rio Grande Valley.
These workers had been paid for the cotton they had picked

during the preceding two or three weeks. However, their employers had withheld $10 to $15 from their pay. Such sums, we discovered, are known as deposits. To redeem this deposit, the wetback was required to re-enter illegally and to reappear on the farm employer's premises within ten days.

Once on the United States side of the border and on the farm, numerous devices are employed to keep the wetback on the job. Basic to all these devices is the fact that the wetback is a person of legal disability who is under jeopardy of immediate deportation if caught. He is told that if he leaves the farm, he will be reported to the Immigration Service or that, equally unfortunate to him, the Immigration Service will surely find him if he ventures into town or out onto the roads. To assure that he will stay until his services are no longer needed, his pay, or some portion thereof, frequently is held back. Sometimes, he is deliberately kept indebted to the farmer's store or commissary until the end of the season, at which time he may be given enough to buy shoes or clothing and encouraged to return the following season.

When the work is done, neither the farmer nor the community wants the wetback around. The number of apprehensions and deportations tends to rise very rapidly at the close of a seasonal work period. This can be interpreted not alone to mean that the immigration officer suddenly goes about his work with renewed zeal and vigor, but rather that at this time of the year "cooperation" in law enforcement by farm employers and townspeople rapidly undergoes considerable improvement. . . .

The wetback is a hungry human being. His need of food and clothing is immediate and pressing. He is a fugitive and it is as a fugitive that he lives. Under the constant threat of apprehension and deportation, he cannot protest or appeal no matter how unjustly he is treated. Law operates against him but not for him. Those who capitalize on the legal disability of the wetbacks are numerous, and their devices are many and various.

Wage rates reflect graphically and dramatically the impact and consequences of the wetback traffic. In 1947, when daily wages for chopping cotton (thinning the rows of cotton plants) in the lower Rio Grande Valley were $2.25 (ten hours), wages were continuously higher at points northward from the border: in the

Sandy Lands of Texas, $3; in the Corpus Christi and Coast Prairie Areas, $4; in the Rolling Plains, $5; in the High Plains, $5.25.

When the commission held hearings in Texas in August 1950, wage rates for picking short staple cotton in the lower Rio Grande Valley were reported as low as 50 cents per hundredweight and as high as $1.75 per hundredweight. From the evidence presented, we conclude that the bulk of the cotton in this area was picked in 1950 for approximately $1.25 per hundredweight. Comparative wage rates for picking cotton elsewhere in Texas were not obtained in the hearings because no other area had yet commenced its cotton harvest. However, the statewide average 1950 rate for Texas is now reported officially by the United States Department of Agriculture to have been $2.45 per hundredweight. Thus, the lower Rio Grande Valley cotton growers got their cotton picked for approximately one half the wages paid by the average cotton grower of Texas.

Wages for common hand labor in the lower Rio Grande Valley, according to the testimony, were as low as 15 to 25 cents per hour. To the north and the west through El Paso Valley, we found a marked tendency for wages for similar work to rise. In southern New Mexico, the prevailing wages for the same type of work were reported to be 40 to 50 cents per hour. Thus, New Mexico was paying twice as much to get its hand labor work done as was being paid in the lower Rio Grande Valley.

Further west in Arizona, wages are still better. . . .

Notwithstanding the strong and clear tendency for wages to rise as one moves westward, with California the highest of the group, we found wages in the Imperial Valley on the Mexican border to represent a complete reversal of this pattern. The going wage rate for common and hand labor in the Imperial Valley was 50 cents per hour. Thus Imperial Valley farm employers pay no more to get their farm work done than do farm employers in southern New Mexico, and probably less than do Arizona farm employers. Direct comparisons in wages paid in cotton cannot be made since Imperial Valley has no cotton, but the comparison in terms of wages paid to hand labor for other types of work leads to this conclusion.

It is thus clear that the Imperial Valley, with its large wetback traffic, represents a substantial contradiction to an otherwise consistent general tendency for farm wages to improve toward the West. . . .

The problem of immigration-law enforcement includes the Mexican national who secures employment and wages through unlawful entry, the smuggler who gains from conspiring in the unlawful entry, the farm employer who gains from the employment of the illegal alien at low wages, and finally the governments of both countries. In illegally crossing the border, the wetback violates the laws of Mexico just as much as he does those of the United States. If Mexican farm workers are to be permitted temporary legal employment in the United States, one of the urgent problems faced by both governments is to devise a legal farm-labor program that will be a decent and orderly substitute for the wetback traffic and not a means of accelerating it. Beyond this first obvious step, which must be principally a matter of intergovernmental negotiation, the problems involved in taking affirmative measures against the respective participating parties require appropriate action by the United States.

When legal action is taken against the wetback, which is done only in very few cases and principally with repeated violators, there is little difficulty of prosecution and conviction. Here the problem is that great numbers make it impossible to proceed against each individual. While there is little difficulty of convicting the wetback, similar actions against those who assist illegal entry are not equally successful. Given the climate of local opinion in the areas of wetback traffic, it is extremely difficult and frequently impossible to prosecute and convict those who conspire to violate the immigration law. Here, as far as the smuggler is concerned, the problem is the enforcement of national law in an area which is unsympathetic to that law. The law against the introduction of excluded aliens is adequate; the problem is enforcement. . . .

DELANO
GRAPE STRIKE

César Chávez's organizational efforts in the early sixties, coupled with the termination of the bracero program, climaxed in 1965 with the Delano grape strike. Early in the spring of 1966, hearings of the U.S. Senate Subcommittee on Migratory Labor aired views of both sides to this dispute. In the following selection, grape grower Martin Zaninovich gives his view of the Delano strike, while Senator Robert Kennedy probes the attitudes of local law-enforcement officials toward the strike and strikers.

. . . Mr. Chairman and honorable members of the committee, my name is Martin Zaninovich. I am a grower of fresh table grapes in the Delano area. . . .

Today I have the privilege of appearing before your committee to present some facts about the highly publicized situation in Delano.

No doubt, like many others not living here and not familiar with the situation, you may have been led to believe that thousands of grape pickers left their jobs last fall. And that they have been out on a so-called strike ever since.

Through a barrage of propaganda, this is the fiction which has been created in the minds of many people. The public has been and is presently being deceived, unfortunately.

The simple truth is, gentlemen, that there is no strike in Delano. More than five thousand of the people who regularly, year after year, have picked our crops stayed on the job. In fact, they picked the largest crop in history. And furthermore, our vineyards were completely pruned by the same people who have performed the pruning operation for a number of years.

From Hearings of the U.S. Senate Subcommittee on Migratory Labor, 89th Congress, 2nd sess. Washington: U.S. Government Printing Office, 1966.

They did all of this despite threats and harassments.

Perhaps a brief review of the chain of events, as I viewed them, which transpired throughout the grape season, would be helpful to your committee.

First, in early September of 1965, the Agricultural Workers' Organizing Committee sought to force the workers into a union by demanding recognition of their organization by the Delano grape growers. At about the time this effort was losing momentum, AWOC was joined by a locally formed and based group known as the National Farm Workers' Association.

For a very brief period these organizations succeeded in frightening perhaps as many as five hundred workers away from their jobs. In many cases, growers told their employees that if they did not want to be exposed to the threats and harassments being hurled at them by a few agitators, they did not need to return to work for the time being. However, most of the workers returned to their jobs within a few days.

The tactics used to scare off workers varied from picketing their homes, threatening them with anonymous phone calls in the middle of the night, and shouting obscenities at them.

Second, having realized that their efforts were failing, the California Migrant Ministry offered the two union organizing forces help to revive the dying cause.

Through the leadership of the migrant ministry, churches throughout the state were urged to support the union against the growers. Many church laymen and ministers took exception to this new role ministers were taking: the role of the union organizer. They felt this role violated the clergy's respected position by pitting Christian against Christian in a pure economic struggle. The Delano Ministerial Association expressed that view in a resolution. The Southern California Presbyteria, of which the migrant ministry director is a member, voted not to support the migrant ministry in its efforts. Other church groups took similar positions, although the migrant ministry commission voted in support.

Despite the highly emotional nature of the migrant ministry campaign, the grape pickers remained on their jobs. One of the young ministers joined the picket lines and called the working pickers "scabs." Because these were regular workers, and not strikebreakers, they greatly resented this name-calling and resolved even more firmly their determination not to join the union.

Claims that our grapes were picked by strikebreakers or imported workers are false. The only deviation from long-standing and standard recruiting practices was the recruitment of seventy workers from outside the Delano area.

Having failed again, and looking for new ways to pump life into the organizing efforts, the leaders next called upon members of the Congress of Racial Equality, the Students for Democratic Society, the Students Non-Violent Coordinating Committee, and the W. E. B. Du Bois Clubs, as well as those opposing this country's support of South Vietnam.

Instead of striking workers, the picket lines consisted almost entirely of campus agitators, ministers, paid professionals—all people who were trying to maintain the fiction that a strike existed.

Again failing to attract workers, these agitators in blind revenge tried to organize a boycott of Delano grapes and grape products. That, too, resulted in utter failure. The failure is evidenced by the fact that fresh table-grape shipments from this area increased by 54 percent since the announcement of the so-called boycott.

Their attempts to foment racial tensions in Delano, a community noted for racial harmony, outraged everyone.

The means used by these outside agitators to gain publicity in the news media have veered from the absurd to the pitiful.

Recently, we were treated to the spectacle of a publicity-seeking comedian giving a press conference in Delano.

At Christmas time, these self-appointed organizers obtained donations of food and clothing from kindly but unsuspecting people from various parts of the state for distribution among the thousands of striking grape pickers. We wonder what those donors thought when the word went out from the local charitable agencies that there were not more than fifty needy families in the Delano area—and they were being taken care of by local groups. Such attempts at deception backfired.

We have been asked: Why don't you negotiate with the unions? Our answer is simply this: It has been apparent from the beginning of the organizational effort that our workers are not interested in becoming part of these unions. They have rejected all of their efforts, and we respect their decision.

We cannot, in good conscience, and will not, enter into any type of negotiations with these unions and thereby force our workers into something that is not of their own free choice.

We have also been asked: Why don't you submit to an election to prove your point?

The workers voted every day of the harvest. How? The size of our crop and the efficiency with which it was harvested are votes that even the most prejudiced person cannot ignore or submerge with half truths and false or misleading statements. They have voted with their feet, so to speak, by going to work regularly in our vineyards.

The proof is that some five thousand of our regular workers stayed on the job and picked the largest crop of grapes in history. Recent figures from the State-Federal Market News Service, a governmental agency, prove this. These figures show that, as of March 13, 1966, the shipment of table grapes by rail from the Kern district totaled 9,228 as compared with 8,441 on the same date in 1965, the year before. This is a 9 percent increase over 1965. It is also interesting to note in an attachment to this statement that the shipment of fresh table grapes from the Delano area shows an increase in every reported period.

Wages are frequently mentioned as a cause for this agitation. Under hourly guarantees, plus incentive rates, harvest workers during the past season were earning upward of $2 per hour. A survey of some of the high-labor-using growers in this area revealed an average wage of $1.73 per hour for the table-grape harvest season. This does not include the free housing that is provided. The survey was based on an audit of 578,303 hours and a payroll of about $1 million. A further sample of wages was taken from the records of 460 men and women field workers. This particularly large ranch showed an average pay of $2.06 per hour.

The harvest of wine grapes returned to the worker as high as $2.77 per hour. A survey was also conducted in this operation to determine average hourly pay. The figures show that during this period the average was $2.43 per hour. This includes part-time housewives and teenagers. Payroll records involved in these surveys will be made available to any member of this committee for your personal examination if you desire.

Remember, gentlemen, this is well above the national minimum industrial wage of $1.25 per hour and is considerably higher than the state average of $1.51 per hour. Our workers know that their earnings in the grape-harvest activities are above those earned in vineyards anywhere else. Many fresh grape growers and shippers, in this area, provide free, year-round housing to single male workers and many families. I have photographs which will show that this is good housing. I'd like to present these to the committee. In addition, growers provide all utilities and pay the salaries of cooks selected by the workers themselves. Those not living in the grower-supplied dwellings are paid a higher hourly base.

For the record, I think it is important to point out two facts:

1. Growers of grapes, as well as other fruits, receive no government price supports.

2. Since we do not use the farm-labor service of the state department of employment, we see little use for the farm-labor office in Delano. We also recommend that the activities of the U.S. Department of Labor in California be ended.

Finally, I would like to repeat:

There is no strike among Delano farm workers. The so-called strike is pure myth, manufactured out of nothing by outside agitators who are more interested in creating trouble in the United States than in the welfare of the farm worker.

SENATOR KENNEDY: There was one incident that was reported to the committee about the arrest of twenty-five of the pickets. Any of you know about that?

SHERIFF GALYEN: Twenty-five? That probably was me.

MR. NELSON: I think it's forty, isn't it?

SENATOR KENNEDY: I don't want to go into it in great detail.

MR. NELSON: I might comment just briefly. I can't go into it too seriously, and if I might even interrupt the sheriff, if I might, Sheriff, because this is a matter that's coming to trial, and to go into the facts might put me in jeopardy, as far as future actions of our superior court and so forth.

I merely can say that there was an arrest made, and this is a matter of record, for unlawful assembly for some forty people in one particular area where the officer in charge felt that the noise had reached the state that was beyond normal, peaceful picketing and numbers involved caused him to feel, and some of the things that were being said, caused him to feel that perhaps a riot might be imminent and he took the action, which is a difficult one for an officer in the field, that he felt was necessary under the circumstances. That case is coming up, however. And, of course, the court will decide what the facts be. . . .

SENATOR KENNEDY: Could I just ask you a question before you go? Have you taken pictures of the people that are picketing— Sheriff, have you been taking pictures?

SHERIFF ROBERTSON: Oh yes, there have been pictures taken at various times.

SENATOR KENNEDY: Why do you take pictures of them?

SHERIFF GALYEN: Well, you have people who come in from other places that we don't know, and we keep in touch, find out who they are, why they're here.

SENATOR KENNEDY: Have you sent pictures of people—have you sent these pictures all over the country?

SHERIFF GALYEN: No.

SENATOR KENNEDY: What are you taking their pictures for?

SHERIFF GALYEN: Just in our files so we will know who they are in case anything happens.

MR. BALLENTYNE: May I answer, Senator? This is one of the big problems in any situation that might arise, to identify the defendant. We ran into this situation with the Hell's Angels in Porterville. It's very difficult when you get into a melee situation to identify the people involved.

SENATOR KENNEDY: Yes. But let me ask, have there been riots?

MR. BALLENTYNE: No, there have been potential riots on occasion.

SENATOR KENNEDY: I'll tell you this, I've never heard of police departments in other communities that have been going around taking pictures of people walking around with picket signs.

MR. BALLENTYNE: This is a big problem. Pictures were taken of the demonstrations in Berkeley.

SENATOR KENNEDY: I understand. I mean, I think there are such places where they do take them, where the situation got out of hand at Berkeley. What I don't understand is going by with a camera and taking pictures of people picketing.

MR. BALLENTYNE: No, this is not being done.

SENATOR KENNEDY: I asked of the sheriff if he was taking pictures of people.

MR. BALLENTYNE: Not in Tulare County.

SHERIFF GALYEN: We had a deal where there was a bunch of growers, I think it was, beating a bunch of pickets, and then we couldn't identify them.

SENATOR KENNEDY: You couldn't identify whom?

SHERIFF GALYEN: The people that got beat up or that never showed up, or we don't know who the growers were. Nobody could tell us. So we started taking pictures.

SENATOR KENNEDY: Did you take pictures of growers?

SHERIFF GALYEN: We took pictures of growers, we took pictures of all the pickets, and we can identify them.

SENATOR KENNEDY: I can understand you want to take pictures if there's a riot going on, but I don't understand why if someone is walking along with a sign you want to take pictures of them. I don't see how that helps.

SHERIFF GALYEN: Well, they might take pictures of us, too.

SENATOR KENNEDY: Sheriff, I don't think it's responsive. It's not a question of them wanting to take pictures of you. You're a law-enforcement official. It is in some way an act of intimidation to go around and be taking their pictures.

SHERIFF GALYEN: I've got to identify those people through my district attorney. I've got to identify, that is the man.

SENATOR KENNEDY: That is the man that what?

SHERIFF GALYEN: That caused this trouble.

SENATOR KENNEDY: Let's separate the two points. I'm not suggesting that you not take pictures of this trouble that's occurring. We're talking about your taking pictures of somebody walking along with a picket sign.

SHERIFF GALYEN: Well, he's a potential, isn't he?

SENATOR KENNEDY: Well, I mean, so am I.

SHERIFF GALYEN: Well, the farmer out there, we want to know who he is.

SENATOR KENNEDY: Do you take pictures of everybody in the city?

SHERIFF GALYEN: Well, if he's on strike or something like that.

SENATOR WILLIAMS: Where do you take these pictures? Where is the individual when you take pictures of him?

SHERIFF GALYEN: Well, he's either on the strike line or he's a worker out there in the field.

SENATOR WILLIAMS: Never down at the police station?

SHERIFF GALYEN: Oh, we take them, naturally we take them at the police station, when we make an arrest. That's an identification picture, too.

SENATOR KENNEDY: Have you brought anybody down to the police station?

SHERIFF GALYEN: Forty of them.

SENATOR KENNEDY: Other than those, have you brought anybody down?

SHERIFF GALYEN: No; just once in a while, a lot of citations issued.

SENATOR KENNEDY: What?

SHERIFF GALYEN: A lot of citations issued where you don't have to appear. You can appear within five days or ten days or you can appear in court.

SENATOR KENNEDY: Have you brought them down?

SHERIFF GALYEN: No, no, we didn't. They appear. It's a minor thing—but a little easier—it doesn't amount to anything.

SENATOR KENNEDY: Have you brought anybody in for fingerprinting, any of those who have been striking?

SHERIFF GALYEN: Yes.

SENATOR KENNEDY: For what reason?

SHERIFF GALYEN: Where they violated and wouldn't move out on a particular section of the law which provides an unlawful assembly.

SENATOR KENNEDY: Have you charged them with an offense?

SHERIFF GALYEN: It came up through the idea that we had news from the inside, that there was going to be some cutting done if they didn't stop saying certain things, so I'm responsible to arrest them as well as anyone else.

SENATOR KENNEDY: What did you arrest them for?

SHERIFF GALYEN: Why, if they got into a riot and started cutting up the people—

SENATOR KENNEDY: I'm not talking about that. Once you got into a riot, I understand that, but before, when they're just walking along, what did you arrest them for?

SHERIFF GALYEN: Well, if I have reason to believe that there's going to be a riot started and somebody tells me that there's going to be trouble if you don't stop them, it's my duty to stop them.

SENATOR KENNEDY: Then do you go out and arrest them?

SHERIFF GALYEN: Yes.

SENATOR KENNEDY: And charge them?

SHERIFF GALYEN: Charge them.

SENATOR KENNEDY: What do you charge them with?

SHERIFF GALYEN: Violation of—unlawful assembly.

SENATOR KENNEDY: I think that's most interesting. Who told you that they're going to riot?

SHERIFF GALYEN: The men right out in the field that they were talking to said, "If you don't get them out of here, we're going to cut their hearts out." So rather than let them get cut, we removed the cause.

SENATOR MURPHY: Do I understand you, Sheriff, that it's your opinion that it's better to take precautionary moves before the trouble starts, that this is in the best interests of the community and the peaceful interests of the citizens?

SHERIFF GALYEN: Who wants a big riot on his hands? And if you can stop it, why, let's stop it before it gets to that point. And I think you'll find all down the line that we've had wonderful cooperation between all of them, and the longer we went along, you'll find nobody say we beat anyone, or anything like that. This is not Selma, Alabama.

SENATOR KENNEDY: Senator, could I finish my questioning here? This is the most interesting concept, I think, that you suddenly hear or you talk about the fact that somebody makes a report about somebody going to get out of order, perhaps violate the law, and you go and arrest them, and they haven't done anything wrong. How can you go arrest somebody if they haven't violated the law?

SHERIFF GALYEN: They're ready to violate the law.

SENATOR MURPHY: I think it's a shame you weren't there before the Watts riots.

SENATOR WILLIAMS: We will recess—

SENATOR KENNEDY: Could I just suggest that the district attorney and the sheriff reconsider their procedures in connection with these matters, because it really is of great concern to me. In the last five minutes, it's a considerable concern to me.

SHERIFF GALYEN: Before I do anything, I ask the district attorney what to do. Just like these labor people out here, they ask their attorney, "What shall we do?"

SENATOR KENNEDY: Can I suggest in the interim period of time, the luncheon period of time, that the sheriff and the district attorney read the Constitution of the United States? . . .

COMMUTERS

Filling a void created by elimination of the bracero program, border commuters became increasingly important in the 1960's as cheap labor. This report describes the history of commuter traffic and explains why it generated considerable opposition in the Mexican American communities along the border.

People have commuted across both borders of the United States to work since the borders were established. Until 1921 there were no numerical limitations on immigration and aliens were free to come to employment in this country so long as they did not infringe the contract-labor restrictions or fall within the classes of aliens excluded by law. When numerical limitations were placed on immigration in 1921, aliens resident in Mexico and Canada for

From Report by the Select Committee on Western Hemisphere Immigration. Washington: U.S. Government Printing Office, 1968.

more than one year were exempted from those restrictions and no special problems involving commuters were encountered before 1924.

The temporary legislation of 1921 was succeeded by the act of May 26, 1924, which established a permanent system of quota allocation and control. While natives of Western Hemisphere countries were not subject to the quota limitations, immigrants from those countries were thereafter required to obtain and present immigrant visas to enter the United States. In administering the 1924 act, commuters were first considered temporary visitors for business and were free to continue to come to their employment in this country. However, on April 1, 1927, the immigration authorities reversed their former position and declared that aliens coming to work in the United States were to be classified as immigrants. This interpretation by the immigration authorities was immediately challenged in the courts, but in 1929 it was upheld by the Supreme Court.

In studying the problem at that time, the immigration authorities concluded that Congress had not intended to interfere with the established pattern of regular border crossings by workers from Mexico or Canada who commuted to jobs in the United States. While such aliens could obtain immigrant visas without difficulty, they would be faced with an impossible task if they were required to obtain a new visa for each daily re-entry. Consequently, the immigration authorities devised a border-crossing identification card which could be used by aliens who frequently cross the international boundary. The issuance and use of such border-crossing cards received express sanction by Congress in the Alien Registration Act of 1940.

Thus a commuter was able to procure an immigrant visa and subsequent lawful admission as an immigrant. Thereafter he would obtain a border-crossing identification card, and with that card he could enter each day to go to his job as returning to his immigrant status in the United States. This arrangement was in harmony with the established good-neighbor policy with Mexico and Canada, facilitated travel across the Mexican and Canadian borders, and avoided serious dislocations in the border areas.

The commuter program was well known to the Congress and

was discussed and endorsed, by implication, in the comprehensive study by the Senate Judiciary Committee which preceded enactment of the 1952 Immigration and Nationality Act. Nothing in the Immigration and Nationality Act or its legislative antecedents indicated that the Congress was dissatisfied with the commuter program or desired to change it in any way. In June 1963 Subcommittee No. 1 of the Committee on the Judiciary of the House of Representatives made a comprehensive study of commuter workers and there was no indication that the committee was dissatisfied with the commuter program as it was then administered by the service. The commuter program is an administrative application of the legislative design to our Mexican and Canadian border areas. . . .

The first legal challenge to the commuter program arose out of a strike at the Peyton Packing Company plant in El Paso, Texas, in 1960. Under the then-existing law, the Secretary of Labor certified that the admission of aliens for employment at the struck plant would adversely affect wages and working conditions in the United States. The Immigration Service enforced the certification except with regard to aliens who had been lawfully admitted for permanent residence and who were returning from a temporary absence, since such aliens were exempt from the bar to readmission by the statute. The service held that commuters were within this exempt class. In the court case the presiding judge took issue with the latter conclusion. He reviewed the commuter program and took no position as to its legality. However, he held that commuters could not be regarded as returning residents for the purposes of the certification. In his view, a contrary holding would "make a shambles" of the aim of the provisions of law designed to provide safeguards for American labor. The presiding judge's decision was rendered in denying the government's motion for dismissal of the complaint and for summary judgment. However, when a proposed final judgment was presented, the presiding judge declined to issue a mandatory order against the Attorney General, since by that time the case virtually had become moot and no appeal was taken. . . .

The number of commuters increased rapidly along the Mexican

border during the years of the bracero program. United States employers assisted the best of the braceros in obtaining immigrant visas and status as permanent residents. These workers retained their domicile in Mexico and became commuters, forming a pool of legal agricultural workers near the border. It was this pool of available legal labor which played a major role in the termination of the bracero program.

In recent years a large number of agricultural workers enter the United States each spring and remain in the United States for several months, following the crops to various parts of the country. These workers go to Mexico during the winter months. Some take up residence near the border and continue to commute to work in the United States, while others go to homes in the interior of Mexico and do not re-enter the United States again until the spring planting begins. Included in this group are some entire families. The spouse and children accompany the principal alien, with the children attending school in the United States when school is in session and attending school in Mexico during the winter months. All members of such families have status as lawful permanent residents. These migrant workers are not commuters in the generally accepted sense, since they actually remain in the United States several months out of each year without returning to their homes in Mexico. Yet they are considered commuters by those who oppose the commuter program.

At places such as San Ysidro, Calexico, and El Paso, there are several hundred commuters who enter each morning to look for work on a day basis. At El Paso there are a number of employment offices (operated independently and not a part of the Texas Employment Service) within two or three blocks of the port of entry. These offices have large blackboards outside the door on which job offers are entered each day. While the job offers are generally made by local employers seeking unskilled labor for relatively short periods of time, during certain seasons of the year employers from as far away as California utilize these offices to obtain agricultural workers. While this group of commuters is comprised primarily of unskilled workers, it does include artisans such as carpenters and masons. In addition to the employment offices, the commuters gather in groups near the port of entry and prospective employers come to these groups to bargain for workers each morning. The employers follow a procedure much like the "shape-up" of stevedores at the piers in port cities. The prospective employer will look over the group of workers available and will select those he wants for his particular job. Most of the yard work and home-improvement work in the cities mentioned above is done by such commuters. . . .

There has always been some opposition to commuters by United States residents who must compete with them for employment, particularly during periods of general unemployment, but until recent years there was little organized opposition. At this time there is little, if any, opposition along the Canadian border. The majority of the commuters are concentrated in the Detroit area and in that area they are union members and are well integrated into the regular work force.

Along the Mexican border the situation is quite different. There is considerable organized opposition to commuters due, in large part, to the wide disparity in the cost of living in Mexico as compared to the cost of living in the United States. The commuter residing in Mexico has a much lower cost of living than his co-worker resident of the United States. The opponents of the commuter program point to this fact and argue that the commuter has little incentive to seek higher wages or better working conditions.

There is considerable opposition to the commuter program in the Mexican American community in the state of Texas. In the west Texas area, those who oppose the program are usually the skilled or semiskilled workers who are native-born citizens. In the lower Rio Grande Valley and San Antonio area, the opposition is spearheaded by organized labor and certain of the civil-rights groups. There is little opposition in the states of New Mexico and Arizona, probably because the number of commuters in those two states is very low, except for the commuters who work in the Yuma area in Arizona. There is some opposition in the Imperial Valley in California, where there are a great number of commuters working in agriculture. However, in the San Diego area there is very little opposition, even though there are a large number of commuters employed in industry and service occupations. The lack of opposition in this area is due to the fact that the commuters employed in industry and service occupations are largely union members. In fact, several locals in the San Diego area hold periodic meetings in Tijuana because so many members of the local reside in the latter city.

At the present time, labor organizations are attempting to organize agricultural workers in the Southwest, and much attention has been focused on commuters because the labor organizers have alleged that commuters are used as strikebreakers. Although the labor organizations sought to terminate the commuter program through court action in 1963, recent news accounts indicate that stronger efforts will be made to organize the commuters. . . .

It can be assumed that the employers of commuter workers would oppose any action designed to restrict or eliminate the commuter program. In those areas where commuter workers are union members and are well integrated into the regular work force, the labor unions concerned would oppose any action which would be detrimental to their members. This would be particularly true in the Detroit area and possibly in the San Ysidro, California, area.

Along the Mexican border, it is believed that American business interests in the border communities would vigorously oppose termination of the commuter program. These businessmen, particularly those engaged in the retail trade, rely to great extent on trade with Mexican nationals and would fear that any curtailment of the commuter program would result in retaliatory action by the government of Mexico which could adversely affect their business. Furthermore, although commuters reside in Mexico, they spend a considerable portion of their income in the American community for goods and services. The recent news report of a study of the commuter situation at Laredo, Texas, stated that 80 percent of Laredo's retail sales, which approximated $86 million in 1966, are made to citizens of Mexico. . . .

There are two recent developments which, although not

directly related to the commuter question, highlight the importance of consultation with the Department of State before taking
any action to change or modify the commuter program. After his
first meeting with the President of Mexico in April 1966, the
President appointed a special envoy to make a detailed study of
the Mexican border area with the objective of improving trade
relations between the two countries as a step toward improving
the economy of both sides of the border area. In addition, the
Joint Presidential statement of April 16, 1966, called for the
establishment of a Joint United States–Mexican Commission on
Economic and Social Development of the Border Area to study
conditions in the border area and come up with recommendations
to improve the standard of living on both sides of the border. . . .

VI
A NEW BREED

Development of Mexican American or Chicano organizations is not new but dates back to the 1800's. Historically, Chicanos have made many efforts to organize themselves politically, but repeatedly have encountered opposition and repression. However, World War II introduced a new period in which Chicanos were more productive and successful in securing social and political rights long overdue. In the vanguard of this new thrust, returning Mexican American veterans, no longer willing to accept second-class citizenship, began to develop aggressive organizations to achieve their rightful place in society. This postwar effort had limited success through the 1950's.

However, in the sixties, Mexican American youths, calling themselves Chicanos, demonstrated considerable signs of impatience, especially with older leaders, and took a more militant approach toward solving their problems. This youth-oriented movement rejected a subservient and inferior role in American society with its accompanying segregation, poor schooling, deteriorating housing, and other aspects of individual and institutional racism.

By the mid-sixties, this movement had given birth to a new breed of activists and a new, dedicated leadership. Among these new leaders four have gained national prominence: in California, César Chávez, who developed his United Farm Workers' organization; in Colorado, Rodolfo "Corky" Gonzales, who organized his Crusade for Justice; in New Mexico, Reies López Tijerina, who established his Alianza Federal de Mercedes; and in Texas, José Angel Gutiérrez, who created a Chicano political party, La Raza Unida.

Although all four continue to have wide support within Chicano communities, each appeals strongly to specific sectors. César Chávez, with his emphasis on non-violence, undoubtedly has the broadest following, based on his vision of elementary justice for all human beings. "Corky" Gonzales, appealing strongly to Chicano youth's sense of idealism, attracts much of his following from high-school and college campuses. Tijerina in his effort to regain lost land grants looks to the past for redress of Chicano grievances; he has a divided following of older Hispanos from northern New Mexico and youthful activists who admire his revolutionary rhetoric. José Angel Gutiérrez emphasizes the development, organization, and use of political-power channels and appeals widely to Chicanos who believe that their future lies in Raza unity as a means to achieving social and political justice.

Besides these four principal leaders, in recent years many other regional and local Chicano leaders of importance have emerged in the political arena. Differing in means rather than in goals, this leadership includes seasoned veterans who have survived the turbulent sixties as well as representatives of the new breed—products of the Chicano movement. Thousands of dedicated Chicano high-school and college students provide a moral goad to this new leadership and thereby render valuable service to their communities. Determined activists, they often challenged their hesitant elders and pressured administrators and institutions into establishing and developing Chicano studies programs in high schools, colleges, and universities. Through such organizations as MECHA (Movimiento Estudiantil Chicano de Aztlán), UMAS (United Mexican American Students), MASC (Mexican American Student Confederation), MAYO (Mexican American Youth Organization), FECH (Frente Estudiantil Chicano), and many others, they have set Chicano goals and obtained programs and resources to implement them. Demanding that all Mexican Americans be treated with dignity and humanity, Chicano organizations insist on complete equality and justice for all citizens.

While this new philosophy of Chicanismo has set new directions, it has also divided Mexican American communities. Not all Mexican Americans espouse the militant stance of Chicano activists; many find the mere term "Chicano" unacceptable and are offended by its use. Even some old-time fighters in the struggle for Mexican American equality find it difficult to adopt the name Chicano and to accept all views of Chicano militants. Moreover, not all Mexican Americans agree on the future course La Raza should follow; but most of them feel that they should be accepted completely as American citizens without having to surrender their distinctive cultural heritage. Standing firm in their convictions, they believe that all Americans benefit from contributions made by La Raza to a pluralistic society.

Although Chicanos have been Americans for over one hundred years, they remain at the bottom of the ladder in employment, social acceptance, and political influence. Stereotyping and racial stigma continue to segregate them from full participation in American society. Mexican Americans today continue to face many problems in all regions of the United States. While they have realized some progress since World War II, their social and economic status remains virtually the same. What the future holds in store for Chicanos will be determined by the attitudes and commitments of all Americans today.

MEXICAN AMERICANS IN UPHEAVAL

Although some amelioration of economic and social conditions has taken place, Chicanos remain at the bottom of the ladder and still experience economic, social, and political discrimination. José Antonio Villarreal interprets the contemporary Mexican American scene and enumerates

From "Mexican Americans in Upheaval," by José Antonio Villarreal. *West* magazine, *Los Angeles Times* (September 18, 1966). Reprinted, with deletions, by permission of the author.

important elements that express its current moods and aspirations. Villarreal is author of Pocho, *an important novel about La Raza set in Santa Clara, California, in the 1930's.*

No minority group in California today suffers the same type or degree of social neglect known to the Mexican American of this state. The discrimination directed against him is not so overt as the discrimination the Negro finds, but the depth of the exploitation practiced against him is far greater. The facts are: that 76 percent of the Mexican adult population in California is employed in unskilled occupations, that they are two years behind the Negro in scholastic achievement, and that they are four years behind the non-minority citizens of the state.

Most appalling, the situation is not improving; it is worsening. A recent study at UCLA showed, for example, that the Californian of Mexican descent lives today on a smaller per capita income than any other group in the population, including Negroes. Although *median* family income among Mexican Americans is higher than non-whites, the study showed, the larger average Mexican American family cuts into this advantage measurably. Thus, the average child of such a family is reared on $1,380 a year, compared with $1,437 for non-whites and $2,108 for the total population. . . .

The history of inequities suffered by California's citizens of Mexican descent is long and is still being written. The great mass of Mexicans in California arrived, or were born to those who arrived, during the years from 1910 through 1930. Much of today's prejudice still stems from that period, when the United States was caught up in a wave of fear over the immigrants from southern and eastern Europe that flooded into the East Coast, or the Orientals who were arriving in the West in increasing numbers. Public sentiment pushed through legislation to prohibit Japanese from becoming naturalized citizens. Behind the slogan of "America for Americans," Congress enacted the Johnson Immigration Act, which President Coolidge signed in 1924.

Despite this widespread attitude, the Mexican's position within the framework of the California society is a study in paradoxes.

Although the Mexican in a legal sense is a Caucasian (many Mexicans here and in Mexico come of European stock), it is common practice to use the term "Mexican" to denote race. Even sociologists and educators, as well as sophisticated Anglos who are *simpatico* to the cause and should know better, have been known to make the distinction between "Mexican" and "white." Still, this does not impede the Mexican, if he can pay the price, from enjoying every right his white neighbor enjoys, even though he is continually reminded of the plight faced by most people of his ethnic background. He knows that the Mexican is discriminated against more for his educational and economic shortcomings than for his ancestry. . . .

Yet there remain areas in California where ostracism, discrimination, and prejudice are as prevalent as ever. Even the Church— both Catholic and Protestant—sometimes helps to perpetuate the caste system, usually in agricultural areas. Here in farm towns of from one to five thousand people, communication between whites and Mexicans is virtually nonexistent. Here can be found the same social conditions that so many Mexicans knew forty-five years ago: stereotyped attitudes toward the Mexican as an inferior being who is incapable of learning and is going to be a stoop laborer anyway, segregated seating in school and church, and special treatment for the white Anglo-Saxon Protestant (WASP) students. The teacher rejects the Mexican student, subtly or overtly, carrying him only as long as the law demands it. By the time he reaches the eighth grade, the Mexican child is legally allowed to drop out and join his father in the fields. Unbelievable, but it happens today in the great, progressive state of California. (In the Salinas area last year, Mexican political activists uncovered the fact that school authorities planned to hold segregated classes for the children of migrant laborers in house trailers rather than bus them to WASP schools nearby.)

Ironically, this portion of the Mexican community, although subjected to the worst prejudice and the most overt discrimination, is most neglected by the reformers from their own ethnic group, simply because they are not an important political force. This is essentially why César Chávez, disenchanted by the emphasis placed on the needs of the urban Mexican community, gave up a directorship in the Community Service Organization in Los Angeles to lead the Delano grape strike.

The semiprofessional man, the professional man, the business-man attracted to the CSO paid little more than lip service to the needs of the farm worker. Not until he began to organize the National Farm Workers' Union did Chávez find the action he desired. . . .

There is another group that is not concerned with politics or social reform. A large group of citizens of Mexican descent in the medium-income level are apathetic simply because they do not now know discrimination. They have been able to assimilate, yet retain a part of the culture of their fathers. They may live in the middle-class areas of Oakland, San Francisco, Los Angeles, San Diego—or in a subdivision in the Santa Clara Valley, or near Norwalk. Many are ex-GIs, or children of ex-GIs. Like their lower-middle-class Anglo neighbors, they may not even be interested in voting, although in traditional American spirit they will be vaguely disturbed about taxation and the size of govern-ment. They are usually buying their homes and share with most of their Anglo friends the fear that the Negro may come into their neighborhood and depreciate values. . . .

But they know they are Mexican. And, with a smugness that would never permit them to deny it, call themselves Mexican. Twice a year, on the fifth of May and sixteenth of September, they attend Mexican national patriotic events with a Mexican pride that is formidable, dressing their children (usually two or three, because they have also adopted the middle-class Anglo fear of overpopulation) in the traditional costume of the *charro* or *china poblana*. . . .

Another group within the framework of Mexican society in California is the professional man: the doctor, lawyer, engineer, the businessman and the educator. And from this group with its academic or economic advantages come the majority of the political activists. . . .

The idea that social and economic reform for the Mexican in California could best be achieved by his participation in local and state government and by the consolidation of a voting bloc stemmed from the disillusion of the veteran of Mexican descent after World War II. Rightfully proud of the distinguished record those of his ethnic group had compiled in conflict around the world, the Mexican American ex-GI had hopes that many of the old rancors at home had dissipated. He was disillusioned when he attempted to get a GI deal on a home and found that his background barred him from living in specific areas. He was disillusioned again when he tried to find employment, and the final hurt was inflicted when he tried to collect the five years of college the federal government and the state of California guaranteed to him under Public Law 346 and he found that the third-rate schools in his barrio had not prepared him for college. He had no direction. . . .

There is the angry, militant young intellectual, usually a lawyer or educator, driven not only by a zeal to deliver his people but also by personal ambition. Typical is Robert E. Gonzales, a San Francisco attorney, who, while still young, has already made a good run for County Supervisor. . . .

There is also the older, embittered veteran who has fought the hard fight (many times alone), whose ambition has been thwarted by the passage of time, and who sees the newcomers receiving state appointments and otherwise reaping the fruits of his labor. Or he may be an old lawyer with years of service to his community who has also struggled long and has been more than once passed over for a younger man when a judicial vacancy came up. Either of them may feel that it's time for a change.

There is also the other ancient, who has given his time and himself to the cause but has no ambition for either wealth or position. He just wants his world made better. And yet he is not without the qualities of leadership, or the cunning and the wisdom of age. Such a one is Eduardo Quevedo, immediate past state president of MAPA, a *manito* from New Mexico with an authentic Mexican accent, an actor. Although not particularly literate, and not especially articulate in either English or Spanish, he is self-made, self-assured, competent, and astute. He is idolized by many of the younger men, who approach him solicitously because he is aging and ailing and they have been trained to respect age. Although he plays the part of a democratic leader, he is often arbitrary and bulldozing. A Franklin Roosevelt Democrat, he is the force that helps keep MAPA, although expressly a bipartisan organization, also expressly committed to the Democratic party.

There are also crooks, those who are out only for what they can get, quickly but not necessarily honestly. They are not a force in the Mexican American community, any more than they are a force in the Anglo community. They are an irritant to both, but that is all.

Finally, there is the tool, the *Tío Tomás* (Uncle Tom), who, for an appointment to a minor office or responsibility, will betray his people, while professing that he is doing good for them. There is for the politician, after all, a value to having a Spanish surname listed on his staff. And for the Mexican staff member, it is justified as being proof that Mexicans can improve themselves. But to him, this is the limit of the improvement. For he has believed the propaganda that he is an inferior being, that the Mexican has neither the capacity to learn nor the native ability to compete with the Anglo on intellectual or creative terms. A leading official of the city of Los Angeles has such a man on his staff. He is not there to serve as a link between the official and the Mexican community, to provide meaningful expression to the official of this community's needs, but rather to keep alive the idea of a democratic city government which would place even one of Mexican descent in such a position of trust. The man's greatest sense of pride is the fact that no Mexican became a turncoat in Korea and that none has given his community a bad name by becoming a prominent Communist.

CHICANO NATIONALISM

Ethnic identity forms the unifying basis for contemporary Chicano movements, however diverse their objectives. This article from The International Socialist Review *briefly describes the genesis of this most important development for the future of Chicanos.*

From "The Struggle for Chicano Liberation," *International Socialist Review* (November 1971). Copyright © 1971. Reprinted by permission of the *International Socialist Review*.

Many of the developments which led to the worldwide youth radicalization of the 1960's also affected the Chicano people and helped facilitate the emergence of a new generation of militant young Chicanos.

The colonial revolution showed that peoples long oppressed could rise up and win their freedom. The Cuban revolution, especially, had an impact in the Chicano community.

The first mass reflection of the colonial revolution in the United States was the movement of the Afro-American people. The struggles of this oppressed nationality shook up the political equilibrium, helped to inspire the youth radicalization, and served as a model for subsequent insurgent movements it helped set into motion. The student movement, the antiwar movement, the Chicano movement, and more recently the women's liberation movement owe much to the initiating role of the black movement, the lessons of its successful and unsuccessful strategies and tactics, and the experiences of black organizations and leaders.

The Chicano movement has benefited from the experiences of these movements, and in turn, it has taught lessons in its own right, surged ahead in some aspects, and now provides examples especially for the black movement.

Two efforts were begun in 1962 that were to influence the initial stages of the new Chicano movement and inspire subsequent developments. These were the farm workers' movement and the land-grant organizing efforts led respectively by César Chávez and Reies López Tijerina.

César Chávez resigned from his position of leadership in the Community Service Organization in 1961, when conservative elements blocked his efforts to use the CSO to support the struggles of Chicano farm workers. The following year he formed the Farm Workers' Association, which was to become a social movement, a union of farm workers that could fight for collective bargaining with the rich growers but would also deal with medical, language, and other problems faced by farm workers.

In 1965 the association joined forces with a Filipino farm workers' group to form the United Farm Workers' Organizing Committee, based in California. The expiration of the bracero program at the end of 1964 (although it partially continued under the Green Card program) had created a new opportunity to organize farm workers with less likelihood that strikes could be broken by the massive importation of Mexican labor. A strike of grape workers began in the fall of 1965, and though it won some initial concessions, it was necessary to carry out a protracted grape boycott campaign before substantial victories were won and consolidated.

The organizing efforts and achievements in California had a major impact upon the barrios and farm-labor camps around the country and led to similar developments in Arizona, Texas, Washington, Colorado, and other states.

It was *la Huelga* (the Strike), together with the land-grant movement in New Mexico, that first forced into the public eye the existence of this "forgotten minority" and the recognition that a new civil- and human-rights movement was emerging. The migrant laborers, who were said by racists to be naturally endowed for such "stoop labor" because they were "built low to the ground," were challenging racist stereotypes and asserting their humanity. Chicanos shouting *"Huelga"* and *"Viva la Causa"* and demanding *"Justicia y Libertad"* added another powerful element to the struggles of the oppressed and exploited.

The farm workers' movement has been led for the most part by pacifist reformists like Chávez, who supports liberal Democrats. Nevertheless, this movement has had an independent nationalist dynamic which has helped set other sectors of La Raza into motion.

This independent dynamic has been incomplete and blunted by the refusal of the Chávez leadership to break politically with the Democratic party and initiate an independent Chicano party. Such a development is a necessary step for the success of the farm workers' struggle. It could result in rapid electoral victories in the cities and towns of the rich farm country in the valleys of California, and in other states where Chicanos are a majority. These victories, in turn, would give fresh impetus to unionization efforts, the fight for higher wages, better conditions, health and child care, and other demands.

The growth of La Raza Unida Party in 1970 and 1971 has

exerted considerable pressure on the farmworkers' movement to embark on the road of independent Chicano political action. This may be seen in Chávez's recent statement in favor of La Raza Unida candidates. If the farm workers' union should begin to stray from the Meany-approved subordination of the labor movement to the Democratic party, the AFL-CIO bureaucracy can be expected to exert considerable pressure on the farm workers by withdrawing financial and other support.

In violation of the provisions of the Treaty of Guadalupe Hidalgo, which ended the United States war with Mexico in 1848, the property of the Mexican inhabitants of what is now the Southwest United States was not respected.

Reies López Tijerina investigated the original land-grant titles and exposed the processes by which they were stolen. The Alianza Federal de Mercedes (Federal Alliance of Land Grants) was formed in 1962 in New Mexico to publicize the claims of the "Indo-Hispanos" to the land now occupied by Anglos and by the National Forest Service.

A series of events beginning in 1966 brought the Alianza to public attention nationally. A march from Albuquerque to Santa Fe with petitions to the governor of New Mexico and the President of the United States was followed by attempts to occupy parts of National Forest lands in the fall of 1966 and summer of 1967. This was answered by military force and frame-up charges against Alianza leaders.

Included in the program of the Alianza was the idea of internationalizing their struggle by appealing to the United Nations and Cuba to recognize their claims to the land and their right to establish an independent republic based on the land grants.

The Alianza participated in a "New Politics" Peace and Freedom-type formation, the People's Constitutional party of New Mexico, during the 1968 elections, running Tijerina for governor. They, along with the Crusade for Justice of Denver, and the farm workers' union, joined the Southern Christian Leadership Conference's Poor People's March on Washington in 1968.

Tijerina and other Alianza militants, after frame-up trials, were imprisoned, and the Alianza has declined.

With Chicanos constituting more than one third of New Mexico's population, and a majority in some areas, considerable potential exists for building an independent Chicano party there, although no such efforts have been undertaken thus far.

An urban civil rights and cultural movement called the Crusade for Justice was formed in Denver, Colorado, in the mid-1960's. While located solely in Denver, the crusade's influence was to be more widely felt as its principal spokesman, Rodolfo "Corky" Gonzales, a former official of the Democratic party, emerged as one of the central leaders in the Chicano movement.

The Crusade for Justice organized and supported high-school strikes, demonstrations against police brutality, and legal cases in behalf of Chicanos framed by the police. It also supported mass actions against the Vietnam war.

One of the most important roles played by the crusade has been organizing the Chicano Youth Liberation conferences. The 1969 and 1970 conferences brought together large numbers of Chicano youth from the Southwest, the Northwest, and the Midwest, as well as some Puerto Rican youth from the Midwest and the East Coast. Out of the first conference came *El Plan Espiritual de Aztlán* (the Spiritual Plan of Aztlán), a program for the mass mobilization of Chicanos for community control. The Plan of Aztlán raised the concept that the liberation of the "mestizo nation" would ultimately require "a nation autonomously free, culturally, socially, economically, and politically." The formation of an independent Chicano party was projected "since the two-party system is the same animal with two heads that feeds from the same trough."

The second Chicano youth conference (1970) represented a further step forward for those forces who supported a mass-action perspective and the formation of an independent Chicano political party. Following the conference, the Crusade for Justice and other Chicanos launched the Colorado Raza Unida Pary.

The schools have been a place where Chicano youth have been politicized by many of the factors that fueled the international youth radicalization, as well as by many specific grievances. By the 1960's the number of Chicano youth in the high schools had dramatically increased. There are approximately 2 million Spanish-surnamed elementary- and secondary-school students in the United States, 70 percent of them in the Southwest. More Chicano students are now going on to college, but not in the same proportion as the rest of the population.

The Chicano student movement developed to combat oppressive school conditions. High-school and elementary students were prohibited from using Spanish in the classroom or on the school grounds; the true history of the Chicano people was not taught; Anglo principals and teachers directly and indirectly expressed their racist concepts and attitudes; and Chicano students not pushed out of the schools were tracked into vocational rather than academic courses, often into the army rather than college. Students were not allowed to freely organize political or cultural groups in the schools. Corporal punishment was meted out to those who objected to these repressive conditions. Disciplinary suspensions and expulsions were common.

To change these conditions a wave of Chicano high-school "blow-outs" (strikes) occurred all over the Southwest and in other places like Chicago, with the largest and most effective taking place in 1968 in Los Angeles, where fifteen thousand Chicano students walked out of the barrio schools and triggered similar actions among students in some predominantly black and several mostly white schools. A Chicano sit-in at the Board of Education brought to public attention the demands of Raza students for "education, not contempt," "education, not eradication," and posed the need for Chicano control of schools in the Chicano community. The actions of the high-school students engendered support from college-student groups as well as parent and community organizations.

Concessions have been granted in the face of these high-school struggles, one of the most important being the repeal or easing of the prohibition against the teaching of regular classes in Spanish in the schools. But the Chicano people still face the problem of how to take control of the schools in the Chicano communities. Elements of control have been won in some school districts in south Texas, where student strikes have been combined with the formation of independent Chicano parties which have elected candidates to office.

Chicano college students also began to organize on the campuses for Chicano studies programs, open admissions, and community control of higher education—the Brown University. Chicano students played a leading role in the Third World Liberation Front strikes at San Francisco State College, the University of California at Berkeley, and elsewhere in 1968 and 1969. A Latin and Mexican American studies department was won at Merritt Junior College in Oakland and some form of Chicano studies was won at many other colleges.

A conference of Chicano students and educators in 1969 at Santa Barbara, California, issued *El Plan de Santa Barbara* which "set out to formulate a Chicano plan for higher education." Some elements of the concept of the Brown University are present in this document as summed up in the statement: "We do not come to work for the university, but to demand that the university work for our people."

No single Chicano student organization exists as a national or Southwest-wide group. UMAS (United Mexican American Students) is strong in Colorado, MECHA (Movimiento Estudiantil Chicano de Aztlán—Chicano Student Movement of Aztlán) in California, MAYO (Mexican American Youth Organization) in Texas. In the Midwest, Chicano students have in some cases united with Puerto Rican students in Latino groups such as the Latin American Student Organization in Chicago.

In many urban areas Chicano youth formed groups like the Brown Berets. These groups have played a role as organizers and monitors in high-school strikes and in actions against police brutality. The Brown Berets vary from place to place, from being non-political or antipolitical, to revolutionary nationalists, to ultraleft sectarians.

In those areas where independent Chicano political parties have been formed, student groups have often provided activists and leaders. This has been especially important in Texas, where MAYO-led student strikes helped lay the basis for the formation of La Raza Unida parties in south Texas. . . .

MECHA

Movimiento Estudiantil Chicano de Aztlán (MECHA), the outstanding contemporary student organization, grew out of a critical need for a vehicle to voice needs of Chicanos in education. In El Plan de Santa Barbara, *the Chicano Coordinating Council on Higher Education describes in considerable detail the philosophy, organization, and function of MECHA.*

MECHA is a first step toward tying the student groups throughout the Southwest into a vibrant and responsive network of activists that will respond as a unit to oppression and racism and that will work in harmony when initiating and carrying out campaigns of liberation for our people.

As of the present, wherever one travels throughout the Southwest, one finds that there are different levels of awareness on different campuses. It is the function of MECHA to further socialization and politicization for liberation on all campuses. The student movement is to a large degree a political movement and as such must not elicit from our people the negative responses that we have experienced so often in the past in relation to politics, often with good reason. To this end, then, we must redefine politics for our people for it to be a means of liberation. The political sophistication of our Raza must be raised so that it does not fall prey to apologists and *vendidos* whose whole interest is their personal career or fortune. In addition, the student movement is more than a political movement, it is cultural and social as well. The spirit of MECHA must be one of *hermandad* and

From *El Plan de Santa Barbara*. Oakland, Calif.: La Causa Publications, Inc., 1969. Copyright © 1970 by La Causa Publications. Reprinted, with deletions, by permission of the publisher.

cultural awareness. The ethic of profit and competition, of greed and intolerance which the Anglo society offers must be replaced by our ancestral communalism and love of beauty and justice. MECHA must bring to the mind of every young Chicano that the liberation of his people from prejudice and oppression is in his hands and that this responsibility is greater than personal achievement and more meaningful than degrees, especially if they are earned at the expense of his identity and cultural integrity.

MECHA, then, is more than a name, it is a spirit of unity, of brotherhood, and a resolve to undertake a struggle for liberation in a society where justice is but a word. MECHA is a means to an end. . . .

Other students can be important to MECHA in supportive roles; hence the question of coalitions. Although it is understood and quite obvious that the viability and amenability of coalition varies from campus to campus, some guidelines might be kept in mind. These questions should be asked before entering into any binding agreement: Is it beneficial to tie oneself to another group in coalition which will carry oneself into conflicts for which one is ill prepared or into issues on which one is ill advised? Can one safely go into a coalition where one group is markedly stronger than another? Are the interests of MECHA and of the community being served? Does MECHA have an equal voice in leadership and planning in the coalition group? Is it perhaps better to enter into a loose alliance for a given issue? How does the leadership of each group view coalitions? How does the membership? Can MECHA hold up its end of the bargain? Will MECHA carry dead weight in a coalition? All of these and many more questions must be asked and answered before one can safely say that he will benefit and contribute to a strong coalition effort.

Supportive groups. When moving on campus, it is often well advised to have groups who are willing to act in supportive roles. For example, there are usually any number of faculty members who are sympathetic but limited as to the number of activities they will engage in. These faculty members often serve on academic councils and senates and can be instrumental in academic policy. They also provide another channel to the academic power structure and can be used as leverage in negotiation. However, these groups are only as responsive as the ties with them are nurtured. This does not mean compromising MECHA's integrity; it merely means laying good groundwork before an issue is brought up, touching bases with your allies beforehand.

Sympathetic administrators. This is a delicate area since administrators are most interested in not jeopardizing their positions and often will try to act as buffers or liaison between the administration and the student group. In the case of Chicano administrators, it should not a priori be assumed that because he is Raza he is to be blindly trusted. If he is not known to the membership, he must be given a chance to prove his allegiance to *la Causa*. As such he should be the Chicano's man in the power structure instead of the administration's Mexican American. It is from the administrator that information can be obtained as to the actual feasibility of demands or programs to go beyond the platitudes and pleas of unreasonableness with which the administration usually answers proposals and demands. The words of the administrator should never be the deciding factor in students' actions. The students must at all times make their own decisions. It is very human for people to establish self-interest. Therefore, students must constantly remind the Chicano administrators and faculty where their loyalty and allegiance lie. It is very easy for administrators to begin looking for promotions, just as it is very natural for faculty members to seek positions of academic prominence.

In short, it is the students who must keep after Chicano and non-Chicano administrators and faculty to see that they do not compromise the position of the student and the community. By the same token, it is the student who must come to the support of these individuals if they are threatened for their support of the students. Students must be careful not to become a political lever for others.

It is a fact that the Chicano has not often enough written his own history, his own anthropology, his own sociology, his own literature. He must do this if he is to survive as a cultural entity in this melting-pot society which seeks to dilute varied cultures into a gray-upon-gray pseudo-culture of technology and materialism.

The Chicano student is doing most of the work in the establishment of study programs, centers, curriculum development, entrance programs to get more Chicanos into college. This is good and must continue, but students must be careful not to be coopted in their fervor for establishing relevance on the campus. Much of what is being offered by college systems and administrators is too little too late. MECHA must not compromise programs and curriculum which are essential for the total education of the Chicano for the sake of expediency. The students must not become so engrossed in programs and centers created along established academic guidelines that they forget the needs of the people whom these institutions are meant to serve. To this end, barrio input must always be given full and open hearing when designing these programs, when creating them, and when running them. The jobs created by these projects must be filled by competent Chicanos, not only those who have the traditional credentials required for the position but those who have the credentials of La Raza. Too often in the past, the dedicated pushed for a program only to have a *vendido* sharp-talker come in and take over and start working for his Anglo administrator. Therefore, students must demand a say in the recruitment and selection of all directors and assistant directors of student-initiated programs. To further ensure strong if not complete control of the direction and running of programs, all advisory and steering committees should have both student and community components as well as sympathetic Chicano faculty as members.

Tying the campus to the barrio. The colleges and universities in the past have existed in an aura of omnipotence and infallibility. It is time that they be made responsible and responsive to the communities in which they are located or whose members they serve. As has already been mentioned, community members should serve on all programs related to Chicano interests. In addition to this, all attempts must be made to take the college and university to the barrio, whether it be in the form of classes giving college credit or community centers financed by the school for the use of community organizations and groups. Also, the barrio must be brought to the campus, whether it be for special programs or ongoing services which the school provides for the people of the barrio. The idea must be made clear to the people of the barrio that they own the schools, and the schools and all such resources are at their disposal. The student group must utilize the resources open to the school for the benefit of the barrio at every opportunity. This can be done by hiring more Chicanos to work as academic and non-academic personnel on the campus, often requiring exposure of the racist hiring practices now in operation in many colleges and universities. When functions, social or otherwise, are held in the barrio under the sponsorship of the college and university, monies should be spent in the barrio. This applies to hiring Chicano contractors to build on campus, etc. Many colleges and universities have publishing operations which could be forced to accept barrio works for publication. Many other things could be considered in using the resources of the school in the barrio. There are possibilities for using the physical plant and facilities not mentioned here; this is an area which has great potential.

Most colleges in the Southwest are located near or in the same town as a barrio. Therefore, it is the responsibility of MECHA members to establish close working relationships with organizations in that barrio. The MECHA people must be able to take the pulse of the barrio and be able to respond to it. However, MECHA must be careful not to overstep its authority or duplicate the efforts of another organization already in the barrio. MECHA must be able to relate to all segments of the barrio, from the middle-class assimilationists to the *batos locos*.

Obviously, every barrio has its particular needs, and MECHA people must determine with the help of those in the barrio where they can be most effective. There are, however, some general areas in which MECHA can involve itself. Some of these are: (1) policing social and governmental agencies to make them more responsive in a humane and dignified way to the people of the barrio; (2) carrying out research on the economic and credit policies of merchants in the barrio and exposing fraudulent and exorbitant establishments; (3) speaking and communicating with junior-high and high-school students, helping with their projects, teaching them organizational techniques, supporting their actions; (4) spreading the message of the movement by any media available; this means speaking, radio, television, local newspapers, underground papers, posters, art, theaters, in short spreading propaganda of the movement; (5) exposing discrimination in hiring and renting practices and many other areas which the student, because of his mobility, his articulation, and his vigor, should take as his responsibility. It may mean at times having to work in conjunction with other organizations. If this is the case and the project is one begun by the other organization, realize that MECHA is there as a supporter and should accept the direction of the group involved. Do not let loyalty to an organization cloud responsibility to a greater force—*la Causa*.

Working in the barrio is an honor, but it is also a right, because we come from these people, and as such, mutual respect between the barrio and the college group should be the rule. Understand at the same time, however, that there will initially be mistrust and even envy on the part of some in the barrio for the college student. This mistrust must be broken down by a demonstration of affection for the barrio and La Raza through hard work and dedication. If the approach is one of a dilettante or of a Peace Corps volunteer, the people will know it and react accordingly. If it is merely a cathartic experience to work among the unfortunate in the barrio—stay out.

Of the community, for the community. *Por la Raza habla el espíritu.* . . .

LA RAZA
AND REVOLUTION

José Angel Gutiérrez of Texas, a founder of the Mexican American Youth Organization and more recently of La Raza Unida political party, is one of the newest Chicano political leaders to emerge. Gutiérrez's influence has been felt from Crystal City, Texas, to the farthest colonias of Aztlán. In this selection from his thesis, Gutiérrez describes Chicano frustration with Texas politics, Anglo-style.

The political instability in south Texas is manifesting itself in several ways. Having been excluded from participation in the traditional political process, the Mexican American is developing a new approach and viewpoint about political affairs. This new approach is to reject assimilation into the Anglo-controlled political system and seek, through organized political movements, the radical redistribution of political power to include Mexican Americans. These political movements will attempt to produce constituencies of Mexican American voters of sufficient size to elect Mexican Americans to office who will promote the interests of Mexican Americans only. If these constituencies are closely knit geographically and if Mexican American voters constitute the majority, a third political party for Mexican Americans should be formed. The Mexican Americans now view the political system as an Anglo system. They feel that only a Mexican American political system can serve their needs. . . .

Among Mexican American youth, this personal approach to politics is taking a new twist. Research in the four counties revealed that young militants feel it is of little benefit to be polite

From "La Raza and Revolution" by José Angel Gutiérrez. San Antonio, Texas: M. A. thesis, St. Mary's University, 1968. Reprinted, with deletions, by permission of the author.

and inoffensive to the Anglo community. Some feel that few Anglos sympathize with their cause. A commonly used argument is that in order to preserve his socio-economic, political, and cultural background, a Mexican American has to work outside the traditional Anglo Political system. The young people feel that Mexican American protest has fallen on deaf ears because of failure to make demands for specific reforms, and that those few reforms implemented were indicative of the slowness with which goals are achieved through the political process. The rewards from the system are too slow and too meager. The youth is also dissatisfied with the traditional Mexican American organizations, such as LULAC [League of United Latin American Citizens], PASO [Political Association of Spanish-Speaking Organizations], and G.I. Forum. The militants feel these organizations have little political efficacy and give false hopes to the Mexican American. They believe that only through the attainment of economic, political, or cultural power can the Mexican American bargain effectively with the Anglo establishment. As one young man put it: "Why join an organization to do something about the problem? I don't need an organization to go kill Mayor MacAllister or to set fire to his building." Dr. Octavio Romano writes in *El Grito*, a journal of contemporary Mexican American thought, about the social scientists who stay away from the protests of the Mexican American: "They stay away by the tens, twenties, and hundreds. They stay away because people who are 'fatalistic,' [and] 'under-achieving' simply are not supposed to say such things as ¡*Basta!* and ¡*Huelga!*'"

But ¡*Basta!* became the slogan in Crystal City and Mathis, Texas. ¡*Viva la Huelga!* became the slogan from the Rio Grande to Austin, Texas. ¡*Viva la Raza!* became the slogan in San Antonio and Laredo, Texas. These words became slogans motivating men to action. To use these words means to take on a new attitude, to take a new militant course of action. These words are the language of the new Mexican American movement.

Mexican Americans' frustration with the Anglo, with the political process, and with the years of exclusion from political participation is reaching a peak. Due to the economic development and a growing middle class among Mexican Americans, the meager political gains and rewards no longer seem satisfactory. For example, every ten years some 300,000-plus Mexican Americans are added to the total Spanish-speaking population. . . .

Yet, with a majority of the population in two counties and close to a majority in two others, the Mexican Americans still cannot gain representation in proportion to their numbers. For example, Kleberg County has no Mexican American officeholders on the county level, Zavala County has two Mexican American office-holders, and Brooks County has four.

Does the Mexican American population register to vote? In terms of the number of voters registered among the Mexican American population in 1968, the same counties that have a Mexican American majority population have the majority of voters, and the other two have significant numbers registered.

If the Mexican American has significant numbers of voters, why is he not able to change the existing personnel in public office? Perhaps Mexican Americans do not vote after they are registered, or perhaps some other legal means are used to curtail the effect of the Mexican American vote.

As was mentioned earlier, Texas has an annual registration that opens in October and closes on January 31 of the election year. The deadline for filing for public office is the first Tuesday in February of the election year. Consequently, voters must register without knowing who the candidates will be. Also, they must register from four to eight months before a primary election is held and from ten to thirteen months before the general election in November. Registration is conducted at a time when there is little, if any, political interest. For those Mexican Americans who do register, frequently the only candidates who appear on the ballot are Anglos. Hence, many Mexican Americans see little point in registering and voting solely for the purpose of electing Anglos to office.

In addition, another legal obstacle for the Mexican American exists in the form of commissioner precincts. It was found that the Mexican American community or barrio is concentrated in one section of the city. Accidentally or by gerrymandering, the barrio was located in only one precinct. Three of the four counties had two precincts located in the city and two located in the rural area of the counties. One of the precincts in each of the three counties took in the Mexican American community, and the other precinct took in the predominantly Anglo community.

San Antonio is the only city that has all four commissioner precincts within the city. In other words, the city is the county. One precinct in Bexar County takes in the bulk of the Mexican American barrio. This situation does not allow the Mexican Americans to exercise voting influence in the other precincts. Of the precincts in the four counties, only those in San Antonio are representative of equal percentages of the total population. In the other three counties, the precincts in the city itself had a greater concentration of the population of the county than did the other precincts in the county. The "one-man one-vote" principle on the county level does not exist in three counties in south Texas.

Other factors that serve to exclude the Mexican American from political participation are the mechanics of voting and the actual date of the primary election. Those Mexican Americans who cannot read frequently vote for the wrong candidate. This occurs because the Texas ballot requires a voter to delete those candidates he does not want, leaving the candidate he does want. This is a difficult task for an illiterate person. Also, lack of expertise among the Mexican American poll watchers handicaps them in checking for irregularities, illegalities, and interpretation of the election code. Lack of familiarity with the political process is evidenced by the small number of Mexican Americans who are aware of the precinct conventions held after the elections; as a consequence, few attend and even fewer participate actively. Further, the dates of the primary election, the possible runoff elections, the precinct convention, the county convention, and the state convention are not the best times for the thousands of migrants in the four counties. The migration of farm workers from Texas begins around April and ends around November.

In summary, the *patrón* system; the manipulation of votes through illegal means; the several legal obstacles, such as registration and precinct boundaries; the expense of politics; the fraud, irregularities, intimidation, and outright cheating; the peculiar political behavior of the Mexican American and his distrust of the political system; the dissatisfaction with the system; the lack of representation of his numbers; and the militancy of the youth all help to explain the low degree of trust the Mexican American has in the political system. The situation in the four counties of south Texas is a very unstable political situation.

The traditional means used within this political system to effect change are viewed skeptically by Mexican Americans. For example, petitions, resolutions, voting, public opinion, elections, and pressure politics are political devices rejected by the Mexican American.

Direct political action is replacing more traditional methods of political problem solving. The political style of the militants is to express openly and verbally hostility toward the Anglo, the Anglo political system, and the Anglo political institutions. The militants question the value of working within the existing political system or engaging in traditional political activity. They question the political efficacy of the traditional Mexican American leadership, because it does not represent them, their views, or their interests. They accurately point out that Mexican American leaders who have worked with the Establishment have conformed to the norms of that power structure. The youth feel that these leaders leave as representatives *of* the Mexican Americans and return as representatives *to* the Mexican Americans. Militants argue that past experience has shown that the rewards obtained in terms of educational, social, political, and economic benefits from working within the political system are too meager.

Political instability exists in south Texas!

REIES LÓPEZ TIJERINA

Reies López Tijerina is unquestionably the most dramatic of contemporary Chicano leaders in his claim (for fellow La Raza members) of millions of acres originally belonging to New Mexican communities. The following article describes the gestation and growth of the Alianza Federal de Mercedes and Tijerina's difficulties with the law. Following is a letter in which Tijerina explains his view of the Alianza movement.

TIJERINA TRIAL

The Reies Tijerina trial, a spin-off of swirling issues, appears well on its way toward becoming a controversy itself.

Whatever the outcome, the trial probably will raise more social and judicial questions than it settles.

The hearings started November 13. Mr. Tijerina and nine other members of a land-grant movement face charges ranging from kidnapping to assault. These arose from the widely publicized "raid" on the courthouse of Tierra Amarilla in the mountain country of northern New Mexico in 1967.

After days of tedious motions and questions put to prospective jurors, District Judge Paul Larrazolo ordered Mr. Tijerina tried alone, as it was apparent the wheels of justice were barely grinding at all.

This brought howls from defense and prosecution lawyers and more calls for mistrial, continuance, and changes of venue. The defense says it cannot find a fair and impartial jury in Albuquer-

From "Social Issues and Politics Swirl about New Mexico's 'Revolutionists'." *The Christian Science Monitor* (December 4, 1968). Copyright © 1968 The Christian Science Publishing Society. All rights reserved. Reprinted by permission of *The Christian Science Monitor*.

que and wants the case heard in the remote town where the
"guerrilla attack" allegedly occurred.

At the outset, Mr. Tijerina asked for and received free,
court-appointed lawyers. He said he had been unemployed since
1960 when he was a cotton picker in Texas.

Later he charged his attorneys were "obsolete" and said he
would act as his own attorney. The court said it would allow this
but ordered legal counsel to stay at his side.

On June 6, 1967, the New Mexico National Guard was called
out to protect the people and capture a band of "revolutionists" in
northern New Mexico. The previous day the courthouse of Rio
Arriba County in the village of Tierra Amarilla had been "raided"
by an armed band.

Law officers had been shot, the building sacked, a newsman
kidnapped, a judge locked in his chambers, and prisoners freed.
The sheriff, Benny Naranjo, was ordered to lie face down,
motionless, on the floor.

The story hit front pages throughout the United States. It
seemed inconceivable that such a thing could happen in the
Southwest in the second half of the twentieth century. But the
one hard fact of the case now being heard in Albuquerque is that
it did, indeed, happen.

Reies López Tijerina—the first and last names may be loosely
translated as "King of the Tigers"—is a figure as shadowy as the
valleys and gullies of Rio Arriba's Sangre de Cristo Mountains. He
says he is from Texas; his activities have been recorded in Arizona
and Mexico.

Just when the Alianza Federal de Mercedes (Federal Alliance
of Land Grants) was organized and when Reies López Tijerina
became its chief are uncertain.

After the "revolution" broke out in the northern counties, the
Alianza supposedly was disbanded, but the group remained
organized under the name of Political Confederation of Free City
States.

Mr. Tijerina has already been convicted of charges arising from
an incident which occurred October 22, 1966, at scenic Echo

Amphitheater, a natural hollow in the side of a sandstone cliff in Carson National Forest.

Two United States forest rangers were "arrested" and held by the band for "trespassing" on the private land of an "independent nation."

Because of the subsequent conviction in federal court, Mr. Tijerina's name was ruled off the ballot of last November's election, in which he had been running for governor. He managed to get a stand-in candidate on the ballot, but he got only a few hundred votes statewide.

Mr. Tijerina continues to acquire assistance and vocal support. The newly organized Brown Berets demonstrated, about sixty strong, on the courthouse steps the weekend after his new trial started.

The Alianza's long-standing argument is that the tens of thousands of acres of former Spanish land grants were transferred to new ownership illegally down through the years. Mr. Tijerina asserts that much of this was done in the nineteenth century and early in the twentieth century during the reign of the so-called Santa Fe Ring.

The argument is based on the Treaty of Guadalupe Hidalgo, which ended the Mexican war of 1848. The treaty supposedly guaranteed recognition by the United States of Spanish land-grant titles in the newly won territories.

It is true that the New Mexico government was at times controlled by a clique of Anglo state officials, judges, and a few other powerful politicians. And it is also true that many of the old land grants were sold or transferred under circumstances which were morally if not legally questionable.

But the hard reality is that few arguments can be seriously weighed toward restoration of the lands to the heirs of their original owners.

In the current hassle, another violent incident clouded the scene and again brought charges and countercharges. In January 1968, Eulogio Salazar, jailer at the Tierra Amarilla courthouse, was kidnapped and beaten to death by unknown assailants.

Mr. Salazar had been seriously injured in the June 1966 raid and was considered a top witness for the eventual trial.

"In my heart I know that Alianza is not to blame," Tijerina said after Salazar's body was found in an abandoned car. Suspects are yet to be arrested in the case.

Rio Arriba County has always been an enigma in the history of modern New Mexico. Ballot boxes are frequently impounded by the courts at election time.

The county seat at Tierra Amarilla is far from the more heavily populated areas. Here there is real poverty, although welfare, which has become a way of life, prevents starvation.

Governor David Cargo has twice been elected because of the support he has among northern Spanish-speaking groups. The Alianza and Governor Cargo had been on friendly terms, and when he first sought the governorship, he appeared at Alianza rallies and conventions.

The Office of Economic Opportunity (OEO) and other government agencies have been prominent in the recent controversies. Members of the OEO defended Alianza members after the courthouse incident.

But agencies such as the U.S. Forest Service have been held up by the Alianza as typical foes of the poor native. The main bone of contention is whether grazing-land permits have been issued or withdrawn on a fair basis with solid conservation plans in mind.

The Forest Service says yes. The Brown Berets, Tijerina, and his followers say definitely not.

A tragic outgrowth of the current issues might be that after centuries of distrust and competition, the Spanish peoples and the Anglos will develop more divisiveness.

But there are hopeful trends in the bigger, more sophisticated urban areas. There one may find many "coyotes," native slang for children of mixed Spanish and Anglo parentage. In Spanish it is pronounced *ko-yo-teh* and is really a term of endearment.

And there are more and more "coyotes" around, symbols of merging cultures.

A LETTER FROM JAIL

Santa Fe Jail, August 15–17 [1969]

From my cell block in this jail I am writing these reflections. I write them to my people, the Indo-Hispanos, to my friends among the Anglos, to the agents of the federal government, the state of New Mexico, the Southwest, and the entire Indo-Hispano world—"Latin America."

I write to you as one of the clearest victims of the madness and racism in the hearts of our present-day politicians and rulers.

At this time, August 17, I have been in jail for sixty-five days—since June 11, 1969, when my appeal bond from another case was revoked by a federal judge. I am here today because I resisted an assassination attempt led by an agent of the federal government—an agent of all those who do not want anybody to speak out for the poor, all those who do not want Reies López Tijerina to stand in their way as they continue to rob the poor people, all those many rich people from outside the state with their summer homes and ranches here whose pursuit of happiness depends on thievery, all those who have robbed the people of their land and culture for 120 years. . . .

What is my real crime? As I and the poor people see it, especially the Indo-Hispanos, my only crime is UPHOLDING OUR RIGHTS AS PROTECTED BY THE TREATY OF GUAD-ALUPE HIDALGO, which ended the so-called Mexican American war of 1846–8. My only crime is demanding the respect and protection of our property, which has been confiscated illegally by the federal government. Ever since the treaty was signed in 1848, our people have been asking every elected President of the United States for a redress of grievances. Like the black people, we too have been criminally ignored. Our right to the Spanish land-grant pueblos is the real reason why I am in prison at this moment.

Our cause and our claim and our methods are legitimate. Yet even after a jury in a court of law acquitted me last December, they still call me a violent man. But the right to make a citizen's

From "Letter from Prison," by Reies López Tijerina. *El Grito del Norte* (September 26, 1969). Reprinted by permission of the author.

arrest, as I attempted to make that day on Evans, is not a violent right. On the contrary, it is law and order—unless the arrested person resists or flees to avoid prosecution. No honest citizen should avoid a citizen's arrest.

This truth is denied by the conspirators against the poor and by the press which they control. There are also the Silent Contributors. The Jewish people accused the Pope of Rome for keeping silent while Hitler and his machine persecuted the Jews in Germany and other countries. I support the Jews in their right to accuse those who contributed to Hitler's acts by their SILENCE. By the same token, I denounce those in New Mexico who have never opened their mouths at any time to defend or support the thousands who have been killed, robbed, raped of their culture. I don't know of any Church or Establishment organization or group of elite intellectuals that has stood up for the Treaty of Guadalupe Hidalgo. We condemn the silence of these groups and individuals, and I am sure that, like the Jewish people, the poor of New Mexico are keeping a record of the Silence which contributes to the criminal conspiracy against the Indo-Hispano in New Mexico.

As I sit in my jail cell in Santa Fe, capital of New Mexico, I pray that all the poor people will unite to bring justice to New Mexico. My cell block has no daylight, no ventilation of any kind, no light of any kind. After 9 p.m., we are left in a dungeon of total darkness. Visiting rules allow only fifteen minutes per week on Thursdays from 1 to 4 p.m., so that parents who work cannot visit their sons in jail. Yesterday a twenty-two-year-old boy cut his throat. Today, August 17, two young boys cut their wrists with razor blades and were taken unconscious to the hospital. My cell is dirty and there is nothing to clean it with. The whole cell block is hot and suffocating. All my prison mates complain and show a daily state of anger. But these uncomfortable conditions do not bother me, for I have a divine dream to give me strength: the happiness of my people.

I pray to God that all the Indo-Hispano people will awake to the need for unity, and to our heavenly and constitutional responsibility for fighting peacefully to win our rights. Already the rest of the Indo-Hispano world—Latin America—knows of our struggle. It is too late to keep the story of our land struggle from reaching the ears of the Indo-Hispano world. All the universities of Latin America knew about our problems when Rockefeller went there last summer. Will Latin America ignore our cry from here in New Mexico and the Southwest? Times have changed and the spirit of the blood is no longer limited by national or continental boundaries.

The Indo-Hispano world will never trust the United States as long as this government occupies our land illegally. The honest policy of the United States will have to begin at home, before Rockefeller can go to Latin America again to sell good relations and friendship. Our property, freedom, and culture must be respected in New Mexico, in the whole Southwest, before the Anglo can expect to be trusted in South America, Mexico, and Canada.

This government must show its good faith to the Indo-Hispano in respect to the Treaty of Guadalupe Hidalgo and the land question by forming a Presidential committee to investigate and hold open hearings on the land question in the northern part of New Mexico. We challenge our own government to bring forth and put all the facts on the conference table. We have the evidence to prove our claims to property as well as to the cultural rights of which we have been deprived. WE ARE RIGHT—and therefore ready and willing to discuss our problems and rights under the treaty with the Anglo federal government in New Mexico or Washington, D.C., directly or through agents.

This government must also reform the whole educational structure in the Southwest before it is too late. It should begin in the northern part of New Mexico, where 80 percent of the population are Indo-Hispanos, as a pilot center. If it works here, then a plan can be developed, based on that experience, in the rest of the state and wherever the Indo-Hispano population requires it.

Because I know WE ARE RIGHT, I have no regrets as I sit in my jail cell. I feel very, very proud and happy to be in jail for the reason that I am. June 8 in Coyote could have been my last day on earth. My life was spared by God, and to be honored by that miracle at Coyote will keep me happy for many years to come. I

am sure that not one of my prison days is lost. Not one day has
been in vain. While others are free, building their personal
empires, I am in jail for defending and fighting for the rights of my
people. Only my Indo-Hispano people have influenced me to be
what I am. I am what I am, for my brothers.

Reies López Tijerina

CRUSADE FOR JUSTICE

*During a symposium on Chicano liberation held at California State
College, Hayward, in November 1969, Corky Gonzales presented his views
on Chicano liberation. Speaking of self-determination and nationalism, he
voiced the need of La Raza to "use more forceful methods" in achieving
an adequate power base.*

What are the common denominators that unite the people? The
key common denominator is nationalism. When I talk about
nationalism, some people run around in their intellectual bags and
they say this is reverse racism. The reverse of a racist is a
humanitarian. I specifically mentioned what I felt nationalism
was. Nationalism becomes *la familia*. Nationalism comes first out
of the family, then into tribalism, and then into the alliances that
are necessary to lift the burden of all suppressed humanity.

Now, if you try to climb up a stairway, you have to start with
the first step. You can't jump from the bottom of this floor to the
top of those bleachers. If you can, then you must be "super-
macho." (I don't talk about superman.) But you can't, so you start

From "What Political Road for the Chicano Militant?" by Rodolfo "Corky"
Gonzales. *The Militant* (March 30, 1970). Reprinted, with deletions, by permission
of *The Militant*.

using those tools that are necessary to get from the bottom to the top. One of these tools is nationalism. You realize that if Chávez, or any popular figure in the Mexicano scene, decided to run, and if he ran for any party, as popular as he is, then out of nationalism we would vote even for an idiot. If his name was Sánchez, if his name was González, you would walk in and vote for him, whether you knew him or not, because you are nationalistic. And we have elected too many idiots in the past out of nationalism, right?

Now, let's take that common denominator, that same organizing tool of nationalism, and utilize it to work against the system. Let's use it to work against the two parties that I say are like an animal with two heads eating out of the same trough, that sit on the same boards of directors of the banks and corporations, that share in the same industries that make dollars and profits off wars. To fight this thing, you look for the tools.

Now, if Tony is a socialist, if my brother here is an independent, if my sister is a Republican—she might hit me later—if one of the others is a Democrat and one is a Communist, and one from the Socialist Labor Party, what do we have in common politically? Nothing. We've been fighting over parties across the kitchen table, wives are Republicans and husbands are Democrats, sometimes, and we argue over a bunch of garbage. And the same Republicans and Democrats are having cocktails together at the same bar and playing golf together and kissing each other behind the scenes.

So you tell me then, what is the common denominator that will touch the barrio, the *campos,* and the *ranchitos?* Are we going to go down there with some tremendous words of intellectualism which they cannot relate to, when they relate on the level of "We need food. We need health care for our children. I need someone to go down to juvenile court with my son. There is no job for my husband." And the revolution of fifteen or twenty years from now is not going to feed a hungry child today. . . .

All right, how do you start this? We start it and call it an independent Chicano political organization. We can use it, as Tony mentioned also, under the FCC code, we can use it as a forum to preach and teach. We can gain the same amount of radio and TV time as any phony candidate. We proved it in Colorado. I ran for mayor as an independent, and I campaigned two weeks. Two weeks, because we were busy directing a play and busy in civil-rights actions. But we had the same amount of time on TV as anybody else, and on radio. We were able to start to politicize people. We were able to start to tell about an idea. We were able, even, to sue the mayor and the top candidates for violating the city charter, for spending more money than the city provided for under its constitution. We had that mayor and the most powerful Republicans and Democrats sitting on their asses down in the courtroom. Our method was to take them to court, to take them to task, to show the public that they were corrupt. And we proved that they were liars, over and over again.

We must start off by creating the structure—the *concilio*—by calling a congress some time this spring, bringing together all those people that believe that it can be done. We understand that when we organize in an area where we are a majority, we can control. Where we are a minority, we will be a pressure group. And we will be a threat.

We understand the need to take action in the educational system. We understand that we need actions such as the "blow-outs," because the youth are not afraid of anything. Because the youth are ready to move. The whole party will be based on the actions of the young and the support of the old.

Secondly, in the communities where we are a majority, we can then control and start to reassess taxes, to start charging the exploiters for what they have made off our people in the past. You can also incorporate the community to drive out the exploiters, to make them pay the freight for coming into the community, and sign your own franchises. You can de-annex a community as easily as they annex a barrio and incorporate it. You can create your own security groups and place a gun here to protect the people, not to harass them, but to protect them from the man who is going to come in from the outside. You can also create your own economic base by starting to understand that we can share instead of cut each other's throat.

Now, what are the tools? We said nationalism, which means that we have to be able to identify with our past and understand our past, in order that we can dedicate ourselves to the future, dedicate ourselves to change. And we have to understand what humanism really is. We can tie the cultural thing into it, but we also have to tie in the political and the economic. We tie these things together, and we start to use the common denominator of nationalism.

Now, for those Anglo supporters, don't get uptight. For the black brothers, they are practicing the same thing right now. And we understand it and respect it. And we are for meaningful coalitions with organized groups.

We have to start to consider ourselves as a nation. We can create a congress or a *concilio*. We can understand that we are a nation of Aztlán. We can understand and identify with Puerto Rican liberation. We understand and identify with black liberation. We can understand and identify with white liberation from this oppressing system once we organize around ourselves.

Where they have incorporated themselves to keep us from moving into their neighborhoods, we can also incorporate ourselves to keep them from controlling our neighborhoods. We have also to understand economic revolution, of driving the exploiter out. We have to understand political change. And we have to understand principle. And the man who says we can do it within the system—who says, "Honest, you can, look at me, I have a $20,000-a-year job"—he's the man who was last year's militant and this year's OEO [Office of Economic Opportunity] employee. And now he's keeping his mouth shut and he ain't marching any more. We have to understand that he is not a revolutionary, that he's a counter-revolutionary. He's not an ally, he becomes an enemy because he's contaminated.

You can't walk into a house full of disease with a bottle full of mercurochrome and cure the disease without getting sick yourself. That's what we say about the lesser of the two evils. If four grains of arsenic kill you, and eight grains of arsenic kill you, which is the lesser of two evils? You're dead either way.

We have to understand that liberation comes from self-determination, and to start to use the tools of nationalism to win over our barrio brothers, to win over the brothers who are still believing that machismo means getting a gun and going to kill a Communist in Vietnam because they've been jived about the fact that they will be accepted as long as they go get themselves killed for the gringo captain; who still think that welfare is giving them something and don't understand that the one who is administering the welfare is the one that's on welfare, because, about 90 percent of the welfare goes into administration; and who still do not understand that the war on poverty is against the poor, to keep them from reacting.

We have to win these brothers over, and we have to do it by action. Whether it be around policy brutality, the educational system, whether it be against oppression of any kind—you create an action, you create a blow-out, and you see how fast those kids get politicized. Watch how fast they learn the need to start to take over our own communities. And watch how fast they learn to identify with ourselves, and to understand that we need to create a nation.

We can create a thought, an idea, and we can create our own economy. You don't hear of any "yellow power" running around anywhere. Because they base their power around their church, their house, their community. They sell Coca-Cola, but their profits go to their own people, you see, so that they have an economic base. We are strangers in our own church. We have got *gachupín* [traditional term of contempt for Spaniards who ruled Mexico for four hundred years] priests from Spain in our communities, telling us, *Vamos a echar unos quatros pesos en la canasta* [let's throw four pesos in the collection dish]. And then he tells you, "I'm your religious leader," and he tries to tell you how to eat, where to go, whom to sleep with, and how to do it right—while he's copping everything else out. You know, we're tired of this kind of leadership.

You have to understand that we can take over the institutions within our community. We have to create the community of the Mexicano here in order to have any type of power. As much as the young ladies have created power in their own community. But they have to share it with the rest of us. They have to be able to bring it together. And we are glad when they sit down instead of retreating. It means that we're all one people. It means that we're all one Raza and that we will work together and we will walk out of here in a positive fashion. . . .

A CONVERSATION
WITH CÉSAR CHÁVEZ

César Chávez, often viewed as messiah or devil, depending upon perspective, is unquestionably the giant in farm-labor unionization. Chávez's philosophy of non-violence has proved a powerful weapon in his organizational efforts. Interviewed by John R. Moyer, the leader of the United Farm Workers' Union explains his concepts of his work.

MOYER: How do you go about building an organization? What do you do at the beginning?

CHÁVEZ: Well, first of all, there has to be a need. Then there has to be someone who is willing to do it, who is willing to take whatever risks are required. I don't think it can be done with money alone. The person has to be dedicated to the task. There has to be some other motivation.

In this country, many have the idea that organizing people is very difficult, but it isn't. It becomes difficult only at the point where you begin to see other things that are easier. But if you are willing to give the time and make the sacrifice, it's not that difficult to organize. Maintaining an organization is much more difficult. I don't look at organizing as something which happens by chance, or as something very complicated. I look at organizing as a lot of hard work. I think that many organizers lose out because they don't have the patience. First of all, people think that you need to have 100 percent participation to be successful; and secondly, they feel it has to happen right away. But really what happens is a chain reaction. If you put one worker together with

From "A Conversation with César Chávez," by John R. Moyer. Excerpted and reprinted with permission from the *Journal of Current Social Issues* (Vol. 9, No. 3, November–December 1970), published by the Division of Higher Education, United Church Board for Homeland Ministries.

another, that reaction is not going to be too noticeable. But when you put a hundred people together, that reaction is going to carry. And it multiplies. When you have people together who believe in something very strongly—whether it's religion or politics or unions—things happen. We are past the stage where it is difficult to get people into the union. That fight has been won. I think the fight right now is to convince the growers that the best thing for them to do is to sign with the union.

At the beginning, up until the strike, everything we did was very deliberate. We had all the time we needed; nobody was pushing us.

Another thing about organizing, you can't wait until you get everything organized and then give benefits; you give benefits as you organize. The group is organized for a purpose. If you tell the worker that he should come into the union, and once it is strong, he will get something—*forget it!*

Organizing is an educational process. The best educational process in the union is the picket line and the boycott. You learn about life. It's the same with education everywhere. When you learn by doing, you learn faster than by other methods. Once you have people who *see* what has happened, they become your best organizers. It's a question of having people turned on, not by gimmickry, but by concrete benefits that they receive when they become members.

MOYER: In the very beginning, when you first try to get people involved, how do you go about finding people? Is it a matter of talking to individuals?

CHÁVEZ: I play the percentages. I know that you can spend a lot of time "chasing the rat," going around in circles and not getting anything accomplished. The name of the game is to talk to people: if you don't talk to people, you can't get started. To establish contacts in a town, I do not believe in going to the "leaders." I want to build leadership loyal to the union and to no one else. I just go to the first house in the labor camp or town and knock on doors. I know there will be at least a few farm workers in every town or camp who will be receptive to me. I also know that you can sell anything you want to sell if you really want to sell it—whether it's good or bad! You knock on twenty doors or so, and twenty guys tell you to go to hell, or that they haven't got time. But maybe at the fortieth or sixtieth house you find the one guy who is all you need. You're not going to organize everything; you're just going to get it started. You are not really looking for members as much as for organizers. But people don't *know* they are organizers when they actually are. Some of the best organizers don't look upon themselves as such.

That's how the process gets started. The evolution of a group is very fast. Once you get people together, you have a different problem.

The other thing is, you don't know everything. And once you realize that, it makes you realize that other people have got to do things. Organizing is a gamble. I'll bet there are more failures in organizing than in any other endeavor you can think of. It's a very risky business. I'm not saying that organizing comes by chance. I'm saying that there are an awful lot of gambles you have to take almost daily. Well, if I'm willing to gamble, I'm willing to gamble on a human being and his ability to do things more than anything else. I like to see people do things, and if they make mistakes, fine, as long as they don't do it intentionally or get into an ego situation. If a guy gets out there and works his head off and draws a blank, fine. It's a learning experience and that will make or break that organizer.

All of us like to have accomplishments. In some cases it has taken us four years to find the right job for the right guy. You will see that someone is dragging and has all sorts of conflicts; he is not producing, he is coming in late. He is not producing because you haven't been able to find the job he can do best. But there *is* a job for everybody. There is something everybody loves to do.

MOYER: In other words, what happens to people in this process is very important.

CHÁVEZ: Sure. People are the raw material. In many cases I know that someone is going to make a mistake, and I point it out. If I get the slightest bit of opposition, I say, Okay, let it be an experience, either for him or for me. Sometimes I will say, "No, it won't work," and I'll argue a lot; but sooner or later I come to the realization that, hell, I don't know everything. Then the guy will go out, and if he fails, I will say to myself, "See, I told you." Then I try to help him see that we went through that road. But even more important, I get surprised sometimes. I say that he shouldn't do it because he will fail, and I'll be damned if he doesn't go ahead with it and he *doesn't* fail. You never get to the point where you know everything.

MOYER: I sense that the style of life of people in the United Farm Workers' Organizing Committee is very important to you. What's going to happen to this as the union gets big? The union is gaining power.

CHÁVEZ: Well, power is not bad. Power is what the game's all about, but a lot depends on how the power is used. We are a long way from there. I think churches can have a lot of power. But I doubt if unions can have power to the extent that it is absolute. The forces working for the devil are not really that marshaled, and they haven't got that much to lose, anyway. But the forces working for the employers are well organized, and they have a lot to lose. So the opposition to labor is much more—it's like politics, except that politics goes in a cycle and it hits a high spot every two to four years. In labor it is constant, day in and day out. I don't think labor unions really have that much power. I really don't, because if they did, there would not be the repressive laws against labor. What has happened is that labor has not been able to keep up with involvement in the total community. You are never strong enough that you don't need help. . . .

MOYER: What constitutes a good support group?

CHÁVEZ: Time is more important than money. An individual who is willing to give us his time is more important than an individual who is willing to give us his money. I think money would be number two. But time is the most important element. Everything you do is predicated on time. On the boycott, for example, if an individual is willing to give us his time, we can teach him and set him in a situation where he can multiply himself many times over in terms of support. That's why the students and the young people are so valuable, because *they have time.* They are not involved in a lot of things yet; their lives are very young. . . .

MOYER: How can you involve people around the country?

CHÁVEZ: We need people right now for the lettuce boycott. We also need people for other work that has to be done. Some work is being ignored because we are concentrating on the boycott. Getting volunteers is the first step. Putting them to work so they get a good experience is the second and even more crucial step. One of the things we have going for us is that we have people in most cases who are satisfied with their experience because they work and they accomplish something. We operate from the theory that a lot of very good people get confused and can't follow because the leaders don't make it possible for them to follow. If I'm going to go on the boycott, I want it to be as simple as possible. So when people come, we say, "Look, that store over there has lettuce, and we want to get the lettuce out." We do this instead of spending time and money in some kind of elaborate orientation, so that by the time we get to the actual job, the volunteer is not so confused that he couldn't possibly make a contribution. I think that one of the great, great problems, probably in education, and I *know* in organization, is confusing people to the point where they become immobile. In fact, the more things people can find out for themselves, the more vigor the organization is going to have. Regimentation does not begin at the point where you ask people to vote for a resolution; regimentation begins when you say that this is the only way it can be done. People get attracted to whatever dominates the scene. If all of the activity of a union is in meetings, people get attracted to meetings and *Robert's Rules of Order*. If there is action, then they get attracted to action. And if they get attracted to action, they will then produce action.

MOYER: What are the implications of the grape-strike victory? Will the union become a national movement?

CHÁVEZ: Yes, I think so. There is enough action going on in other areas by workers themselves that will make the union national, not because we have contracts, but because we have people who look toward California and the experience we have had here and who want to do the same thing. So in that sense, it's national even now. But in a formalized, structural way, we are a long way from that. . . .

MOYER: What is the nature of your relationship to the A F of L? I noticed a small article in *The New York Times* headlined MEANY CALLS OFF GRAPE BOYCOTT. How do you manage to maintain your individual style and your independence within the framework of a big labor organization?

CHÁVEZ: The A F of L is only a federation of unions. The individual unions have a lot of autonomy. They're completely autonomous. But beyond that, we've had a very good relationship with the AFL-CIO. They have assisted us in many ways, but they have permitted us to do our job, because they know that we know best. It would be no fun if we couldn't make decisions, right or wrong. That's what gives us the desire and the drive to continue working and to make the sacrifices, because we have the freedom to act. If we were goofing and fouling things up, I have no doubt that things would be different.

As for George Meany calling off the boycott, I asked him to do it. You see, two things are not generally known. One is that, in 1939, Meany helped charter one of the first farm-labor unions in California. The union lost the strike, but he personally got about $15,000 for them. The other thing is that, of all the people I talked to, George Meany was the only labor leader who recognized that, in this modern age, a boycott is more important than a strike. So when we were ready to call off the boycott, I thought it was a good gesture to ask him to do it. . . .

MOYER: César, what kind of a society would you like to see in this country, and what might be the possibilities of building it?

CHÁVEZ: I've always maintained that it isn't the form that's going to make the difference. It isn't the rule or the procedure or the ideology, but it's human beings that will make it. Society is made up of groups, and so long as the smaller groups do not have the same rights and the same protection as others—I don't care whether you call it capitalism or Communism—it is not going to work. Somehow, the guys in power have to be reached by counterpower, or through a change in their hearts and minds, or change will not come.

MOYER: You seem to be one of the few organizations among the poor today which continues to maintain, deliberately and overtly, a philosophy and strategy of non-violence. How do you manage it?

CHÁVEZ: Non-violence is a very powerful weapon. Most people don't understand the power of non-violence and tend to be amazed by the whole idea. Those who have been involved in bringing about change and see the difference between violence and non-violence are firmly committed to a lifetime of non-violence, not because it's easy or because it is cowardly, but because it is an effective and very powerful way.

Non-violence means people in action. People have to understand that with non-violence goes a hell of a lot of organization. We couldn't be non-violent in Salinas and win unless we had a lot of people organized around non-violence up and down the United States and Canada. We are organizers at heart. Most of us in the movement take great pride in being able to put things together. . . .

THE MEXICAN AMERICAN WOMAN

Chicanas, like all women, historically have been exploited by society. Chicano militancy of the late sixties, coupled with the women's liberation movement, created the movement for Chicana liberation. No longer subservient, Chicanas have emerged as a powerful force. Ms. Enriqueta Longeaux y Vásquez describes their problems.

Today, as we hear the call of La Raza and as the dormant, "docile" Mexican American comes to life, we see again the stirring of the people. With that call, the Chicana woman also stirs and I am sure that she will leave her mark upon the Mexican American movement in the Southwest.

From "The Mexican-American Woman," by Enriqueta Longeaux y Vásquez. In *Sisterhood Is Powerful*, Robin Morgan, ed., New York: Random House, 1970. Copyright © 1969 by Enriqueta Longeaux y Vásquez. All rights reserved by author. Reprinted by permission of the author.

How the Chicana woman reacts depends totally on how the macho Chicano is treated when he goes out into the "mainstream of society." If the husband is so-called successful, the woman seems to become very domineering and demands more and more in material goods. I ask myself at times, Why are the women so demanding? Can they not see what they make of their men? But then I realize: this is the price of owning a slave.

A woman who has no way of expressing herself and of realizing herself as a full human has nothing else to turn to but the owning of material things. She builds her entire life around these and finds security in this way. All she has to live for is her house and family; she becomes very possessive of both. This makes her a totally dependent human. Dependent on her husband and family. Most of the Chicana women in this comfortable situation are not particularly involved in the movement. Many times it is because of the fear of censorship in general. Censorship from the husband, the family, friends, and society in general. For these reasons she is completely inactive.

Then you will find the Chicana whose husband was not able to fare so very well in society and perhaps has had to face defeat. This is the Chicana who really suffers. Quite often the man will not fight the real source of his problems, be it discrimination or whatever, but will instead come home and take it out on his family. As this continues, his Chicana becomes the victim of his machismo, and woeful are the trials and tribulations of that household.

Much of this is seen particularly in the city. The man, being head of the household but unable to fight the system he lives in, will very likely lose face, and for this reason there will often be a separation or divorce in a family. It is at this time that the Chicana faces the real test of having to confront society as one of its total victims.

There are many things she must do. She must: (1) find a way to feed and clothe the family; (2) find housing; (3) find employment; (4) provide child care; and (5) find some kind of social outlet and friendship.

1. In order to find a way to feed and clothe her family, she must find a job. Because of her suppression, she has probably not been

able to develop a skill. She is probably unable to find a job that will pay her a decent wage. If she is able to find a job at all, it will probably be sought only for survival. Thus she can hope just to exist; she will hardly be able to live an enjoyable life. Here one of the most difficult problems for the Chicana woman to face is that of going to work. Even if she does have a skill, she must all at once realize that she has been living in a racist society. She will have much difficulty in proving herself in any position. Her work must be three times as good as that of the Anglo majority. Not only this but the competitive way of the Anglo will always be there. The Anglo woman is always there with her superiority complex. The Chicana woman will be looked upon as having to prove herself even in the smallest task. She is constantly being put to the test. Not only does she suffer the oppression that the Anglo woman suffers as a woman in the market of humanity but she must also suffer the oppression of being a minority person with a different set of values. Because her existence and the livelihood of the children depend on her conforming, she tries very hard to conform. Thus she may find herself even rejecting herself as a Mexican American. Existence itself depends on this.

2. She must find housing that she will be able to afford. She will very likely be unable to live in a decent place; it will be more the matter of finding a place that is cheap. It is likely that she will have to live in a housing project. Here she will be faced with the real problem of trying to raise children in an environment that is conducive to much suffering. The decision as to where she will live is a difficult matter, as she must come face to face with making decisions entirely on her own. This, plus having to live them out, is very traumatic for her.

3. In finding a job she will be faced with working very hard during the day and coming home to an empty house and again having to work at home. Cooking, washing, ironing, mending, plus spending some time with the children. Her role changes to being both father and mother. All of this, plus being poor, is very hard to bear. On top of this, to have a survey worker or social worker tell you that you have to have incentive and motivations—these are tough pressures to live under. Few men could stand up under such pressures.

4. Child care is one of the most difficult problems for a woman

to have to face alone. Not only is she tormented with having to leave the raising of her children to someone else, but she wants the best of care for them. For the amount of money that she may be able to pay from her meager wages, she will be lucky to find anyone at all to take care of the children. The routine of the household is not normal at all. She must start her day earlier than an average worker. She must clothe and feed the children before she takes them to be cared for in someone else's home. Then, too, she will have a very hard day at work, for she is constantly worrying about the children. If there are medical problems, this will only multiply her stress during the day. Not to mention the financial pressure of medical care.

5. With all of this, the fact still remains that she is a human and must have some kind of friendship and entertainment in life, and this is perhaps one of the most difficult tasks facing the Mexican American woman alone. She can probably enjoy very little entertainment, since she cannot afford a baby-sitter. This, plus the fact that she very likely does not have the clothes, transportation, etc. As she cannot afford entertainment herself, she may very often fall prey to letting someone else pay for her entertainment, and this may create unwanted involvement with some friend. When she begins to keep company with men, she will meet with the disapproval of her family and often be looked upon as having loose moral values. As quite often she is not free to remarry in the eyes of the Church, she will find more and more conflict and disapproval, and she will continue to look upon herself with guilt and censorship. Thus she suffers much as a human. Everywhere she looks she seems to be rejected.

This woman has much to offer the movement of the Mexican American. She has had to live all of the roles of her Raza. She has had to suffer the torments of her people in that she has had to go out into a racist society and be a provider as well as a mother. She has been doubly oppressed and is trying very hard to find a place. Because of all this, she is a very, very strong individual. She has had to become strong in order to exist against these odds.

The Mexican American movement is not that of just adults fighting the social system but it is a total commitment of a family unit living what it believes to be a better way of life in demanding social change for the benefit of humankind. When a family is involved in a human-rights movement, as is the Mexican American family, there is little room for a women's liberation movement alone. There is little room for having a definition of woman's role as such. Roles are for actors and the business at hand requires people living the examples of social change. The Mexican American movement demands are such that, with the liberation of La Raza, we must have a total liberation. The woman must help liberate the man, and the man must look upon this liberation with the woman at his side, not behind him, following, but alongside of him, leading. The family must come up together.

The Raza movement is based on brother- and sisterhood. We must look at each other as one large family. We must look at all of the children as belonging to all of us. We must strive for the fulfillment of all as equals, with the full capability and right to develop as humans. When a man can look upon a woman as human, then, and only then, can he feel the true meaning of liberation and equality. . . .

RESPONSE TO CHICANO MILITANCY

Not all Mexican Americans view contemporary Chicano militancy as the proper approach toward alleviating economic and social conditions. Texas congressman Henry B. González expresses his views in the following speech made in the House of Representatives.

Mr. Speaker, we are a nation of immigrants. Every one of us, save the Indian, is either an immigrant or the descendant of immigrants. All immigrants or their ancestors are either members of

From Speech given in the House of Representatives, by Henry B. González. *Congressional Record*, 91st Congress, 1st sess. Washington: U.S. Government Printing Office, 1969.

some racial or religious minority or their descendants have been, at one time or another. There is not a living American who either is, has been, or has a descendant who was not a member of some minority. As it happens, I am myself the member of an ethnic minority and am so classified by the census. I think that there is not a member of this body who is unaware of the effects that minority status can have on an individual life. . . .

An ethnic minority is in a peculiar position. I happen to be an American of Spanish surname and of Mexican descent. As it happens, my parents were born in Mexico and came to this country seeking safety from a violent revolution. It follows that I, and many other residents of my part of Texas and other Southwestern states, happen to be what is commonly referred to as Mexican Americans. That label sums up most of the elements of a vast conflict affecting perhaps most of the 5 million Southwestern citizens who happen to bear it. The individual finds himself in a conflict, sometimes with himself, sometimes with his family, sometimes with his whole world. What is he to be? Mexican? American? Both? How can he choose? Should he have pride and joy in his heritage, or bear it as a shame and sorrow? Should he live in one world or another, or attempt to bridge them both? . . .

The question facing the Mexican American people today is, What do we want and how do we get it?

What I want is justice. By justice I mean decent work at decent wages for all who want work; decent support for those who cannot support themselves; full and equal opportunity in employment, in education, in schools; I mean by justice the full, fair, and impartial protection of the law for every man; I mean by justice decent homes, adequate streets and public services; and I mean by justice no man being asked to do more than his fair share, but none being expected to do less. In short, I seek a justice that amounts to full, free, and equal opportunity for all; I believe in a justice that does not tolerate evil or evil-doing; and I believe in a justice that is for all the people all the time.

I do not believe that justice comes only to those who want it; I am not so foolish as to believe that goodwill alone achieves good works. I believe that justice requires work and vigilance, and I am willing to do that work and maintain that vigilance.

I do not believe that it is possible to obtain justice by vague and empty gestures, or by high slogans uttered by orators who are present today and gone tomorrow. I do believe that justice can be obtained by those who know exactly what they seek and know exactly how they plan to seek it. And I believe that justice can be obtained by those whose cause is just and whose means are honest.

It may well be that I agree with the goals stated by militants; but whether I agree or disagree, I do not now nor have I ever believed that the end justifies the means, and I condemn those who do. I cannot accept the belief that racism in reverse is the answer for racism and discrimination; I cannot accept the belief that simple, blind, and stupid hatred is an adequate response to simple, blind, and stupid hatred; I cannot accept the belief that playing at revolution produces anything beyond an excited imagination; and I cannot accept the belief that imitation leadership is a substitute for the real thing. Developments over the past few months indicate that there are those who believe that the best answer for hate is hate in reverse, and that the best leadership is that which is loudest and most arrogant; but my observation is that arrogance is no cure for emptiness.

All over the Southwest new organizations are springing up; some promote pride in heritage, which is good, but others promote chauvinism, which is not; some promote community organization, which is good, but some promote race tension and hatred, which are not good; some seek redress of just grievances, which is good, but others seek only opportunities for self-aggrandizement, which is not good.

All of these elements, good and bad, exist, and all of them must be taken into account. The tragic thing is that in situations where people have honest grievances, dishonest tactics can prevent their obtaining redress; and where genuine problems exist, careless or unthinking or consciously mean behavior can unloose forces that will create new problems that might require generations to solve. I want to go forward, not backward; I want the creation of trust, not fear; and I want to see Americans together, not apart. . . .

Unfortunately, it seems that in the face of rising hopes and expectations among Mexican Americans, there are more leaders with political ambitions at heart than there are with the interests of the poor at heart; they do not care what is accomplished in fact, as long as they can create and ride the winds of protest as far as possible. Thus, we have those who play at revolution, those who make speeches but do no work, and those who imitate what they have seen others do but lack the initiative and imagination to set forth actual programs for progress. . . .

Not long after the Southwest Council of La Raza opened for business, it gave $110,000 to the Mexican American Unity Council of San Antonio; this group was apparently invented for the purpose of receiving the grant. Whatever the purposes of this group may be, thus far it has not given any assistance that I know of to bring anybody together; rather it has freely dispensed funds to people who promote the rather odd and I might say generally unaccepted and unpopular views of its directors. The Mexican American Unity Council appears to specialize in creating still other organizations and equipping them with quarters, mimeograph machines, and other essentials of life. Thus, the "unity council" has created a parents' association in a poor school district, a neighborhood council, a group known as the barrios unidos—or roughly, united neighborhoods—a committee on voter registration, and has given funds to the militant Mexican American Youth Organization (MAYO); it has also created a vague entity known as the "Universidad de los Barrios," which is a local gang operation. Now, assuredly all these efforts may be well intended; however, it is questionable to my mind that a very young and inexperienced man can prescribe the social and political organizations of a complex and troubled community; there is no reason whatever to believe that for all the money this group has spent there is any understanding of what it is actually being spent for, except to employ friends of the director and advance his preconceived notions. The people who are to be united apparently don't get much say in what the "unity council" is up to. . . .

As another example, the Universidad de los Barrios is operated by a college junior and two others. The "universidad" has no curriculum and offers no courses, and the young toughs it works with have become what some neighbors believe to be a threat to safety and even life itself. After a murder took place on the doorstep of this place in January, witnesses described the place as a "trouble spot." Neighbors told me that they were terrified of the young men who hung around there, that their children had been threatened, and that they were afraid to call the police. After the murder, the "dean" of this "university" said that he could not be there all the time and was not responsible for what happened while he was away. This might be true, but the general fear of the neighbors indicates that the "university" is not under reliable guidance at any time. I note that since I have made criticisms of this operation, its leader says it is ready to enter a "second phase." I hope so.

Militant groups like MAYO regularly distribute literature that I can only describe as hate sheets, designed to inflame passions and reinforce old wounds or open new ones; these sheets spew forth racism and hatred designed to do no man good. The practice is defended as one that will build race pride, but I never heard of pride being built on spleen. There is no way to adequately describe the damage that such sheets can do, and there is no way to assess how minds that distribute this tripe operate. But, Mr. Speaker, I say that those who believe the wellsprings of hate can be closed as easily as they are opened make a fearful mistake; they who lay out poison cannot be certain that it will kill no one, or make no one ill, or harm no innocent bystander. . . .

We see a strange thing in San Antonio today; we have those who play at revolution and those who imitate the militance of others. We have a situation in Denver where the local leader said, "This is our Selma," and not a week later a situation in Del Rio where the local leader said, "This is our Selma." But try as they might, Selma was neither in Denver nor in Del Rio. We have those who cry "brown power" only because they have heard "black power," and we have those who yell "oink" or "pig" at police only because they have heard others use the terms. We have those who wear beards and berets, not because they attach any meaning to it, but because they have seen it done elsewhere. But neither fervor nor fashion alone will bring justice. Those who cry for justice but hold it in contempt cannot win it for themselves or for anyone else. Those who prize power for its own sake will never be able to use it for any benefit but their own; and those who can only follow the fashions of protest will never understand what true protest is.

I believe that a just and decent cause demands a just and decent program of action. I believe that a just and decent cause can be undermined by those who believe that there is no decency and who demand for themselves what they would deny others. I have stood against racists before, and I will do it again; and I have stood against blind passion before and I will gladly do so again. I pray that the day will come when all men know justice; and I pray that that day has not been put further away by the architects of discord, the prophets of violence. I pray that these great tasks that face us in the quest for justice and progress will be taken up by all men; and I know that when all is said and done and the tumult and shouting die down, those who only spoke with passion [will be] cast aside, and those who spoke with conviction and integrity will still be around. I am willing to let time be my judge. . . .

LA LEY—THE LAW

The hearings of the U.S. Commission on Civil Rights, which probed the social anguish of Mexican Americans, were conceived in controversy and born in protest. These San Antonio hearings clearly showed that people indigenous to the Southwest sometimes felt themselves strangers in their own land and alienated from fellow Americans.

Justice is the most important word in race relations. Yet too many Mexican Americans in the Southwest feel with David Sánchez, Los Angeles Brown Beret leader, that "to Anglos justice means 'just us'."

From *Strangers in One's Land*, by Rubén Salazar. Publication No. 19, Washington: U.S. Commission on Civil Rights Clearinghouse, May 1970.

La Ley or the Law, as Mexican Americans call the administration of justice, takes forms that Anglos—and even Negroes—never have to experience. A Mexican American, though a third-generation American, for instance, may have to prove with documents that he is an American citizen at border crossings, while a blue-eyed blond German immigrant, for example, can cross by merely saying "American."

Besides the usual complaints made by racial minorities about police brutality and harassment, Mexican Americans have an added problem: sometimes they literally cannot communicate with the police. A commission report told of a young Mexican American who, while trying to quell a potentially explosive situation, was arrested because the police officers, who did not understand Spanish, thought that he was trying to incite the crowd to riot. . . .

One of the many reasons a Mexican American cannot relate well to *la Ley* is that he doesn't see many of his own in positions of authority serving on agencies which administer justice. The 1960 census indicated that Mexican Americans represent about 12 percent of the Southwest's population. In 1968, only 7.4 percent of the total uniformed personnel in law-enforcement agencies in the Southwest were Mexican Americans, according to those agencies answering a commission questionnaire.

As for policy-making positions, the commission learned in its survey that only ten law-enforcement agencies are headed by Mexican Americans and eight of these are in communities of less than ten thousand in population.

(A commission study of the grand-jury system of twenty-two California counties concluded that discrimination against Mexican Americans in juror selection is "as severe—sometimes more severe—as discrimination against Negroes in grand juries in the South.")

In east Los Angeles, which is the largest single urban Mexican American community in the United States, "friction between law enforcement and the Mexican American community" is on the increase, according to a psychiatric social worker, Armando Morales. . . .

One of the reasons for this increasing friction, Morales told the

commission, was that "gradually the Mexican American community is becoming much more aggressive as to its social demands, its
social needs. It is becoming more active. And at the same time,
law enforcement is becoming much more suppressive, hence
creating that much more friction between the two." Morales also
contended that police aggressive behavior seems to be condoned
by high-level government.

Morales charged "indifference and apathy to the justice and
needs of the Mexican American" by the federal government. He
said his council investigated twenty-five cases of alleged police
brutality, five of which were submitted for consideration to the
FBI. The FBI referred them to the U.S. Department of Justice,
which in turn ignored the matter, according to Morales.

The Reverend John P. Luce, rector of the Epiphany Parish in
east Los Angeles, agreed with Morales that communication
between Mexican Americans and the Los Angeles police had
broken down and said he feared "we are on a collision course in
Los Angeles" along the lines of a "police-barrio confrontation."
Reverend Luce charged that the Los Angeles police and sheriff
departments "refuse to talk with militant and political leaders
with whom they might disagree, with young people, with a whole
variety of activist people who want change."

The Anglo clergyman told the commission that the indictment
of thirteen Mexican American leaders in the March 1968 East Los
Angeles High School walkouts has led to the strong feeling that
"the [Los Angeles] district attorney has singled out the Mexican
community because he thought they were weaker than some other
communities" but that he "miscalculated on this point, because
the Mexican is organizing even that much more."

A commission staff report said that "one of the most common
complaints (throughout the Southwest) was that Anglo juvenile
offenders are released to the custody of their parents and no
charges are brought, while Mexican American youths are charged
with offenses, held in custody, and sent to a reformatory." . . .

The commission's report further stated that it is felt throughout
the Southwest that "the most serious police harassment involves
interference with attempts by Mexican Americans to organize
themselves in order to assert their collective power."

To the advocates of brown or Chicano power, the Texas Rangers, or *Los Rinches*, are the symbols of this repression. The Texas Rangers is an elite 136-year-old statewide law-enforcement agency under the Texas Department of Public Safety. At the time of the hearing, there were sixty-two Texas Rangers, none of them Mexican Americans.

To the Mexican American, especially the poor, such as the farm worker in the Rio Grande Valley, the Rangers in their Stetson hats, fancy boots, hand-tooled revolvers, and holsters personify everything they fear: tough-talking, rancher-grower types who can run you out of town at the slightest suspicion that the Mexican Americans want to assert themselves.

"The Rangers are the cowboys and we're the Indians," say Mexican Americans.

Farm workers, labor organizers, and civil-rights workers testified before the commission that the Texas Rangers break agricultural-worker strikes in the Rio Grande Valley through force and intimidation. The unionization of farm workers is seen as a holy war in Texas, where farm hands get no workmen's compensation, no state minimum wage, no unemployment and disability insurance, and where there are no mandatory standards in farm-worker housing. (In contrast, California requires by law all of these things.)

Reynaldo de la Cruz, twenty-six, a farm worker and father of six children who had been arrested six times for union activities, told the commission he joined the union because of "what every Mexican American farm worker faces, that they have been cheated too long . . . because I had been cheated too many times. [I joined the union] so that we could fight for our rights and for the rights of other people that don't know how to defend themselves."

Asked what the feeling of Mexican Americans is toward the Texas Rangers, José M. Martínez, a farm worker, told the commission:

"Many people hate them, many people are afraid, because the majority of the Mexicans are not armed. They [Rangers] are armed. And when the Rangers are coming, then the people are afraid. They are afraid of being hit, or being pushed around. . . .

The minute that you hear the Rangers are coming, everybody hides. If you are on strike, if you know the Rangers are coming, then they don't want to strike. This is the feeling of the people in the Valley. They are afraid."

Trying to determine what Mexican Americans thought of government as an administrator of justice, Howard A. Glickstein, then Acting Staff Director of the commission, asked farm worker de la Cruz whether in his work as a union organizer he saw the state government and state officials as friends or enemies.

DE LA CRUZ: Well, considering that the Rangers are state officials, I think they are our enemies.

GLICKSTEIN: How do you view the federal government? What do you think of the role the federal government has played or hasn't played?

DE LA CRUZ: Well, I am not too sure about the federal government. But if they were really our friends, then something would have been done when the Texas Rangers were messing with the strike.

Earlier, Pete Tijerina, executive director of the Mexican American Legal Defense and Educational Fund, had noted that the U.S. Attorney General had intervened on behalf of Negro cases throughout the South, but that "not once, not once, has the Attorney General . . . intervened in any Mexican American case." . . .

Arnulfo Guerra, a Rio Grande Valley attorney, charged that local and state government openly opposed the strike and the farm workers' right to organize, and he said that the Rangers in particular "were entirely and completely partial to the growers. And I say this because the people who called them [Rangers] in were the county administration, and the county administration was completely and totally partial to the growers. It was a one-sided affair, and they [Rangers] were excessively partial. . . ."

Ranger Captain Allee, a thirty-six-year veteran of the Texas Rangers, appeared before the commission on the closing day of the San Antonio hearing. . . .

Asked what reputation the Texas Rangers have among Mexican Americans, Captain Allee said: "Among Mexican Americans I think they have a good reputation. I worked around the Mexican people all my life. I had a big percentage of the people of Starr, Texas, of Mexican American people send a petition into Austin and I didn't request it, asking the Rangers to stay there because they feared violence and bloodshed. And that petition is on file. . . ."

Questioned whether there were workers in the fields during the strike, Captain Allee responded: "Oh yes, there were workers in the fields, lots of people working in the fields. I couldn't tell you whether they were from Starr County or not. Some of them were and some of them from across the border, the green-card workers.

GLICKSTEIN: There were a lot of green-card workers?

CAPTAIN ALLEE: I don't know how many.

GLICKSTEIN: They come across [the border] in the morning and go home at night?

CAPTAIN ALLEE: That's right.

It was as if Captain Allee were reminding Mexican Americans what they have known for many years: if they rock the boat, they can always be replaced by cheaper Mexicans from across the border. . . .

THE FUNCTION OF ANGLO-AMERICAN RACISM

Racism is seldom considered a factor in low levels of achievement among Chicanos in American society. Professor Ralph Guzmán describes the social and political implications of this little-recognized reality.

From "The Function of Anglo-American Racism in the Political Development of Chicanos," by Ralph Guzmán. *California Historical Society Quarterly*, 50, 3 (September 1971). Reprinted, with deletions, by permission of the author and the publisher. The *California Historical Society Quarterly* is published four times a year by the California Historical Society in spring, summer, fall, and winter. Contents copyright © 1971 by the California Historical Society. Editorial offices at 2090 Jackson Street, San Francisco, California 94109; office of publication at 1120 Old Mill Road, San Marino, California 91108.

World War II increased the urbanization of the Chicano population; but urban institutions were ill prepared to cope with the
Chicano people. Both public and private agencies saw Chicanos
as problems and rarely as potential contributors to society. . . .

The conditions of social contact between Chicanos and the
larger society were altered by the demographic change from rural
to urban, but they were not improved. Greater social mobility—
meaning freedom to live where they chose, eat at restaurants they
could afford, visit public facilities that offered comfort and
rest—was not forthcoming for all Chicanos.

The ground rules of American society in the cities were often
even more explicit than they were in the agrarian areas. Signs on
house porches and in employment agencies advised Chicanos in
Spanish and in English that they were not welcome. When
written signs were missing, the silent language of the doorman,
the foreman, the school principal, and others made it apparent
that social ingress was not possible.

The state of Texas to this day provides the best examples of
social exclusion. For example, in 1945 a U.S. Senate Subcommittee on Education learned that Chicanos from McCarney, Texas,
traveled forty-five miles to Fort Stockton for a haircut because
Anglo barbers would not cut Chicano hair and Chicanos could not
legally become barbers in McCarney. Other witnesses reported
that they could not use a public street to celebrate a Fourth of
July because the holiday was "for white people only." In a Texas
restaurant a Chicano customer, asked to identify his race,
answered "Misanthrope" and was promptly served.

The war years forced Chicanos to interact widely and intensely
with the larger society. Change had to take place because
Chicanos and other disadvantaged groups were needed in the
defense factories and in the battlefields. The competence of
Chicanos as semiskilled workers modified some stereotype attitudes. At one Los Angeles area aircraft company an enterprising
Chicano rose from the position of custodian to a high administrative post "mostly on nerve and need."

On the battle front, the fighting qualities of Chicano servicemen serving in integrated units similarly influenced majority-
group reservations about their loyalty. While the war years did

not completely reverse majority views of the past, they did bring about increased social interaction between Chicanos and non-Chicanos. For Chicanos, the war years became another important stage in their urban political socialization. The war experience and postwar developments, such as the educational opportunities offered to Chicanos through the GI Bill of Rights, helped Chicanos to see American society more clearly.

The majority's views of Chicano political behavior have, of course, a very direct bearing on the political participation of Chicanos. These views have been a part of the Anglo ideologies as far back as the early years of this century. Among the most important are: (1) that Chicanos in general are submissive and therefore not capable of effective political activity; (2) that Chicanos are deeply imbued with foreign values and therefore cannot understand the American political system; and (3) that Chicanos cannot achieve ethnic unity. These views have more or less persisted to the present day.

It was often said that Chicanos had values that were not consonant with the American value system. In politics, for example, Chicanos were not expected to understand cherished beliefs about the rights of man, freedom of religion, and other constitutional guarantees. Chicanos were considered products of a semifeudal, colonial social system where the poor obeyed the dictates of benevolent employers. Chicano women, Anglo ideologues argued, were shamefully mistreated by their husbands. Finally, it was argued that Roman Catholics, particularly primitive Roman Catholics, could not possibly practice religious freedom.

The assumption of submissiveness carried with it the belief that Chicanos were not interested in the acquisition of political power. It was held that members of this minority were accustomed to the commands of priests and labor *patrones*. Consequently, personal initiative was not a well-developed trait. People without personal initiative, it was rationalized, could not aspire to the control of political institutions.

The conclusion that Chicanos were irrevocably Catholic and eternally foreign was a powerful and pervasive conclusion. The

Roman Catholic Church was, indeed, foreign and totally overwhelming. Fear existed that Chicanos would react according to
the direction of the Church once they acquired political power.
Traditional Anglo mistrust of the Roman Catholic Church found a
new target in the Chicano group. In Los Angeles, civic meetings
held in parish halls reinforced the belief that priests and nuns
guarded the political life of their impressionable but devout
parishioners. The truth is that the Roman Catholic Church,
operated by Anglo nuns and priests, did exercise substantial
political control over devout Chicanos.

Well-meaning individuals who were willing to help the Chicano
people during the early postwar years were openly skeptical about
the ability of these people to organize effectively. Liberal
Democrats in particular were doubtful. In Los Angeles they
greeted the first mass registration of Chicano voters in the country
with aplomb. While viewing the figures that reported great
success, a liberal Democrat said, "So they're registered; will they
vote?"

Ideologies are often inconsistent. For example, in the 1930's a
view diametrically opposed to the assumption of an incurable
ethnic disunity existed. Chicanos were considered to be group-
minded, and thus there was apprehension that they might develop
a Tammany Hall type of organization. Evidence for this fear of
Chicano bloc voting and machine politics came from experience
in the state of New Mexico. Ethnic politics in that state proved to
some observers that Chicanos practiced a religious-ethnic solidarity even within the political system. Only one party, the
Democrats or the Republicans, received the votes of the Chicanos
according to one Anglo scholar. He indicated that New Mexico's
Chicano population would accept whatever political party their
leaders designated. As a consequence, recruitment of Chicano
voters by non-Chicano outsiders was considered difficult. "This is
something our Anglos . . . find extremely irritating," a writer
commented. New Mexico, then, where the political involvement
of the Chicanos was extremely high (when one compares that
state with the rest of the Southwest), justified an ideological
conclusion that was out of phase with judgments about disunity
made in other regions.

Why the Anglo majority would appear to emphasize ethnic unity in New Mexico while underscoring disunity elsewhere is not difficult to understand when region and time are considered. The Chicano population was deeply rooted in New Mexico when American political institutions were imposed. The state's institutions were already in Chicano hands, and group-mindedness and religious-ethnic solidarity were indeed a reality. New Mexicans reacted negatively to outsiders—the conquering Anglos who seized their land with the force of arms. Nevertheless, in terms of time, New Mexico Chicanos had a head start of a few generations over Chicanos from other states, particularly those who came later in the twentieth century. Chicanos in New Mexico represented an original population as opposed to the immigrant population from Mexico that followed. New Mexicans appeared to interact with American society *as a group* with a solidarity that distinguished them sharply from Chicanos living elsewhere.

Still another image of Chicanos was that as a group they were easily controlled. While this notion appealed to many members of the dominant Anglo society, it tended to repel others. In the 1920's and 1930's, fear was expressed that Chicanos would not vote for the "vested interests" in agriculture and industry on which they depended and that rural landlords, in particular, would be able to herd them to the polls with "banners flying." On the other hand, it was said that the group was also easy prey for demagogues. "Socialism, the I.W.W. and Communism find a ready soil for their seed among the Mexicans in our country," said one writer who deplored Chicano "gullibility."

Thus, the apprehensions of Anglo society militated against political activity by Chicanos. Adding to the Anglo majority's fears was a feeling of uncertainty, ambivalence, and frustration with regard to Chicano leadership. Until World War II it was commonly believed that the group was devoid of responsible leaders who could stimulate a sense of collective commitment— part of an Anglo ideology that Chicanos were quiescent and satisfied with life as it was. Typical of this view was an Anglo businessman's statement that Chicanos were a contented and leaderless people "who did not, in the last analysis, know what they wanted. They are like children." Finally, Chicanos were considered to be even more handicapped because socially mobile Chicanos, the economic achievers, tended to forsake life in the barrio, thus depriving lower-class Chicanos of an articulate middle class.

Anglo expectations concerning Chicano leadership have always had a significant impact on the political participation of this minority. This impact became even greater after World War II, when growing urbanization and the return of Chicano veterans who did maintain their contact with people living in the barrio increased the political potential of the group. The importance of Anglo ideologies stems partly from the fact that the validation of Chicano leaders has often come not from the minority itself but from Anglo society—a condition that parallels the political history of other ethnic or racial groups in this country and has only recently been modified in the case of blacks who prefer self-determination. Thus, Anglos would urge Chicanos to find and develop leaders, with the implicit understanding that these would be "acceptable"; or they would express distrust of individuals who represented themselves as Chicano spokesmen. It was the political power structure of the dominant Anglo society that ultimately decided who were legitimate Chicano leaders. The problem of the validation of Chicano leadership has continued to this day.

The aggregated views, judgments, and presuppositions about the Chicano minority held by the larger Anglo society have been described. To recapitulate, they constitute constellations of ideologies that differ from one place to another and from one historical period to the next. In order to clarify what is meant by majority ideologies, the notion of conditions of social contact between the minority and the majority was re-examined in terms of other American ethnic groups. In each instance it was shown that social contact between the minority and the majority generated mutual views that usually hampered and only occasionally assisted the minority group to grow politically. Conditions of social contact on the eastern seaboard were different from those that existed in the Southwest; the ethnic actors were different and so were their reasons for being in this social order. Chicanos initially bypassed the well-known process of urban political socialization. While there were few political machines in the Southwest, fear that they might become common in Chicano areas was expressed. This fear, and other social expressions concerning Chicanos, impinged upon their political experience. They grew politically within an oppressive, racist environment that clearly restricted social opportunity. Within this context of explicit and implicit social discrimination and economic exploration, Chicanos created counter-ideologies that contained judgments of the Anglo social order. The contents of those counter-ideologies and their function in the increased political consciousness of Chicanos remain to be examined.

AFTERWORD: THE FUTURE

A minority is almost by definition a problem as viewed from the outside by the general society. The present generation of Mexican Americans, as an ethnic group, carries the stigma of dependency, which means inadequacy, which implies non-competency, which by degrees leads to the second sense of the word "minority." Minors are persons who have to be dealt with through practical combinations of tolerance, forbearance, persuasion, oversight, firmness, and occasionally force. Minors who number millions and who have grown to adulthood without achieving independence are costly. The deprivations they suffer must be mitigated at the expense of others.

Minority problems have been avoided or abolished by prohibition of immigration, by assimilation, and even by extermination. The last solution is not known to be under consideration for the Mexican American. The second is working by slow degrees from one generation to the next, slowed down by what amounts, in practice, to a rejection of the first. The Mexican American problem, for those who choose to think of it that way, will endure.

This is a predominantly young demographic group. It is likely to sustain the present high rate of reproduction during the next two or three decades, now twice that of the general society. Immigra-

From *Mexican-Americans in the Southwest*, by Ernesto Galarza, Herman Gallegos, and Julian Samora. Santa Barbara, Calif.: McNally & Loftin, Publishers, 1969. Copyright © 1969, 1970 by the Southwest Council of La Raza. Reprinted by permission of the authors.

tion, at the present pace, will add forty thousand or more newcomers each year. By the end of 1970, it is likely that in the Southwest the total population of the Spanish-speaking, the Spanish-surnamed, the Mexican Americans—whatever their designation—will be well over 5 million, and possibly closer to 6 million.

These will be predominantly, one could say overwhelmingly, poor people. Although the Mexican economy is spinning at a high rate of growth, it also shows a chronic incapacity to distribute the new wealth more evenly. Those who are able to cross the border into the United States will gravitate toward the hard-core poverty tracts in which the language, the customs, and the privation will be familiar. The Mexican American barrios will continue to be concentrations of poor people. These will be urban concentrations. In the central cities, where planners are busy, the dislocation of the barrios that presently have the greatest absorbing capacity will certainly continue.

For the new migrants the problem of making a living will depend upon whether there is an upward movement of their predecessors which would vacate manual jobs. The forecast in this direction is not encouraging, to put it mildly. There is no prospect of a grand breakthrough in educational and vocational opportunity.

If risks are to be taken in prophecy, it would be safer to take them on the side of the probability that the cost of social assistance to the Mexican Americans will rise rather than fall at present standards of need and levels of welfare expenditure. The *colonia*, for all its capacity to share its scarcities of housing, food, and employment, has no visible savings or institutions to encourage enterprise or extend charity. Help must continue to come from the outside, and it must be aimed primarily at the Mexican family, under siege by the increasing pressures of urban existence which make even more difficult parental control and protection against the particular stresses of the barrio. If the cost of helping these families is high, the alternative—banishing Mexican dependency to Mexico, as was done thirty years ago when unemployed Mexicans by the thousands were deported—would be even more expensive in terms of international opinion.

As an urban dweller by the hundreds of thousands, the Mexican American will continue to live in or close to the Negro pockets of poverty. If the minorities are pitted against each other, each will be aroused by self-preservation. If they are moved by cooperation, they may yet make common cause.